LIVING ON THE EDGE

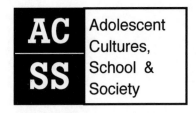

AC / SS
Adolescent Cultures, School & Society

Joseph L. DeVitis & Linda Irwin-DeVitis
GENERAL EDITORS

Vol. 61

The Adolescent Cultures, School & Society series
is part of the Peter Lang Education list.
Every volume is peer reviewed and meets
the highest quality standards for content and production.

PETER LANG
New York • Washington, D.C./Baltimore • Bern
Frankfurt • Berlin • Brussels • Vienna • Oxford

JOHN SMYTH AND TERRY WRIGLEY

LIVING ON THE EDGE

RETHINKING POVERTY, CLASS AND SCHOOLING

PETER LANG
New York • Washington, D.C./Baltimore • Bern
Frankfurt • Berlin • Brussels • Vienna • Oxford

Library of Congress Cataloging-in-Publication Data
Smyth, John.
Living on the edge: re-thinking poverty, class, and schooling / John Smyth, Terry Wrigley.
pages cm. — (Adolescent cultures, school and society; v. 61)
Includes bibliographical references and index.
1. Educational sociology. 2. Social classes. 3. Children with social disabilities—Education.
4. Poor children—Education. 5. Educational equalization. I. Title.
LC191.S637   371.826'94—dc23   2013012584
ISBN 978-1-4331-1653-7 (hardcover)
ISBN 978-1-4331-1685-8 (paperback)
ISBN 978-1-4539-1137-2 (e-book)
ISSN 1091-1464

Bibliographic information published by Die Deutsche Nationalbibliothek.
Die Deutsche Nationalbibliothek lists this publication in the "Deutsche
Nationalbibliografie"; detailed bibliographic data is available
on the Internet at http://dnb.d-nb.de/.

The paper in this book meets the guidelines for permanence and durability
of the Committee on Production Guidelines for Book Longevity
of the Council of Library Resources.

Printed in the United States of America

Contents

Acknowledgments

Sometimes books come about as a result of long processes of professional interaction that culminate in bringing the work into existence. This is not such a book. Before starting to write this book, we had only a cursory relationship, had never met face-to-face, and even now have had only electronic contact with one another. The fact that a text as complex as this one could be written against this background is testimony to the power of ideas and the passion with which we hold them. In an era in which egos are everything, we had an incredibly generous and harmonious professional relationship in bringing this book into existence.

John extends his appreciation to the Australian Research Council for the several grants that supported his thinking lying behind some parts of this book. Appreciation is expressed to the remarkable people at Peter Lang Publishing—Chris Myers and Bernadette Shade in particular—who continue to believe in the importance of our work, and to Joe DeVitis who has been such an academic stalwart as series editor in supporting our work. As always, he is incredibly grateful to Solveiga for her contribution to the formatting aspects and for reminding him that there is more to life than writing books!

Terry wishes first of all to thank Bob Lingard for his ongoing support and in particular for his timely advice to examine the wider sociology before returning to the world of education. Also thanks to Lew Zipin who struggled through the draft text and made many perceptive suggestions for its revision. Finally, to Kathy for being so tolerant: from time to time she tries to explain that retirement from a full-time university post should mean taking things easy, but he is such a slow learner.

We both wish to thank the many committed and creative teachers who have found diverse ways to make a difference to young people's learning and lives in very difficult circumstances. It has been a privilege to see them at work and to listen to the explanations and theories they have formed. Thanks also to academic colleagues in many countries who have helped us clarify our thinking.

Finally, we are very much aware of the political context of our writing. Poverty shows no sign of abating in this Age of Austerity, as governments try to make the many pay for the greed and folly of the few. We continue to be encouraged by the energy and courage and resistance of millions around the world who continue to fight for a better future.

Putting those 'Living on the Edge' at the Centre of Educational Policy and Practice

This is an important book concerning more socially just ways of educating disadvantaged young people. It builds on the influential work that both John Smyth and Terry Wrigley have done over the years. The book re-examines many of the faulty explanations and damaging policies which continue to dominate educational practices and exacerbate the problems of poverty. Never content with simply producing a critique, the authors develop a well-theorized basis for a socially just and pedagogically productive education.

This book is especially relevant in the contemporary geo-political and policy context. Despite the depredations of the global financial crisis, neo-liberalism still remains intact, almost inviolate as the framework for education and other public policies across the globe, albeit vernacularized in its mediated impact in different nations. Associated austerity policies or dogma about surplus budgets as political responses to the crisis have most impact on those with real unmet needs, with unjust effects.

In *Living on the Edge,* Smyth and Wrigley draw on good evidence and analysis of how and why schools produce and reproduce class-based inequalities. They reject 'blaming the victim' accounts of class-based underachievement in schools: specifically, they expose the poverty of accounts based on supposed pathologies, whether located in individual deficits (e.g., low intelligence), family defects (e.g., a lack of aspirations for their children) or community dysfunction (e.g., the underclass myth). They point to material poverty as the root cause, while acknowledging that poverty does have profound psychological and cultural effects.

They also reject accounts that blame teachers and schools located in such communities. A sustained and myopic focus on teachers and quality teaching has become the policy mantra in most societies today. In this policy setting, sharper control of the teaching process and a competitive version of 'accountability' are regarded as the ways towards better learning outcomes for all students, denying contextual influences on student performance. This accountability gaze on teachers and schools distracts from the need to challenge politicians and policy makers and hold them to account on the basis of 'opportunity to learn standards' for impoverished populations, that is, the provision of resources of many kinds necessary to socially just outcomes.

In *Living on the Edge*, Smyth and Wrigley proffer a structural account of the impact of social class and poverty, but one which brings into focus the cultural mediations of class divisions. They make good use of Bourdieu in this respect. In a challenge to much contemporary sociology of education, they bring a relational class analysis back into their account and recognize in so doing the ways in which globalization has affected class structures in relational ways across developed and developing countries. They also rightly acknowledge the intersectionality of class with gender, ethnicity, race and sexuality. We also probably need to think about digital technologies and their effects on contemporary class relations and cultural manifestations of class.

Yet, on the basis of schools they know and have worked and researched with, they nonetheless also proffer a substantiated argument that schools and teachers can make a difference here and now through changed school culture, different leadership practices, through pedagogies of hope—'rich teaching' in their terms. Rather than locating blame with marginalized young people or with those who teach them, they pursue an interactionist understanding of how teaching can reconnect to learners' lives, through school/community engagement and recognition of the deep 'funds of knowledge' embedded in all communities, however disadvantaged they are made by contemporary economics and public policy.

At the same time, they also recognize that a broader political project is needed to move towards more socially just schooling and a more socially just society, particularly in this age of neo-liberal globalization and growing inequality within and between nations. With Anyon (2005) and Hayes et al. (2006), they recognize and outline how schools and teachers can make *a* difference but not *all* the difference: complementary social and economic policies are required that confront cruel social and economic inequalities. This point is also well made by Condron (2011), who writes about inequities in US schooling and the failure of policymakers to recognize the educational effects of an inequitable social structure and inequitable funding of schools. There is an important educational politics, and broader politics, deeply embedded in the analysis provided by John Smyth and Terry Wrigley in *Living on the Edge*, which offers a perceptive critique of contemporary politics, in addition to a practical educational politics of hope.

The educational politics of *Living on the Edge* argues the ethical necessity of redistributive politics so that extra monies are expended on schools in poor communities in response to complex barriers to learning. These politics also acknowledge the need for recognitive justice in such schools, whereby cultural differences are accepted, supported and valorized; schools need to work with and value difference. In terms of school and community engagement, a new representative politics is needed that supports and works with community funds of knowledge, to scaffold a transformative change in school pedagogies and curriculum. Schools need to be in their communities and encourage communities in the school. New horizontal accountabilities are also needed between schools and their communities, and communities and their school.

Smyth and Wrigley also address the negative impact of high stakes testing on pedagogies. High stakes testing serves to restrict the breadth and reach of curriculum, particularly for schools in poor communities, where contemporary policies of accountability have their most reductive effects. This is well exemplified in Australia: the Gillard Government is to be commended for their redistribution of federal monies into schools serving low socio-economic status communities, but unfortunately the accountability for such redistributive monies is framed largely in terms of improved performance on what have become high stakes literacy and numeracy tests. This has seen the introduction of scripted pedagogies— 'pedagogies of poverty' in Smyth and Wrigley's terms—in many schools serving poor communities, thus enhancing curricular inequalities. Smyth and Wrigley are surely correct to argue that, instead, enriching and intellectually demanding pedagogies are an imperative in such schools. Quality of pedagogies is a social justice issue. We also need to think about curricular justice.

In their account of necessary school reform, Smyth and Wrigley challenge the school effectiveness and school improvement literatures for their anodyne politics and failure to challenge reductionist goals for contemporary schooling, especially for young people living in poverty. They suggest both of these reform approaches demand an *intensification* of what schools are *already* doing and that this does not work. Einstein is reported to have said that insanity is doing the same thing over and over and expecting a different outcome. Such a view is central to Smyth and Wrigley's stinging critique of school reform practices to date. They also offer such a critique of the thinned-out 'policy as numbers' approach which accompanies high stakes testing today and which substitutes for the lack of imagination about what schools can and should be aiming to achieve for all students.

Despite the global financial crisis, neo-liberalism appears hegemonic. Implicitly, Smyth and Wrigley argue the need for a new social imaginary to underpin a new politics and educational policy: *other globalizations are possible* (see Rizvi and Lingard, 2010, Ch 9). This is the bigger political project embedded in the argument of *Living on the Edge*, one that challenges the possessive individualism underpinning neo-liberalism and foregrounds instead concerns for the common good. The explication of such a politics would require another book, but the necessity of such a new politics rings loudly from the pages of this one.

There are important lessons here for all involved in education: politicians, policymakers, principals, teachers, students, parents and communities. There are recommendations for changes in practice and policy right now, to provide better schooling for all young people, but especially those young people living in poverty for whom schooling is the only way to a better future. They also argue most persuasively that this is the way to better societies and a better future for all. Darling-Hammond (2010) has argued similarly in *The Flat World and Education*, suggesting that the USA's future depends upon achieving more equitable schooling and a more equal society. Sahlberg (2011) has also argued this position in his *Finnish Lessons*, a book that demonstrates how Finland's high quality and high equity school system correlates to low levels of social inequality, equitable provision of schooling (all students attend government schools), valuing the professionalism of highly educated teachers, early intervention for students in danger of falling behind, and rejection of the neo-liberal policy frame that underpins school reform in Anglo-American countries (see Ball, 2013). John Smyth and Terry Wrigley offer an agenda for a way forward and a progressive politics of education. Their arguments and analyses are vital for all those committed to more socially just schooling. From a social justice perspective, it is difficult to argue with their stance that young people living on the edge should be put at the centre of educational policy and practice.

— Bob Lingard
School of Education and the Institute for Social Science Research
The University of Queensland

Living on the Edge

Rethinking Poverty, Class and Schooling

*L*iving on the Edge examines the relationship between social divisions and school. It concerns the education of young people whose lives have been made precarious by forces beyond their control. It focuses on poverty in affluent countries during a period of increasing economic division, and it seeks to understand why children growing up in poverty tend to underachieve in school. Our title points to the precariousness of their lives, in general, and of their engagement with school.

The book revisits some key arguments developed in previous decades and that continue to resonate. Though many were originally articulated in terms of working-class children, they are now recycled in terms of child poverty. This shift is significant, reflecting in part the current reluctance to acknowledge class division and an unjust economic system. Much easier, perhaps, for policy makers to imagine we are living in a benign meritocracy where talent finds its way upward, with the unfortunate exception of the poor. This opens the way to tackle the problem through newsworthy policy initiatives, interwoven with discourses of denigration about poor parenting and failing schools.

Worn-out theories are constantly being reinvented and new ones are introduced. Explanations for the correlation between social division and academic achievement have ranged across inherited intelligence, language use in the family, parental interactions with young children, low aspiration of young people or their parents, lack of self-esteem, material poverty, disruptive neighborhood cultures, inadequate resources, ineffective schools, indifferent teachers, inappropriate curricula, intellectual and social segregation between or within schools, pedagogical styles, school size and structure, prejudice, and school ethos. It is our contention that many of these explanations are either erroneous or so misleading that they do more harm than good.

A large part of this book, therefore, is devoted to developing a critique of inadequate theory. We have been concerned with these issues for many years and have been able to draw upon extensive knowledge and involvement with practical initiatives in Australia and Britain as well as substantial reading on social justice and school development. We decided it was time to share our thinking and critically evaluate the ideas we had encountered on a theoretical level. This intellectual process of clearing away the muck of ages (Marx & Engels, 1845) is not a substitute for practical engagement but its prerequisite. We hope that it will help avoid the endless recycling of flawed policies, refocus research, and enable committed teachers and social activists to have greater impact.

For all the confusion of explanations, international evidence consistently points to a strong and enduring statistical relationship between social position (income, occupation, parental occupation) and school achievement. The extent of economic disadvantage, and the degree to which that impacts school outcomes, varies between countries, and in some the consequences for educational qualifications and future opportunities are extreme. There is good reason to use the term *reproduction* to describe this process: the school system tends to reproduce social inequalities rather than overcome them.

This does not mean, however, that nothing can change. The authors of this book have seen many fine examples of educational change that really make a difference to children's lives and opportunities.

Class and Schooling

It is no accident that our subtitle refers to class as well as poverty. The official policy discourse, while acknowledging poverty (or at least disadvantage), is virtually silent about class. We made a conscious decision to break that silence. It is our view:

1. that poverty derives from class, in the sense of differences of power and position related to economic ownership and employment; and

2. that class, and indeed capitalism overall, has an impact on learning far beyond people suffering from poverty and stretches well beyond youth into lifelong learning.

In addressing poverty in affluent countries today—and the educational policies and theories that are supposed to mitigate it—we are very much aware of the continuity of current concerns with earlier theories articulated in terms of working-class children. This usually meant, in fact, the children of manual workers, particularly those with lower levels of skills. Parents in these families tend not to have gained high levels of school qualifications or attended university. In many locations, manual workers have been particularly vulnerable to chronic unemployment following industrial closures. We are also acutely aware, however, that there have been massive changes in patterns of employment and that large numbers of low-paid service sector employees are now on insecure contracts and levels of pay that throw them into poverty.

The nature of employment can also have a major impact on the quantity and quality of lifelong learning, and some modes of work constrain intellectual development as Adam Smith (2005[1776]), the founding father of capitalist economics, pointed out two centuries ago in *The Wealth of Nations*:

> The man whose whole life is spent in performing a few simple operations, of which the effects, too, are perhaps always the same, or very nearly the same, has no occasion to exert his understanding, or to exercise his invention, in finding out expedients for removing difficulties which never occur. He naturally loses, therefore, the habit of such exertion, and generally becomes as stupid and ignorant as it is possible for a human creature to become. (p. 674)

While taking issue with the derogatory adjectives in his final sentence, we can see in our own day the limiting effects of repetitive and tightly regulated work over which workers have no control. This is compounded by the intellectual damage of many forms of commodified entertainment, starting with the worst kinds of commercially funded children's television. All of this is pedagogical, albeit in a negative sense.

It is impossible to understand recent changes in educational policy and practice without reference to the cultural and ideological impact of neoliberalism—an attempt to purify capitalism, restoring it to its (supposed) earlier coherence. Though few neoliberal ideologues nowadays believe that nineteenth-century conditions can be restored in terms of the complete removal of state provision, we are witnessing comprehensive and multilevel attempts to ensure that the state prioritizes servicing the needs of the capitalist economy, to the neglect of other purposes such as social welfare.

Summarizing this policy shift, Stephen Ball (2008) argues:

> The social and economic purposes of education have been collapsed into a single, overriding emphasis on policy making for economic competitiveness and an increasing neglect or sidelining (other than in rhetoric) of the social purposes of education. (pp. 11–12)

This is reflected, for example, in curriculum reforms in England that overprivilege the basics of literacy and numeracy, especially in primary school, and in secondary schools give priority to what are now called the STEM subjects (science, technology, engineering, and mathematics). Furthermore, often under the pretext of making schooling more relevant, many working-class pupils are encouraged to follow a vocational curriculum from the age of 14, abandoning, for example, the wider human formation associated with humanities and creative arts. It is important, however, to add that this emphasis on functionality is applied differentially: cultural enrichment and intellectual challenge are preserved for pupils from families with higher socioeconomic status, whatever their career ambitions.

The ascendancy of neoliberal politics and increasing globalization have increased class divisions and, in particular, led to a massive increase in child poverty. This has occurred despite the vastly increased takings of the global super-rich and the dramatic improvement in productivity as a result of the introduction of computer technologies. It has also been accompanied by increasing global migration of workers, with new challenges for families and schools.

Although, as we argue in chapter 1, the differences between manual and nonmanual employment do not constitute a *class* division as such, such differences may impact on children's chance of school success. The children of parents in professional employment requiring university education have generally been able to achieve higher than most other groups. This is the result of various factors, including parental education, the forms of communication required in work environments, greater opportunities to enhance the child's cultural experience, and a more skillful navigation of systems of secondary school choice.

An even greater difference occurs, however, toward the top of the social scale. In England, for example, just 7 percent of children attend fee-paying independent schools, but these schools account for half the students of Oxford and Cambridge universities. Private school fees typically exceed many other families' total income. They buy not only small classes and grand buildings but also an ethos of ambition and a rich menu of sporting and cultural activities. It has even recently emerged that half the British medal winners at the 2008 Beijing Olympics were former pupils of these elite fee-paying schools (BBC News website, August 3, 2012). These schools are typically attended by children of capitalists and company executives, along with high-ranking professionals such as barristers and top civil servants.

Despite the differences between what are sometimes called class fractions (unskilled manual workers, professional white collar, etc.), we should note that the vast majority of pupils attending state schools become employees of one kind or another, whether manual, white collar, or in professions such as teachers or nurses. The differences in educational attainment between the (unskilled or semiskilled) manual and the professional groups have been a particular concern of educational sociology, but it would be a mistake to assume that the latter are unaffected by the structures of capitalism. Though the children of professional parents are clearly in a better position to gain advantage from systems of choice (Power, Edwards, Whitty & Wigfall, 2003), they are also damaged by capitalism, whether through intense competitive pressure to succeed or from a fear of falling

(Ehrenreich, 1989). Even higher achievers are being socialized into a narrowly instrumental engagement with education, seeing it overwhelmingly in terms of the accumulation of credentials.

Of course, economic social divisions also connect with and are compounded by racial divisions. A recent study of the backgrounds of medical students in the UK in the past five years discovered that children from social class I were 30 times as likely to study medicine as children from social class V; it also found that no Black people from social class V were admitted to medical school from 1996 to 2000 (Seyan, Greenhalgh & Dorling, 2004). These paragraphs summarize only the sharp distinctions of social position and school outcomes but serve to illustrate the extent of correlation. We should recognize, however, that some education systems actually seem designed to maintain and exacerbate this correlation.

The history of mass schooling in England and the United States provides ample evidence that the public school systems were originally designed to keep working-class children in their place; intense professional and political struggle has since moderated this, but the legacy has continuing effect. Robert Lowe, the politician responsible for compulsory schooling in Britain, proclaimed:

> We do not profess to give these children an education that will raise them above their station and business in life . . . We are bound to make up our minds as to how much instruction that class requires, and is capable of receiving. (cited in Tropp, 1957, p. 89)

Or witness the contemptuous disrespect shown by the Boston School Committee toward immigrants in the nineteenth century, predominantly Irish at that time:

> taking children at random from a great city, undisciplined, uninstructed, often with inveterate forwardness and obstinacy, and with the inherited stupidity of centuries of ignorant ancestors; forming them from animals into intellectual beings, and, so far as a school can do it, from intellectual beings into spiritual beings. (cited in Katz, 1971, p. 40)

Locating the Causes

One of the inspirations for this book was the "conceptual synthesis" of the field undertaken by Carlo Raffo and colleagues at Manchester University (Raffo et al., 2010, p. 18 seq.). Their bold attempt to develop a map of the multiple explanations linking poverty to low school attainment was an important impetus for us, but it is important to outline here our reasons for making different choices.

1. The strength of Raffo and colleagues' model is its utilization of spatial scale to organize and locate causal explanations as macro, meso, or micro. However, we regard it as essential to distinguish clearly between school and neighborhood factors; each side of the boundary fence has its macro, meso, and micro scales. Thus, at a macro level on the school side, we can consider national education policy and accountability regimes, or at a

micro level, classroom teaching and the activities belonging to it. This makes it easier to spot the silences, for example the systematic gaps in the mainstream school improvement literature, which focuses on (meso level) leadership and management to the neglect of classroom pedagogies (micro) or national policy frameworks (macro) (Wrigley, 2003; Thrupp & Willmott, 2003).

2. It is particularly important to examine how the macro-level structures relating to class work down through meso- and micro-level experiences, and we must be particularly sensitive to the ways in which macro-level structures exert power down the line. Isolating the lower levels, or exaggerating their autonomy or power over the macro, very easily slides into assumptions that young people are essentially held back by their own 'culture of poverty' or low aspirations.

3. Clear distinctions should be made between causes and interventions. A causal factor might be located at the meso level such as the family, whereas the most effective intervention might involve micro-level interventions such as mentoring. Further, the preferred official response might differ from that which would be most appropriate.

4. Finally, we rejected the idea of providing a neutral summary and undertook to develop a critical analysis of the various explanations and theories.

As we worked to untangle this, it became increasingly apparent that seeking to locate issues, though organizationally convenient, was leading us away from crucial issues of interaction. Consequently, though many of our chapters are organized around explanations pertaining to a particular level or location, our aim is to develop an understanding of the dialectical and symbolic interactions among the various levels and between schooling and society, including the complexity of students' daily transitions between the classroom and their other lifeworlds. Paradoxically then, our method involves separating factors internal and external to school in order to explore their interaction.

A Dialectical Approach

Our title, *Living on the Edge*, addresses the precariousness of life for large numbers of young people and their families, including some of the world's most affluent countries. It also speaks to the precariousness and fragility of their school experience and the deep sense of disaffection and alienation that many of them feel. In rethinking explanations of the link between low socioeconomic position and poor school attainment, we have drawn particular guidance from sociological and educational thinkers whose work particularly focuses on border situations and encounters, and on the fragility of relationship between marginalized young people and traditional schooling.

Some of the most interesting insights into young people's experiences of schooling concern the pedagogical interactions with their teachers. The term *pedagogical* refers not only to methods of teaching and learning but also to the entirety of what young people learn from their encounters with adults (the hidden curriculum, self-esteem, a place within the pecking order, learner identity, and so on).

Bourdieu's work in particular has encouraged us to take a relational perspective, though we take issue with aspects of his model of class. His concept of cultural capital addresses an important facet of student-school interaction, and it is crucial to emphasize that his use of the term can only be properly understood relationally in terms of interactions and interpersonal perceptions. A lack of cultural capital does not imply that some young people lack culture but that their cultural characteristics and activities go unrecognized or are even denigrated by powerful defining institutions such as school. Similarly, *social capital*, for Bourdieu, is an explanation of how some young people gain scholastic and economic advantage through their parents' social affiliations and connections, including the deployment of these connections to overcome any obstacles in the school environment. This is fundamentally different—more dialectical—than Putnam's view of social capital as something quantifiable, though his more specific *bridging capital* partly converges with Bourdieu's sense.

Teachers make all kinds of explicit and tacit judgments about children's abilities and characters that are at least partly based on their perception of nonacademic qualities, including assumptions about children's family lives. In some schools and school systems, these judgments become institutionalized in terms of internal selection into particular streams or tracks, leading to different curricula, styles of teaching, and outcomes. Such interpersonal perceptions, structured by socioeconomic and cultural difference, affect how people behave toward one another, including circumscribing the ambitions and pathways teachers deem realistic for each student to pursue.

Erving Goffman is less well known now, but his work is of enormous significance. Goffman comes from a social sciences paradigm known as *symbolic interactionism* (Blumer, 1969), concerned with the ways in which people perceive one another, shape each other into particular roles, interpret one another's actions and responses, and struggle to maintain the respect of others and their own self-respect. Goffman's interactionist work focusing on one-to-one relationships provides invaluable tools for classroom ethnography: for example, *Stigma* (1963) or *The Presentation of Self in Everyday Life* (1959) with concepts derived from drama such as face, role, performance, and the maintenance of expressive control. Even more interesting, for our purpose, is his book *Asylums: Essays on the Social Situation of Mental Patients and Other Inmates* (1968 [1961]).

Asylums examines similar interactions in the particularly strained context of *total institutions*. Goffman (1968) defines these as "a place of residence and work where a large number of like-situated individuals, cut off from the wider society for an appreciable period of time, together lead an enclosed, formally administered round of life" (p. xiii). His examples include prisons, mental hospitals, boarding schools, and convents. All of these place strong and often idiosyncratic expectations on inmates or residents, which require a strained adjustment to role expectations that are different from the outside world and may appear absurd. They require an acceptance of arbitrary authority, rituals of admission and daily life, punishments for failure to conform; inmates often develop stratagems of pretending to conform.

Total institutions impose particular ways of speaking to those in authority and the learning of behaviors that make little real sense but are required by the institutional culture. Identities established in the outside world have to be replaced and indignities passively accepted. Only the staff have the right to make judgments and set rules, though inmates develop (often unproductive or self-destructive) forms of resistance in the struggle to maintain respect of self and that of others.

Readers will already recognize some important similarities between Goffman's total institutions and regular day schools. Yet for all the difficulties of initial adjustment that total institutions such as boarding schools impose on new pupils, the issues of adjustment for pupils attending day schools may be even more acute. This is especially the case where there is a serious cultural gap between the school and students' lives outside. It may prove difficult for students to make sense of required behaviors and modes of interaction that their teachers simply regard as normal. Students have to adjust on a daily basis to different expectations; their easy interaction with parents and grandparents at home may be treated as disrespectful and rude by their teachers. Their teachers may have very limited understanding of their lives beyond the school fence and, indeed, regard them as deficient compared to their own home lives and the norms of the school.

Day schools in some countries have an equally strong set of idiosyncratic norms as boarding schools and other total institutions—especially in Britain and its former colonies where day schools were, to a considerable extent, styled in imitation of nineteenth-century elite boarding schools—yet urban youth are expected to make a calm and trouble-free transition into that environment on a daily basis. The problems are particularly acute for many young people growing up in poverty, who have little reason to trust what the school claims to offer in exchange for conformity and assimilation. Reprimands from adults are often experienced as humiliating by these students, especially when they occur in full view of their peers; they feel compelled to respond in ways that sustain the respect of those peers, albeit at the cost of antagonizing their teachers.

Bourdieu and Goffman both offer ideas and methods for investigating the difficult symbolic interactions between marginalized students and their schools. We find these two theorists particularly enlightening, but let us briefly continue the argument in relation to the chapters that follow.

In chapter 1 we express the need to understand social classes not simply as categories with differing lifestyles but as opposing forces related to each other according to their different role and power in production. Culture is important to this argument but cannot be separated from, or exalted over, the dynamics of its relation to economics.

In chapter 2 we explain how poverty derives from class position. The poor are not a separate class but workers who for various reasons (racism, disability, single parenthood, location, unemployment) are particularly hard hit. Their poverty is not the result of their own deficiencies but of the wealth and power of a minority of others. Again, we relate economics to culture by looking at the stigma attached to poverty, the stereotypes, the degree to which media and politicians seek to blame the victims. This, along with the economic pressures, has a deep effect on educational engagement and outcomes.

In chapter 3 we focus on poor neighborhoods, or rather places made poor, damaged not primarily by the actions of their residents but by macro-level structural forces, whether they are U.S. ghettos, former industrial centers that have become rustbelts, or the mushrooming slums of the global South. Their residents are not marginal but actively marginalized. They despair, not due to a lack of moral fiber but because of a lack of opportunity. In this chapter we also expose the myths associated with social capital theory (in Putnam's and Coleman's versions), and the short-termism of area-based interventions that attempt to overlook the destructive power of macro-level economic forces. A sound understanding of places made poor, and of the blighted communities who inhabit them, is crucial if we are to develop new ways for schools to connect with communities.

Chapter 4 deals with the fallacious theory of inherited intelligence, which not only blames the victims but makes low achievement seem inevitable. This theory, built on social prejudice rather than rational science, diverts our attention from the interaction of human beings with their environment and of children with their parents—in favor of an outdated view of genes as hard-wired carriers of fixed characteristics.

In chapter 5 the blame shifts from the individual's supposed innate stupidity onto working-class parents for initiating their children into deficient modes of language use. The highly flawed research upon which such ideas are based reaches conclusions based on language structure rather than meaningful use in context, and it treats linguistic difference as deficit. The chapter continues by looking at wider aspects of early upbringing, focusing on various kinds of stimulus from parents (reading, play activities, places of interest). A simplistic statistical contrast among different types of parents, based implicitly on deficit assumptions rather than a genuine interest in different patterns of parenting, simply reinforces a sense of parental deficit, and encourages forms of early years provision that exclude parents rather than enriching parenting skills.

The discussion of aspirations in chapter 6 questions the assumption that young people growing up in poverty lack ambition. Aspirations can only be understood dynamically and contextually in terms of realistic opportunities to fulfill them: low aspirations might actually turn out to be high aspirations frustrated by bad experiences and difficult circumstances. We look at how ambitions are nurtured in elite families and schools and examine research that points not to a lack of parental ambitions in poorer working-class homes but to parental uncertainty on how to help and what routes are available.

While chapters 3–6 deal with out-of-school explanations of the poverty-underachievement link, chapters 7–9 focus on schools. Chapter 7 makes clear the difficulties that have arisen from attempts to "improve" schools that tacitly assume that they operate independently of the outside world and of their students' lifeworlds. School Effectiveness research and related versions of School Improvement (together known as SESI) not only leave neoliberal economistic aims and government surveillance methods unchallenged, but also treat each school as an autonomous manageable entity in competition with other schools.

Chapter 8 continues the discussion of 'official' School Improvement theory that seeks to operate in isolation from neighborhoods and wider cultures. It points to a more engaged and critical conceptualization of key terms such as *school culture*. It then highlights the damage done by forms of academic segregation, including streaming, setting, and tracking; the messages delivered by these forms of differentiation can only be understood in terms of their interaction with messages of denigration of working class and particularly poor or ethnic minority families, which are circulated by mass media and the political establishment in the wider society (Jones, 2011). The chapter ends with some alternative thinking about school reform that is oriented to social justice and respect-based community engagement.

Chapter 9 begins by returning to older debates about curriculum. While supporting radical initiatives that seek to engage with the concerns of working-class students, it rejects a simple appeal to immediate relevance. Schools must bridge between students' experiences and the body of academic knowledge in order to develop a critical understanding of the world. We also raise serious questions about the recourse to vocationalism as an alternative rather than a complement to academic learning. In our discussion of pedagogy in the second part of this chapter, we look at limited kinds of teaching that tend to predominate in schools serving areas of poverty. We critique nondialogic authoritarian modes of teaching that are overwhelmingly abstract and draw on the practice and theory of Paulo Freire and Harold Rosen, among others, as a stimulus for reform.

Remaking the Link

Our concluding chapter connects some of these strands and makes reference to new and further examples. Building theoretically on sociologists such as Bourdieu and Goffman, and educators such as Freire and Rosen, as well as the rich theory-in-practice emerging from innovative school change, we point toward new possibilities for a socially just education. In doing so, we are very much aware that high levels of social division and child poverty will constantly undermine schools' attempts to improve achievement (Mortimore & Whitty, 1997). Teachers who are committed to social justice often engage in wider community and political struggles. However, we do not believe that schools must remain as they are until wider political change occurs.

We point to practices that reengage disaffected and disappointed young people; school cultures that are posited on the notion that their pupils are at *promise* rather than at risk; leadership to turn around the school—literally—to face its community; and curriculum and pedagogy that are dialogic, collaborative, critical, creative, and concerned.

We do not wish to give the impression that education for work is unimportant; preparation for a productive and creative engagement with nature and society will always be an important part of education. However, in the present utilitarian climate engendered by neoliberal macropolitics, we all need to insist on a wider vision—that schools are also a place for growing up, for cooperation, for developing social concern and solidarity, for critical thinking, physical activity, and creative and cultural development.

If we are serious about democracy and social justice, schools must become a site for critical and engaged thinking about the world's big problems, including climate change, racism, hunger, and war. If we truly wish to generate wisdom, we need to help young people to become more critical about the goods and values promoted by a consumer society, the commodified pleasures, and the mass media's bizarre and trivial "regime of truth."

In particular, for young people whose lives are damaged by poverty, marginalization, and restricted opportunities, we must consider how to honor their right to know *why*. Capitalism, for its part, needs workers who are "clever enough to be profitable but not wise enough to know what's really going on" (Wrigley, 2006, p. 8). For educators committed to social justice, one of the most challenging questions is how to assist young people to an understanding of the economic structures that generate poverty. The challenge from nineteenth-century socialists to ruling class utilitarians remains relevant: the socialists demanded "really useful knowledge . . . concerning our conditions in life, and how to get out of our present troubles" [cited in Johnson, 1979, p. 84).

Accountability in the form of political bullying does nothing to promote greater equality of achievement, let alone engagement or enjoyment. Drawing on our previous publications and the inspiring work of the teachers described in them (e.g., Wrigley, 2000; Wrigley, Thomson & Lingard, 2012; Smyth & McInerney, 2007a; Smyth, Down & McInerney, 2010), we hope this book will help to keep alive a more fruitful and just understanding of educational change.

Understanding Class and Poverty

Part 1 provides an important conceptual and sociological foundation for the rest of the book. It aims to clarify some of the complexities and ambiguities of class and poverty, in terms of economic and social structure, personal experience, and symbolic significance. The impact of class and poverty on educational engagement and achievement is both economic and cultural.

It has become increasingly difficult in recent decades to conceptualize the relationship of education to social class. This is partly because of the recurrent claims that class is no longer a meaningful concept. In part, this relates to changing patterns of production and employment, but the difficulties also stem from the fashionable academic meta-narrative of Postmodernism that other differences are more important.

In chapter 1 we undertake a critical discussion of class as structure and experience. It draws on educational sociology but critically, taking odds with its Weberian tendency to foreground lifestyle over economic relationships and raising questions about its preferred binary of 'working class' versus 'middle class'. By applying the intellectual resource of classic Marxism to our contemporary situation, we develop a model of class that better reflects the economic reality and its relationship to schooling. While our view is that class is fundamentally an economic category, we do not divorce this from the cultural experience of class identification, relationship, and consciousness. We examine the myth of classlessness, the floating signifier 'middle class', and the media myth of an 'underclass'.

We discuss Pierre Bourdieu's understanding of class *reproduction* and Nancy Fraser's application of *recognition*, before outlining the relevance of class to schooling.

Chapter 2 builds on this by explaining how poverty derives from class division. It is constantly produced by capitalist exploitation and dispossession, nationally and globally. We discuss definitions of absolute and relative poverty as well as personal experiences of adults and children. Parts of the chapter examine the intersections with race, gender, and disability, and the geography of poverty involving both migration and urban concentration.

The chapter takes serious issue with attempts to blame people thrown into poverty for their own distress and with the discourse of denigration used by sections of the media and political establishment. Contrary to these stereotypes, we introduce evidence to highlight the skills and persistence needed to survive.

A critical lesson from ethnographies of working-class life, particularly in deindustrialized conurbations characterized by chronic unemployment and unreliable, poorly paid jobs, is the widespread sense of shame (humiliation, stigma, etc.) and a sense of futility or hopelessness that life can be improved. These terms will recur throughout the book as they have a profound impact on young people's experience of education.

CHAPTER ONE

Making Sense of Class

Marxism has not been put out of business because Etonians have started to drop their aitches . . . While the chief executive smoothes his jeans over his sneakers, over one billion on the planet go hungry every day.

—Eagleton, 2011, pp. 261–63

We are frequently told that class is dead or, alternatively, if we are not all equal, at least we enjoy equal opportunities within a meritocracy. As we demonstrate in this chapter, nothing could be further from the truth. What we provide here in terms of a sociological framework for the book is a critique of dominant views of class found in many academic texts as well as the mass media and everyday common sense. Rather than focusing on surface appearances based on lifestyles or occupational categories, what we offer is a more robust historical and structural account. We argue that many of the labels attached to groups and individuals operate to obfuscate the workings of capitalism and how it produces social stratifications.

This is crucial to understanding how the disadvantaging of young people occurs and how it impacts their educational lives and identities. In short, our argument is that class is deeply infused with economic, historical, and political dimensions that operate to create and sustain inequality and how that works educationally. While we draw heavily on the British situation to explain and exemplify this, the lessons are equally applicable to other Western countries.

While we hold that class is essentially rooted in economic positions linked to production, and to an economic structure based on exploitation, it is vital to explore the cultural expressions and ramifications of this. We draw, for example, on Nancy Fraser's thinking (Fraser & Honneth, 2003) to examine the relationship between the distribution of resources (economic) and forms of (mis)recognition and (dis)respect (cultural).

We use this critical scrutiny of the sociological literature pertaining to class to set the stage for three priorities later in the book: (1) to create a more pedagogically respectful approach toward young people; (2) to prevent some young people being treated as surplus to requirements within the schooling and education system; and as a result (3) to establish some principles for a socially just curriculum that recognizes and gives young people a voice.

The Relationship between Poverty and Class

The class analysis developed in this chapter forms an important foundation for sorting out the multiple confused explanations of school disengagement and low achievement. Class divisions and class power have direct and mediated effects on schooling, profoundly restricting young people's learning and development. Within this, a sound understanding of class is also essential for understanding poverty and its impact on schooling; this chapter, therefore, serves as a basis for the discussion that begins in chapter 2. A clear understanding of both is essential for untangling some of the complex explanations of educational difficulties and differences.

Class and poverty are distinct issues but strongly related; they have distinct but cumulative influences on education. Poverty in the modern world is not accidental misfortune or degrees of disadvantage but the product of an economic system that employs people only so long as they generate profit. It is no longer possible to regard poverty as a remnant of an earlier historical period, the teething troubles of an immature capitalism that it would eventually outgrow through increased productivity. Poverty is the consequence not of weak production but of unjust patterns of ownership and distribution within a class-divided economic system. Indeed, despite massive increases in productivity and dramatic technological progress, poverty and insecurity are constantly generated in a system that seeks to maximize profit by cutting wages and reducing the size of the workforce, that shops around the globe for cheaper workers, and where numerous people are declared redundant even though others desperately need their work and skills to house and feed and teach and care for them.

In countries that have implemented neoliberal policies most strongly, notably Britain and the United States, financial inequalities have increased dramatically during the recent decades of unprecedented technological advance. Computer technologies have not resulted in the promised age of leisure but in mass youth unemployment. Simultaneously, in their attempt to purify capitalism and return to its (supposed) nineteenth-century golden age, neoliberal policymakers have cut the public spending that for a time offered a safety net to the most vulnerable members of society.

A Historical Overview

Because class is frequently represented in terms of consumer choices, lifestyles, and attitudes, we must begin with a brief clarification of the origins and development of the concept. This is by no means straightforward. To quote Raymond Williams' (1983[1976]) classic understatement, "class is an obviously difficult word" (p. 60). Though used in Ancient Rome to refer to divisions of the population for taxation purposes according to the amount of property people owned, class only acquired its modern meaning around the early nineteenth century during the Industrial Revolution. Even after that, older words such as *rank, estate,* and *order,* belonging to a tightly hierarchical society, survived into the twentieth century. Initially the rising capitalist class (factory and mine owners, merchants, etc.), along with high-status professionals such as lawyers, began to call themselves proudly the middle or middling class, thus distinguishing themselves on the one hand from the landowning aristocracy, who they saw as unproductive and profligate, and on the other hand from the common people or lower classes, who they deemed incapable of self-governance. Subsequently, from 1818 onward, the term *working classes* was used to distinguish workmen from their employers. As Williams (1983[1976]) explains, the term *working class,* though originally assigned by others, was eventually appropriated by that class and used as proudly as middle class had been: for example, "the working classes have created all wealth" (p. 64). One of the early socialists, Bronterre O'Brien, was making a revolutionary claim on its behalf to "a complete dominion over the fruits of their own industry" (p. 64).

On these foundations Marx and Engels, in the *Communist Manifesto* (1996 [1848]), developed their understanding of modern society as driven by conflict between two major classes they called the *bourgeoisie* ("the class of modern Capitalists, owners of the means of social production and employers of wage labor") and the *proletariat* ("the class of modern wage-laborers who, having no means of production of their own, are reduced to selling their labor power in order to live") (p. 3, including footnote by Engels). They saw this emergent division as replacing earlier ones such as slave owners and slaves in the ancient world, or aristocracy and serfs in feudal Europe. Marx predicted the demise of in-between middle-class groups: professionals such as doctors and scientists would themselves become wage laborers, and the "petit bourgeoisie" of small-scale shopkeepers and peasants would also "sink into the proletariat" because they were unable to compete with large-scale producers (p. 8 & p. 13).

Thus, industrialization did not mean the end of social struggle but new battle lines, and increasingly on a global scale. In Marxist theory, because the relationship between employers and workers is one of exploitation (the extraction of profit), conflict inevitably arises between these two classes, and hopefully the class of employees will take over and run society for themselves.

Toward the end of the nineteenth century, however, other social theorists were proposing different usages of the word *class*. In particular, Weber sought a more sophisticated and elaborate division of society that included consideration of skills, social status, consumption patterns, and cultural habits—though crucially losing the notion of *exploitation leading to class struggle*.

Government officials also became interested in class and began to record it statistically (Rose, 1995). Initially it was related to issues such as infant mortality, but in the early twentieth century a dominant concern was Eugenics, that is, the fear that the "British race" might degenerate because workers were reproducing faster than their social superiors. The official class scheme sees society as a graded hierarchy of sets of occupations. For most of the twentieth century in Britain, the official hierarchy was:

I   Professional and Executive

II   Managerial and Technical

IIIN   Skilled Non-Manual

IIIM   Skilled Manual

IV   Partly-skilled

V   Unskilled

Apart from the absurd idea that anyone can earn a living without any skills, this classification, like its more sophisticated successor the National Statistics Socio-Economic Classification used since 2001, muddles together employers with professional workers such as teachers and nurses in the upper groups.

In parallel to this, similar schemes have been used for marketing purposes but with a focus on lifestyle and educational levels. For example, the National Readership Survey (originating with newspaper publishers) has the following categories:

A   upper middle

B   middle

C1 lower middle

C2 skilled working (i.e., manual)

D   working (i.e., semi- and unskilled)

E   "those at the lowest level of subsistence" (i.e., state pension, unemployed)

A middle with no upper is strange indeed, as is the notion that all employees of manual occupations are of lower status or at least buy different goods than white-collar workers.

Enormous confusion has been generated by these multiple conceptions of class, used interchangeably in ordinary speech and more formal texts. The confusion has been exacerbated in recent decades by claims that we now live in a classless society or that "everybody is middle class now." Both these proposals hide capitalism's global super-rich from view.

Postmodernist academics share responsibility for this confusion with their belief that class has no greater relevance than other divisions such as ethnicity or sexuality, a trend that has muddled rather than enriched social analysis. As Beverley Skeggs remarks of some feminist academics, class "may not be recognized as a problem for those who have the privilege to ignore it" (1997, p. 6).

Bourdieu and Wacquant (2001) complain that in "Neoliberal Newspeak" the terms *capitalism, class exploitation, domination,* and *inequality* are conspicuous by their absence. The myth of classlessness has coincided with a period in which capitalism's attack on workers' living standards has become increasingly acute:

> Progressives of all stripes seem to have caved in to neoliberal thinking since it is one of the primary fictions of neoliberalism that class is a fictional category that exists only in the imagination of socialists and crypto-communists. . . . The first lesson we must learn . . . is that if it looks like class struggle and acts like class war then we have to name it unashamedly for what it is. (Harvey, 2005, p. 202; see also 1993)

The common-sense notion that class is basically a matter of style is equally confusing, allowing the casualization of ruling-class taste to distract from deepening divisions of wealth and power as alluded to in our prefacing quote to this chapter:

> Marxism has not been put out of business because Etonians have started to drop their aitches. . . . There is a telling contrast between the dressed-down matiness of the modern office and a global system in which distinctions of wealth and power yawn wider than ever. . . . While the chief executive smoothes his jeans over his sneakers, over one billion on the planet go hungry every day. (Eagleton, 2011, pp. 161 & 163)

Economics and Culture

Since this confusion is widespread in educational sociology, it is important to emphasize that the Marxist version is clearly built on an economic relationship, and it rests fundamentally on relations of production rather than the fashions we adopt or the attitudes we display. Deborah Kelsh (2010) has coined the word *Cultureclass* to critique the way sociologists have shifted away from this economic foundation into viewing class as a free-floating cultural phenomenon. Kelsh complains that educational sociologists, drawing on Weber, neglect issues of exploitation inherent in the binary opposition between capitalists and workers and invert the relationship between economics and culture; culture is mistakenly regarded as the cause, not effect, of class division. She argues that by erasing exploitative relations of production from the theoretical imaginary, such academics make it impossible to think beyond life under capitalism.

This is a telling intervention, as it puts a finger on so many problems of sociological theory, but there are also dangers of a dogmatic exclusion of culture from class thinking that, in fact, would be equally un-Marxist.

Though Marx grounds his concept of class in the economic relations of employment, his driving interest is how to change society. Mostly he speaks of class as something to be *formed*; classes are based on economic relationships but involve collective human action. For example, the *Communist Manifesto* speaks of "the organization of the proletariat *into a class.*" Thompson (1980[1963]) took up this theme in *The Making of the English Working Class*, with its memorable claim that the working class was "present at its own making." In other words, there was not a ready-made economic entity that then started to struggle, but rather it was a long process of development with politics and culture involved at every stage. Indeed, a collection of workers employed by capitalists but without skills or songs, location or language, tastes or traditions, is simply unimaginable, a meaningless abstraction:

> The class experience is largely determined by the productive relations into which men are born—or enter involuntarily. Class-consciousness is the way in which these experiences are handled in cultural terms: embodied in traditions, value-systems, ideas, and institutional forms. If the experience appears as determined, class-consciousness does not. We can see a logic in the responses of similar occupational groups undergoing similar experiences, but we cannot predicate any law. Consciousness of class arises in the same way in different times and places, but never in just the same way. (Thompson, 1980[1963], p. 10)

Nor is class formation ever finished:

> Classes must be seen, not as veritable geological formations once they have acquired their original shape, but as phenomena in a constant process of formation, reproduction, re-formation and de-formation. (Therborn, 1983, p. 39)

Recent British history provides a dramatic example. The Thatcher government brought about a significant readjustment of the class structure, in the process of weakening the power of workers to resist capital. This included the widespread destruction of heavy industry and much of its strongly unionized workforce; the shift of many manual workers into self-employment, placing them in a petit bourgeois rather than working-class relationship; the marginalization of large numbers of industrial workers into chronic unemployment or insecure low-paid work (the so-called underclass); and the proletarianization of public sector professionals such as teachers through new forms of surveillance and management imported from the private sector. These are structural shifts that have had deep effects on education in Britain, though the opposition between capitalism and the working class, broadly conceived, remains central.

Culture is imbricated throughout the process of class formation, connecting economic relations and structures of employment and production to changes of consciousness, forms of social organization, the creation of a sense of common identity, and so on. In an important sense, this is a thoroughly educational process.

There is no smooth shift from class structure to class consciousness to class action (the so-called S-C-A model: structure-consciousness-action; see Pahl, 1989, p. 711), and sociologists have deployed various categorizations to articulate this process. Skeggs (1997) asks: "For instance, do we mean class structure, identity, consciousness, action, and so on when we speak of class?" (p. 6). Thrift and Williams (1987) distinguish five major levels: "class structure, the formation of classes, class conflict, class capacity and class consciousness." (p. 5). Mann (1973, p. 13) argues that class consciousness can be further divided into class identity, class opposition, class totality and conceptions of an alternative society; to illustrate this, workers may be conscious of themselves as part of a class but fatalistic about the potential for change. Within the field of education, Ball (2003, p. 9) traces the exercise of class advantage through:

- economic context—the state of class relations
- structure
- dispositions
- aspirations, responsibility, and anxiety
- practices
- choice, distinction, and closure
- the impact of state policy formation.

Each level or aspect is capable of further qualitative distinctions. Trade union actions can be envisaged in terms of striking for immediate benefit or as part of a broader social struggle for socialism, and the two are often entangled. Workers can be conscious of themselves as a class at a more or less instinctive level—the common sense level of "them and us"—or in more politically aware terms. As well as class consciousness, Bourdieu argues that people's conditions of life and social situation can generate a more instinctive and embodied "class *unconsciousness*" in terms of a habitus or set of attitudes, dispositions, and behaviors (Bourdieu, 1977, p. 78). Such distinctions also carry through into schools; for example, instinctive and embodied attitudes to social difference deeply affect how teachers react to different children.

The complexity of class—the many aspects involved in the development of a society divided by class—has its counterpart in the tangled interrelationship between education and a class society. Both are deeply cultural, which is not in opposition to the economic but culture and economy interwoven with each other. Culture does not stand in opposition to or apart from economics, for various reasons:

- culture is itself generally material—tools, houses, pottery, TV shows, dancing;

- markets are themselves a social construct and exchange—employment and ownership can only take place if we share a basic understanding of the terms of such social relations (Skeggs, 2004, p. 28);

- cultural work and consumption now form a significant portion of the economy;

- capitalist production processes and relations are a central constituent of our way of life.

In a certain sense, culture does go all the way down. The word's origins lie in agricultural labor, the cultivation of the land (Williams, 1983[1976]), and culture is thoroughly material as well as spiritual when used in its modern anthropological sense of a way of life. A good working definition would be *matter with meaning* or *activity that signifies*, though it also extends to thoughts and beliefs. As Eagleton (2000) argues, "In Marxist parlance, it [culture] brings together both base and superstructure in a single word" (p. 1).

A Classless Society?

Though the myth that we live in a classless society is certainly not prevalent in educational sociology, the field is ideologically marked by a confusion about class. Sociology of education devotes enormous attention to the binary of *working* versus *middle* class, that is, manual versus clerical or intellectual workers, but rarely discusses directly the impact of capitalism. Indeed, it is remarkable how infrequently the relationship between capital and labor appears even when popular themes such as globalization, risk, or the knowledge society are discussed. Furthermore, it has also become unusual, in comparison with the 1960s through 1980s, for educators or educational theorists to mention class when discussing curriculum and pedagogy.

The illusion of classlessness, over several decades, was itself a consequence of a flawed understanding of class. Many theorists misread changing work patterns and the temporary reduction of severe poverty in developed countries as the end of capitalist relations per se. Lack of clarity about relations of production as the bedrock of class is evident throughout. The disintegration and disappearance of the working class were already under discussion in the 1950s. Indeed, it became a common explanation for the defeat of the Labour Party in the 1959 general election in Britain:

> The most popular formula was that the defeat was inevitable because Labour is identified with the proletariat and the proletariat is breaking up. This is extremely doubtful. It is true, of course, that modern houses, modern furniture, television sets and washing-machines and, in some cases, cars, are increasingly available to many wage-earners. But what is meant by calling this process "deproletarianization," as the *Economist* has done? (Williams, 1965, p. 353)

As Devine and Savage explain:

> Affluence in the late 1950s and 1960s, it was argued, undermined the unique way of life and the values and beliefs associated with it among the working class. . ... A new working class of privatized workers and their families saw themselves as middle class and distanced themselves from the trade unions and the Labour Party. Goldthorpe et al. (1968b, 1969), in the Affluent Worker series based on research in Luton, quickly refuted what became known as the "embourgeoisement thesis." Affluence was enjoyed but at the price of long hours of overtime doing dull repetitive work. (Devine & Savage, 2005, pp. 5–6)

Moreover, as Savage (2005) showed in his re-examination of this data, the Luton car workers may have been relaxed about manual-clerical worker differences but they were acutely conscious of the existence and power of a capitalist ruling class. In educational sociology we find Entwistle (1978) writing of a "shift in advanced industrial societies away from manual and towards non-manual, white-collar occupations at either a professional or quasi-professional level," a process that he unfortunately evaluated in terms of workers becoming middle class (p. 40).

Although the concentration of workers into factories created important conditions for class action, much confusion arises from the spurious equation of capitalist exploitation with heavy industry. As Eagleton (2011) reminds us:

> In Marx's own time, the largest group of wage laborers was not the industrial working class but domestic servants, most of whom were female. The working class, then, is not always male, brawny and handy with a sledgehammer. . ..
> Marx himself did not consider that you had to engage in manual labor to count as working class. In *Capital*, for example, he ranks commercial workers on the same level as industrial ones. (pp. 169–71)

The intensity of work and the oppressive nature of work discipline in call centers is arguably worse than on the car factory production line, because at least in the car plant you can fix your mind on something else.

Many economic and cultural changes have occurred in the transition from industrial to late or postmodern capitalism, but the essential nature of capitalist relations of production remain despite those who speak of the replacement of a class-divided industrial society by a classless *knowledge society* (e.g., Drucker, 1994, p. 64). Exploitation does not depend on the heaviness of the product or production process, nor is the argument diminished by the postmodern emphasis on *surfaces*. Capitalism extracted profits from workers who painted flowers on crockery in the nineteenth century, as it exploits those who produce images on computer screens in the twenty-first century. Capitalism is promiscuous in the ways it can extract profit—in the production of solid objects, surfaces, energy, or ideas.

This blurring of class in public discourse has inevitably affected attempts to understand educational disadvantage. For example, In British educational statistics eligibility for free school meals is used as a proxy for poverty and (even more confusing) for working class. This is misleading in various ways. First, many children below the poverty line do not have a statutory entitlement to free meals. Second, their parents may be low-paid white-collar workers rather than manual workers. Third, many manual workers are quite well paid. The equation of working class with either poverty or manual occupations is deeply flawed and increasingly archaic. Such confusion also makes it difficult to examine with any clarity the nature of interactions between different young people and their teachers, the extent to which class differences are reproduced by the education system or how the school curriculum might be made more relevant.

Bourdieu, Cultural Capital, and Class Reproduction

While many people see education as a way of overcoming working-class disadvantage, it is also widely agreed that class is reproduced by schools, though there is little consensus on how this occurs. One of the most influential theorists of class reproduction is Pierre Bourdieu, perhaps the most cited social theorist internationally in educational sociology. It is important to understand his ideas but also identify where they might be problematic.

Much of his work was an attempt to move beyond what he saw as the one-dimensional nature of Marxism's emphasis on the economic by looking at how it connects with other aspects of our lives including cultural and educational activity. He explained how power and advantage are exercised through various other kinds of assets in addition to economic ones; by analogy with capital in the economic sense, Bourdieu refers to other capitals such as cultural, social, linguistic, educational, and symbolic.

His concept of cultural capital has been particularly influential in explaining some of the ways in which the education system reproduces class structures and membership. Basically, the argument is that elites can convert the institutional and public recognition of their cultural activities into an economic advantage. Thus, to give a crude example, a pupil who is learning the cello might be regarded by teachers as more intelligent, placed in higher ability groups, and ultimately move on to better paid employment than his classmate who plays bass guitar.

Unfortunately Bourdieu sometimes appears to put the power of economic and cultural capitals in contemporary society on a par with each other. We see this at its most graphic in *Distinction* (1984a, p. 128), in diagrams in which the vertical axis represents differences in power and status (the highest ranking at the top) and the horizontal axis distinguishes between those with more economic capital and those who rely mainly on cultural capital. Bourdieu's explanation is that individuals owe their position within social space to an aggregate of economic and cultural capital; some members of the ruling class are there because of the wealth they deploy in the production process and others because of cultural assets, including education and qualifications. Bourdieu claims to locate occupational groups on the vertical axis by calculating the total of their capitals, though it is unclear what quantum of cultural capital might equate with, say, an economic capital of $1 million.

It is worth noting that Bourdieu is more concerned here with social status and cultural tastes than with class per se. In other words, his aim is to account for how people in particular occupations are seen by others and the relationship of these judgments to cultural preferences with economic power and position. There are various reasons why cultural or social capitals cannot simply be seen as on a par with economic capital:

1. Though capitalists might rely for their legitimacy on lawyers, musicians, professors, and newspaper editors, these cultural legitimators would not survive without the processes of material production and the power of the capitalist class.

2. The production and circulation of dominant ideologies operate within the broad constraints of capitalism, whereas the reverse does not hold true.

3. The owners of economic capital invariably buy education for their children to ensure that they also acquire cultural capital. Conversely, it is more difficult to acquire the highest level of educational qualifications, to enter the highest status professions, and so on without a certain amount of finance. Money is crucial in both cases.

4. Those located at the bottom of the social scale generally possess neither economic nor cultural capital; they don't divide into two fractions. (However, immigrants may arrive with cultural assets they are able to pass on to, and activate in, the next generation.)

5. Internationally renowned poets and pianists with very high levels of cultural capital have minimal power over the rest of the population and

certainly do not exploit them. The same can hardly be said of the top 100 chief executives.

Bourdieu's (1984a) division of the population into classes is, to say the least, dubious. He speaks broadly of three classes and each includes various fractions. His dominant or upper classes include secondary school teachers alongside industrial and commercial employers; his middle classes include primary teachers and technicians alongside craftsmen and small shopkeepers (p. 526). Within middle classes he includes a fraction that he inappropriately calls the "new petite bourgeoisie," an eclectic mix of "junior commercial executives, the medical and social services, secretaries, and the various cultural intermediaries" (p. 14); indeed one of his illustrations of the tastes and attitudes of this group is based on a nurse living on a shoestring budget with her daughter in a two-room flat.

The metaphor of multiple capitals beyond the economic has brought important insights into the complexities of how power is exercised, using capital to mean assets that bring returns in a kind of exchange, but we should beware of reading too close an equivalence between them. In some texts, Bourdieu (1984b) does assert that these other capitals are indeed subordinate to the economic:

> The economic field tends to impose its structure on other fields. (p. 230). . . .

> In reality, the social space is a multi-dimensional space, an open set of relatively autonomous fields, fields which are more or less strongly and directly subordinate, in their functioning and their transformation, to the field of economic production. (p. 245)

With these reservations, then, we can draw upon Bourdieu's extensive explorations of social power while avoiding defining *class* in terms of cultural assets. His concept of habitus, for example, focuses our attention on the ways in which social positions can lead to unconscious attitudes and behaviors that leave unjust social relationships unchallenged. This is clearly one of the ways in which the power structure of capitalism is maintained or reproduced and is pertinent to a discussion of educational aspirations:

> Closer to a class unconscious than to a "class consciousness" in the Marxist sense, the sense of the position one occupies in the social space (what Goffman calls the "sense of one's place") is the practical mastery of the social structure as a whole. . . . They incline agents to accept the social world as it is, to take it for granted, rather than to rebel against it . . . The sense of one's place, as the sense of what one can or cannot "allow oneself," implies a tacit acceptance of one's position, a sense of limits ("that's not meant for us"). (1984b, p. 235)

Bourdieu (1984b) also explains that such a conservative outcome is not inevitable: by bringing these relationships into the open and talking about them, people's "disquiet, anxiety, expectation, worry [become] objectified, visible, sayable, and even official"(p. 236). People see what they have in common and how they might rebel against the established order. This can involve challenging what had previously seemed obvious, for example, racist assumptions of white superiority: "The most marked objective differences may be hidden behind more immediately visible differences (such as, for example, those which separate ethnic groups)" (p. 237). Bourdieu's argument comes close to Gramsci's analysis of hegemony and how it can be contested. He speaks of a "symbolic struggle for the production of common sense or, more precisely, for the monopoly of legitimate naming as the official . . . imposition of the legitimate vision of the social world" (Bourdieu, 1948b, p. 239). An overemphasis on the unconscious nature of habitus can, however, lead to a new fatalism: "As many commentators have observed, his emphasis on the adaptation of the habitus to actors' circumstances exaggerates actors' compliance with their position" (Sayer, 2005, p. 23).

Modifying Bourdieu's notion of habitus so as to open up possibilities of liberation and resistance, Sayer (2005, pp. 22–51) insists that we can block or override the dispositions we have been socialized into, that our habitus can be modified, that tensions can arise through being pulled in different directions, that we have internal conversations, become conscious, listen to other people's arguments and ideas, consider the ethics of forms of action, feel our own pain and that of others, and so on. He points out that Bourdieu's later research is inconceivable if we believe that human beings are simply habitus conforming to habitat:

> It is evident from the interview transcripts presented in Bourdieu et al.'s *The Weight of the World* that some actors churn through their moral narratives in their internal conversations almost obsessively (Bourdieu et al., 1999). (Sayer, 2005, p. 29)

> Some of the younger interviewees . . . seem to have resisted their first habitat from the start. (p. 34)

Again, this question of inevitability or resistance is an important consideration when seeking to understand how young people (dis)engage with schooling or make educational choices.

What Is the Middle Class?

In the *Communist Manifesto*, Marx and Engels (1996 [1848]) argue that class structure would be simplified into a binary opposition between employers and wage laborers. Already in 1848, they predicted the disappearance of two large sections of the middle class, those who we now call *professionals* and the small-scale business people they called the petit bourgeoisie. As they express it rhetorically and in a sweeping prophetic style: "It [the bourgeoisie] has converted the physician, the lawyer, the priest, the poet, the man of science, into its paid wage-laborers" (p. 8). More prosaically:

The lower strata of the middle class—the small trades people, shopkeepers, and retired tradesmen generally, the handicraftsmen and peasants—all these sink gradually into the proletariat, partly because their diminutive capital does not suffice for the scale on which Modern Industry is carried on, and is swamped in the competition with the large capitalists, partly because their specialized skill is rendered worthless by new methods of production. (p. 13)

However, many sociologists and newspaper columnists suggested the reverse was happening as the living standards of manual workers improved in the 1950s and 1960s—workers were becoming "bourgeoisified." Subsequently the increasing proportion of white-collar and professional employees in the knowledge economy led to suggestions of the death of the working class and the arrival of a classless society. As the number of white-collar jobs and particularly managerial and professional ones increased, it was proposed, contrary to Marx's prediction, that the middle class was actually growing—perhaps everybody was becoming middle class apart from an underclass of no-hopers.

The differences in average school attainment between manual and nonmanual workers' children is an important issue, but we need to interrogate some of the assumptions of an educational sociology that is built upon a binary of working class versus middle class. The difficulties become clear as soon as one begins to ask how this fits with Marx's class model. Stephen Ball's (2003) book on education and the middle class manages to avoid definitions until the appendix, where he calls it a service class of *employees*. In other words, within Marx's model, any of these occupations belong to an expanded working class, albeit as different fractions whose interests may not always appear to coincide. Ball (2003) regards these occupations as more advantaged than other workers because they have "pension rights, increments, employment rights and career opportunities" and "some degree of professional autonomy," though acknowledging that both kinds of relative advantage are under threat (p. 181). His actual research informants all had some form of higher education and were homeowners, but this seems a tenuous basis on which to classify them objectively as a separate class. After all, many manual workers have to exercise a degree of autonomy at work; many private sector manual workers used to pay into company pension schemes until employers began to loot the funds; and home ownership is scarcely a middle-class preserve in the context of sub-prime mortgages and a lack of public housing.

Savage and colleagues (1992) speak in terms of three distinct middle classes: the petite bourgeoisie or small businessmen who hold property assets; managers; and professionals with cultural capital and operating in collectively organized occupations licensed by the state (see Power, Edwards, Whitty & Wigfall, 2003, p. 118). This composite divorces public sector professionals such as teachers or nurses from workers directly employed in privately owned industry or commerce, while suggesting they have a coherence of interest with managers and small businessmen.

A more fruitful way of understanding the position of public sector professionals is in terms of their role of maintaining and forming other workers as human capital. In Marxist terms, nurses are paid to keep labor power healthy, and teachers are employed to produce the next generation of workers. This is part of the process that increases the profit extracted from labor power, and it is reflected in the emphasis that neoliberal policy places on education as human resource production.

However, workers in health and education also care for the minds and bodies of their fellow human beings in ways that transcend capitalism's view of their role. For teachers, the power to shape a new generation of workers involves ethical dilemmas and demands, in class terms as well as those of a shared humanity. It inevitably raises questions of how education can be something more and other than the production of labor power or human resources. This contradiction is at the heart of the long historical struggle for education reform.

Of course, managers and supervisors, who are paid employees too, also have a role of intensifying the productivity and profitability of others' labor through a combination of organizational, motivational, and (in a limited sense) developmental activity. Moreover, many of those carrying the title of manager are nowadays themselves quite low paid and with limited autonomy. However, the power many of them have over other workers' employment, as a proxy for the owners, makes it almost impossible for them to become part of a working class in struggle; nor is there the same kind of tension in their role as for medical and education workers. At the same time, it is inconceivable that they, by themselves, could form a separate middle class with any kind of independent orientation or political autonomy.

There are two errors in the considerable emphasis that recent educational sociology has placed on educational ambition as a middle-class way of securing advantage over working-class children: first, it overlooks the aspirations of many manual worker parents to ensure their children enjoy a better life; second, the anxieties of middle-class parents can also be interpreted more defensively in terms of a "fear of falling" (Ehrenreich, 1989) in an increasingly precarious employment market. This perspective is articulated by Ball (2006), where insecurity rather than a search for advantage explains intense anxieties about school choice, the uncertainty of the knowledge available even to those with greater cultural and social capital, and a clinging to traditionalist curricula and disciplinary regimes they believe to be required for academic success. Ball (2006), citing Beck-Gernsheim(1996, p. 143), relates this to the notion of a risk society: "The extent of parents' ethical and social responsibility today . . . is historically unprecedented . . . The contemporary family is under a pressure to educate" (p. 272). But capitalism and the ruling capitalist class are significantly absent from this argument, or at best remain implicit. This is ironic given that the same sociologists who assume a working–middle-class binary are often highly critical of neoliberal accountability regimes and education markets. The capitalist ruling class is an unacknowledged absence in both bodies of work.

All of this is operating, of course, in the context of technological change, leading to a polarization between higher-skilled knowledge economy work and low-waged, low-skilled work of a nonindustrial kind; both have grown massively. Brown (2006), however, points out that the increase in knowledge economy jobs has not kept pace with increasing numbers of well-qualified young people, which creates further pressure to acquire advanced qualifications. Though graduates earn more than nongraduates, Brown (p. 388) argues that this is largely due to the decline in the earning power of non-graduates.

Despite the better chance of middle-class children attaining higher qualifications, it is important to recognize that they also suffer as education becomes more pressured, instrumental, and alienating. The shift to high-stakes accountability systems is not in their interests but designed to serve economic interests at the top. Indeed, increasing regulation and standardization of school learning in many developed countries (Au, 2009; Taubman, 2009) coincide with the diminishing autonomy of professionals in the workplace (an autonomy which is supposedly characteristic of middle-class employment):

> The power shift in the direction of knowledge workers has been greatly exaggerated. Most 'knowledge' workers are only able to capitalize on their knowledge within employment. . . . While employees are free to change employers, they are not free from the need to make a living in a wage economy. (Brown, 2006, p. 388)

This does not diminish the importance of research by Ball, Reay, Power, Whitty, and others in studying how parents in professional occupations are better able to ensure their children's educational success through deploying social and cultural capital, for example, in the process of choosing secondary schools. It does, however, place a question mark over presenting them as a separate class engaged in a struggle against a working class of manual and routine white-collar workers. This is to misunderstand the fundamentals of wealth and power. By regarding what these sociologists call the middle class or middle classes as *fractions* of a greater Working Class, in a Marxist sense, we recognize that differences of behavior or attitude exist (just as they sometimes emerge between skilled and unskilled workers) but can be overcome, and that it would be in the best interests of each group to act together in solidarity.

Raymond Williams (1965) had already reached a similar conclusion in the early 1960s:

The ordinary salary-earner, thinking of himself as middle class because of the differences between himself and the wage-earners already noted, fails to notice this real class beyond him, by whom he is factually and continually exploited. . . . We can see the supposed new phenomenon of classlessness as simply a failure of consciousness . . . there can be [no real classlessness] until social capital is socially owned.

Is the working class becoming middle class, as its conditions improve? It could as reasonably be said that most of the middle class have become working class, in the sense that they depend on selling their labor and are characteristically unpropertied in any important sense. (Williams, 1965, pp. 351–52)

The practice of middle class-ness increasingly appears as a cultural project and discursive construction that lacks a viable economic foundation; as soon as we ask how particular groups of employees relate to capitalism, we begin to see the recent strikes against public service cuts and the loss of pension rights by civil servants and teachers not as the result of middle-class selfishness but as the valid resistance of a section of an extended working class (;proletariat,' in Marx's words).

This is not to suggest that all white-collar professionals form part of the working class; there clearly do exist newspaper editors who go horse riding with prime ministers; doctors who acquire ownership of highly profitable old people's homes; and high-ranking civil servants who float through revolving doors to become executives and consultants in private-sector companies with lucrative government contracts. But these elite individuals, however powerful and well connected, scarcely constitute a class with interests separate from capitalists. At most, even when merged with the managerial group, they probably constitute less than a tenth of the working-age population; though they do appear to have an influence on the political establishment that is greater than their size, they have little scope to strike out in an independent direction from the capitalist class. This elite group certainly does not amount to the third of the population that Stephen Ball (2003, p. 5) groups together as middle class. It is also completely unhelpful when academic researchers fail to make it clear whether the interviewees they quote are top civil servants or low-paid staff in the local benefits office.

Underclass: The Politics of Class Contempt

While identification of relatively advantaged workers as a separate middle class is unhelpful, labeling the most vulnerable section of the working class as an 'underclass' is intensely destructive. There is a particular venom in the way those who have been pauperized by deindustrialization and austerity politics are blamed for their own suffering. Families struggling to survive in places where no work is to be had are blamed for a lack of aspiration. Though poverty clearly does have cultural manifestations, it only suits the rich to turn the relationship upside down and see culture as cause rather than effect.

This has serious implications for educators and sociologists who struggle to explain the poor educational outcomes of the majority of young people growing up in poverty, particularly given the tendency for the attainment gap to grow even larger during their teenage years.

In 1989, after years of Thatcher, the *Sunday Times* invited Charles Murray, proponent of the *Underclass* concept in the United States, to visit two of Britain's poorest council estates for half a day each. Predictably, he pointed to "drugs, crime, illegitimacy, drop out from the job market, drop out from school, casual violence" (Murray, 1996, p. 25) as the causes of poverty. This found its way into Blairite discourse in more hybrid forms (Levitas, 2005) before a new crescendo during David Cameron's bid for power. Owen Jones' (2011) book *Chavs: The Demonization of the Working Class* describes dramatically and with carefully referenced evidence how an ideological class war accompanied the economic one:

> With the help of Tory briefings, newspapers left their readers in no doubt as to what Cameron was getting at. "David Cameron tells the fat and the poor: take responsibility," as the *Times* put it. (p. 74)

Cameron became prime minister accompanied by a chorus of media denigration against "benefit scroungers," unmarried mothers, young men who were "making lifestyle decisions" not to work. Naturally the riots of 2011 in England were blamed on bad parenting, absent fathers, criminality, idleness, immorality, greed and gang culture:

> The chav caricature is set to be at the heart of British politics in the years ahead. After the 2010 general election, a Conservative-led government dominated by millionaires took office with an aggressive programme of cuts, unparalleled since the early 1920s. The global economic crisis that began in 2007 may have been triggered by the greed and incompetence of a wealthy banking elite, yet it was working-class people who were—and are—expected to pay the price. But any attempt to shred the welfare state is fraught with political difficulties, and so the government swiftly resorted to blaming its users. (Jones, 2011, p. 11)

This is part of a wider and complex process whereby

> class is being increasingly defined as a moral cultural property of the person, related to their attitudes and practices (not named and known directly as class) . . . the shift from class as an economic categorization to one based on cultural practices. (Skeggs, 2005, p. 50)

> The working class are positioned as stuck, with nothing to offer culturally except as an indication of the difference between the civilized and the uncivilized. Their difference is marked through cultural-moral value, through scrounging, being yobs and breeding too much. (p. 57)

Of course the ideological displacement of economic oppression by moral and cultural explanations isn't new. Blaming poverty on fecklessness and promiscuity has been a constant trope in explanations of class differentiation and social suffering since Victorian times. It came as no surprise, therefore, to hear Prime Minister David Cameron insisting that the riots of August 2011 were caused by moral breakdown rather than a sense of hopelessness felt by many young people about their future. Cameron, heading a government packed with millionaires, saw fit to denounce the rioters' greed and their expectation of reward without effort. (Presumably he didn't regard inherited wealth as reward without effort!)

Robert MacDonald's (1997) research on the experience of young people in Teesside, previously a thriving center of shipbuilding and steel and chemical industries, shows how much they still want reliable work and a stable family life. Those left behind by deindustrialization cannot be written off as the "irresponsible, welfare-draining" single mothers and "feckless" young men (p. 19) who epitomize Murray's culture of poverty.

Even when a more charitable view is taken that avoids blaming poverty on its victims, a failure to locate this group within the working class remains problematic: They are inevitably represented as incompetent and defective, inviting a response of charitable paternalism at best. This 'charitable' stance comes fundamentally from a failure to locate poverty within the economics of capitalism. As MacDonald (1997, p. 195) argues, they are not a separate underclass but workers struggling through the shifting sands of unreliable low-paid work alternating with spells of unemployment.

Having an economically based understanding of poverty is, we argue, essential if teachers are to avoid either stigmatizing disadvantaged students or patronizing them.

Recognition and Redistribution

Some interesting research has developed in recent years around notions of respect, recognition, and identification in addition to the above mentioned studies of stigmatization. This is now beginning to be applied to educational theory. A central figure has been Nancy Fraser (2000) examining the relationship between redistribution of resources (economic) and recognition, that is, treating people with respect (cultural). In other areas of social justice work, such as race equality and the struggle against homophobia, recognition may be the most important issue, but not so with class. Fraser states:

> This move [in social theory] from redistribution to recognition is occurring despite—or because of—an acceleration of economic globalization, at a time when an aggressively expanding capitalism is radically exacerbating economic inequality. In this context, questions of recognition are serving less to supplement, complicate and enrich redistributive struggles than to marginalize, eclipse and displace them. (p. 108)

At the same time, Fraser does not ignore recognition and its role within the struggle for working-class self-emancipation:

> As a result of repeated encounters with the stigmatizing gaze of a culturally dominant other, the members of disesteemed groups internalize negative self-images and are prevented from developing a healthy cultural identity of their own. (p. 109)

This explanation is clearly of fundamental importance to educators. Just as adult workers need a positive sense of themselves in struggle—hence the tradition of trade union banners, reports of victories won, and so on—so do their children need to know they are not only cared for but also respected. Fraser also suggests a further meaning of recognition in terms of social status and the ability to participate on a par with others, so the struggle for recognition includes overcoming a sense of inferiority and subordination and developing the confidence to participate in a democratically run school.

Beverley Skeggs (1997) has added substantially to our understanding of the cultural workings of class through her detailed study of working-class women training for care work in the aftermath of Thatcherism. She describes their struggle to dis-identify as workers and claim membership of the 'middle class'. Skeggs explains this in terms of a reaction against the traditional denigration of working-class women unless they could prove themselves as respectable. Victorian hypocrisy, unable to legitimize denigrating them simply for being working class, managed to reframe the issue as one of morality:

> The reports of the great Parliamentary commission, which in the 1830s and 40s investigated working conditions in the factories and mines, were saturated with an obsessive concern with the sexuality of the working class, the social order, displacing in the end an acute social crisis from the area of exploitation and class conflict where it could not be coped with, into the framework of a more amenable and discussible area of "morality" (Weeks, 1981, pp. 19–20, quoted in Skeggs, 1997, p. 43).

Until reading this, I (TW) had always wondered why my grandma, after spending all day Monday washing and drying the family's clothes by hand and ironing everything from sheets to hankies, insisted on mopping her doorstep and coloring it with sandstone before putting her feet up.

Skeggs's (1997) interviews with trainee care workers show clearly how they associate working class-ness with being "rough," "poor," "on the dole," "a fag in their mouths," "common as muck," and "battering their kids" (p. 75). They are desperate to show, by assuming the identity of responsible care givers, that they do not fit this stereotype:

> In the women's claims for a caring/respectable/responsible personality class was rarely directly figured but was constantly present. . . . It is a study of doubt, insecurity and unease: the emotional politics of class. (pp. 74–75)

These young women engage in a desperate struggle to adopt what they feel is a middle-class aesthetic, constantly fearful of getting it wrong:

> Mary: I do get dressed up, I get dressed up. I call it getting tarted up but I'm not tarty. Karen will ring up and say "are you getting tarted up tonight?" I'm aware that I can't wear certain things that are too tarty say mini-skirts, they're tarty . . . I wear classy clothes. I don't want to sound snobby but I like classical dresses, things that don't go out of fashion. (p. 84)

Skeggs spots the signs of embarrassment and anxiety, the desire for approval, as her interviewees are afraid of being caught out in their adoption of middle-class tastes: "When a visitor enters the house they see their most intimate environments through the eyes of the other and they apologize. They continually doubt their own judgments." (p. 90)

This has profound implications for teachers. The time is long past when the working class was more visible—when workers walked to work together, when the whole town could afford football on Saturdays, when trade union branches and working men's clubs and women's groups at the local church provided a visible basis for solidarity and the assertion of a collective identity. This suggests that breaking the silence, within schools, about class, poverty, and the impact of deindustrialization is an important part of the struggle to work on young people's identity, aspirations, and hope for a future. The alternative is that many hardpressed young people will seek more dangerous and destructive sources of self-esteem through school disruption, teenage gangs, racism, and macho or *raunch* sexualities.

The Consequences for Educational Theory

As we argued above, the binary between 'working class' and 'middle class' is endemic in educational sociology. This is not to suggest that the distinction is meaningless but to insist on locating differences between manual and white-collar or professional workers within a larger frame that recognizes they are different kinds of workers living and working in a social configuration determined by the interests of capitalism. Use of this larger frame also prevents us from confusing teachers and university lecturers with commercial executives and industrial managers, even though some of them might occasionally attend the same dinner parties.

The failure to hold on to this wider structural dynamic has serious consequences for educational theory, influenced by a more general Weberian sociology. Bisseret (1979) argues, for example, that Bernstein, despite frequent allusions to power relations, "thinks of his society as a diversified, stratified reality without class conflicts" and sees social relations predominantly in terms of intersubjective relations (pp. 104–5).

We referred earlier to Bourdieu's (1984a) messy classification in *Distinction*, showing a spurious tripartite division in which those with a degree of ownership and control of production merge with various grades of employee. In general, however, while Bourdieu refrains from explicit classification, he gives the impression of a world divided between an elite cultural milieu (professionals educated at the *hautes écoles*, France's equivalent of Oxbridge or the Ivy League) and a severely marginalized precariat of less skilled and unemployed workers, including many migrants. There is little mention of skilled and organized manual workers or the majority of nonmanual employees.

Bernstein (1972) bases his work on language deficit (see chapter 5) on a distinction between working class and middle class, though he further defines the former as semi-skilled and unskilled manual workers. Rosen's (1972) critique points to the gaps and distortions in this model: first, Bernstein ignores the large body of skilled manual workers and communities that have a long history of class struggle; second, Bernstein's exemplars of the middle class are actually a small group of high culture professionals. They are, as Rosen puts it, "Hampstead man, not Orpington man," (p. 11), that is, those who later came to be known as London's "chattering classes" rather than the bulk of white-collar suburbia.

This problem seems to affect even the brightest lights in the field of sociology of education. Discussions of school choice within a marketized public school system include blanket references to the 'middle class' as having plentiful social and cultural capital; the desire to secure the best possible education for your offspring is seen as a middle-class attribute, suggesting that working-class parents are somehow indifferent. A frequent suggestion is that these middle-class parents should feel guilty. The ruthless ambitions of some are generalized into a characteristic of all. Such analyses can deflect attention from the truly powerful class who largely educate their own children outside the state system in expensive fee-paying schools.

Other texts describe the very small number of parents who can afford to buy a private education for their children (around 7 percent in England, 4 percent in Scotland) as the middle class (Riddell, 2010); similarly, the even smaller proportion of parents in China who reject provincial universities for prestigious institutions in Peking, Shanghai or overseas are labeled "the middle class" without further qualification (Ciupak & Stich, 2012).

Why Class Matters

In the social and cultural workings of class, we find the complex and messy interweaving of class identification, dis-identification, and misidentification; consciousness and unconsciousness; habitus and reflection; lived experience on a day-to-day basis and through crises; collusion and resistance; struggles for short- and long-term goals; ethics and aesthetics; ideology and theory; structure and reproduction. The workings of class are also inextricably bound up with the complexities of race, linguistic and religious diversity, gender, and sexuality. To argue that these processes are thoroughly cultural is not to deny the centrality of economy and class relations. These are deeply pedagogical processes in our social activity and development.

Within the field of formal education, questions of class reproduction are of crucial importance; there is a very strong correlation between poverty and poor qualifications, but also there is a significant relationship between qualification levels and whether your parents are manual or white-collar workers. It is not the attainment gap per se that matters but the barriers experienced and the impact on future lives. Underachievement is about large numbers of young people being denied the knowledge and intellectual capacity they need to live well and to understand, participate in, and change their world.

School culture—ethos as well as curriculum—is also an important issue for teachers concerned about social justice, and it needs to be related to questions of class in its Marxist sense. The insistence by government-approved experts over the past twenty years on tight discipline as a way of turning around underachieving urban schools overlooks how this interconnects with the pervasive denigration and stigmatization that these families and young people already suffer. The many case studies in *The Power to Learn* (Wrigley 2000), a study of thriving and successful inner-city schools, show that respect rather than discipline is the keyword characterizing the positive relationships being fostered in these exemplary schools.

As Charlesworth (2000) and others show, the experience of long-term unemployment and insecure work in deindustrialized areas generates a psychological outlook of (1) shame, as people internalize their situation and (2) futility, as they realize that plans simply do not reach fruition and further training does not bring them work. It is important to understand how these emotions are reinforced by traditionalist patterns of schooling. First, children from poorer families are likely to be placed in low ability groups and consigned to tedious and unchallenging tasks. Second, alienated forms of learning (see Wrigley, 2006), whereby students simply follow instructions to produce something of no apparent benefit to anyone, are particularly unmotivating for young people growing up in a climate of hopelessness. This is a neglected aspect of education's reproduction of class relations.

The struggle for dignity and respect studied by cultural sociologists such as Beverley Skeggs is highly pertinent to the reproduction of class relationships by the school system. The regular and exhausting conflicts in schools in disadvantaged areas are saturated with young people's sense that they are disrespected and stigmatized. Students quickly come to understand themselves as surplus in schools where exclusions are common; this mirrors a society blighted by monstrous levels of youth unemployment. Sennett and Cobb (1977), in their book *The Hidden In-*

juries of Class, point to the long-term damage brought about by the ways in which schooling draws on ideologies of fixed (in)ability and (un)intelligence. We need to look at the combination and reciprocity of economics (being surplus to requirement) and culture (feeling stigmatized) in order to understand the relative attractions of rioting, teenage gangs, fascists, early motherhood, or joining the army as alternative sources of self-esteem. This requires an educational sociology that is underpinned by a Marxist class analysis rooted in ownership and exploitation, rather than a fixation on the lifestyle-based binary of 'working' versus 'middle' and the devastating mythology of an 'underclass'.

For those concerned with social justice in the field of education, class is a central issue, though for many years neglected in comparison to race and gender. Even within the limited and generally conservative horizons of School Effectiveness researchers, and within the regulatory systems linked to international testing, poverty has now become a major concern. However, it needs to be adequately located within a framework of capital and labor. To reiterate the argument at the beginning of this chapter, poverty isn't accidental misfortune or degrees of disadvantage, it is the product of a system that employs people only so long as they produce profit. Despite the possibilities of freedom from economic pressures generated by the amazing advances of science and technology within a single generation, an economic system driven by the need to maximize profit produces poverty by cutting wages and reducing the size of the workforce. The liberation of mind and body that globalization could entail degenerates into the destructive forces of multinationals shopping around the globe for cheaper workers and the global casino capitalism of the financial markets.

But class and capitalism also impact curriculum, teaching, and learning. An increasingly instrumental mode of education, in terms of its supply of human resources to the economy and the brutal competition in a spurious meritocracy, damages a very wide section of society. As Freire (1972) constantly argued, education is either for liberation or for domestication. This applies, albeit in ways that may be experienced differently, to the children of white-collar and professional employees as well as manual workers and the chronically unemployed. The reproduction of class by the school system goes beyond the distribution of qualifications and involves the acquisition and exercise of voice and agency. Socially committed educators must attend to culture as well as economics, because their key interest is to transform society, not just analyze how it is divided.

These questions will be discussed at greater length in the next chapter, which concerns poverty, and later in the book in a more detailed scrutiny of the explanations that have been developed for links between class, poverty, and education.

CHAPTER TWO

Understanding Poverty in the Twenty-first Century

Not economically marginal but exploited, not socially marginal but rejected, not culturally marginal but stigmatized, and not politically marginal but manipulated and repressed.
—Janice Perlman, 1974, p. 195

Poverty is another misunderstood phenomenon, and in this chapter we challenge some misleading ideas. Officially, of course, there is a tendency to deny
its existence, to imagine it is contained within isolated geographic pockets, or to
explain it in terms of poor lifestyle choices, familial defects, and indolence. We
want to puncture these myths by insisting not only on the reality of material deprivation but rather that its occurrence is systematic not accidental. Moreover, it
is generally accompanied by disrespect, humiliation, and exclusionary discrimination. These serve as a diversion to make the underlying causes of poverty invisible,
by deflecting responsibility onto the alleged deficits of individuals, families, and
communities.

What is missing from these dominant and demonizing representations of
poverty is any sense that the people who are experiencing it might perhaps have
some ideas about what the experience actually means. Even worse, people who
find themselves in poverty are portrayed as incompetent failures in the market-
place: They have simply not been able to work out how to present themselves in
a marketable way.

We argue vehemently that there are structural causes for poverty in the fundamental inequalities of exploitation and dispossession, exacerbated by the seismic

shifts of globalization and neoliberalism. Large sections of the population, even in many affluent countries, are treated as collateral damage or cheap and dispensable fodder for the economy (see Chadderton & Colley, 2012, on disposable youth).

The reason this kind of analysis is so important for us is that children and young people are particularly exposed, through the economics of family life, the neighborhoods they are consigned to, and at their point of attempted entry into the labor market. Untold damage is wreaked educationally in all kinds of ways, not the least of which is "learning [how] to be poor" (Ridge, 2002, p. 140). These young people are made to feel complicit in their own misfortune for having limited aspirations. These are crucial issues that have to be confronted if we are to understand how poverty does its ugly work of educational disfigurement.

The Changing Face of Poverty

In the 1960s and 1970s it was possible to believe that poverty was something that belonged to distant times and places. In either case, it was seen as a residual or receding problem. So it was assumed that African countries were undeveloped, that is, they had not yet become modern like ourselves. Most people understood that there had been dire poverty in Britain during the Industrial Revolution, but, apart from a short come-back in the 1930s Depression, they believed it had almost disappeared as a result of industrial modernization and the Welfare State. Anybody still complaining of poverty could only have themselves to blame: they should get off their backsides and look for a job and stop having kids or come off the booze.

Few can still believe this in the early twenty-first century. Despite the dramatic advances in productivity associated with computer technologies, and a boom time for the mega-rich, child poverty statistics are scandalously high. Statistics for the UK show the extent of child poverty more than doubled during the 1980s, fell only slightly around the turn of the century, and will doubtless rise again in the Age of Austerity following the financial crash (Child Poverty Action Group, 2011).

Apologists for the rich and powerful are once more arguing that paying taxes has a disincentive effect on the rich. They argue that the poor must suffer their fair share of cuts, however close they are to disaster. Even now, on the surface, the visible signs of poverty are not as clear as in the 1930s. My 96-year-old aunt (TW) tells me about walking to school along the bank of the canal and regularly seeing bodies of unemployed men who had drowned themselves. She hopes those times will not return but cannot see the same visible signs of poverty, and she has read newspaper stories about benefit cheats who simply do not want work. It is not just the elderly who become confused, so this chapter aims to present an account and explanation of the causes and experiences of poverty and its impact on young lives.

Defining Poverty

Reformers campaigning to alleviate poverty in the nineteenth century relied on proofs of absolute need; the research of Booth and Rowntree in Britain used the cost of basic foodstuffs to convince the public that many of those in poverty could not conceivably meet their basic physical needs and that "the life-style of the poor was at least in part caused by low income and not by improvidence," as was widely believed (Veit-Wilson, 1986, p. 69). For example, in 1899, Rowntree's hypothetical diet, which he posited to show the impossibility of living below a certain income, consisted of bread and porridge for breakfast, potatoes with milk or vegetable broth for dinner, and bread and margarine for supper. This is not because Rowntree was only concerned with physical survival since he also spoke of secondary poverty. His response to the question "Why do poor people spend their inadequate incomes on social recreational activities instead of food?" showed an understanding that basic needs are social, not just physical:

> The explanation is that working people are just as human as those with more money. They cannot live on a "fodder basis." They crave for relaxation and recreation just as the rest of us do. But . . . they can only get these things by going short of something which is essential to physical fitness, and so they go short. (cited in Veit-Wilson, 1986, p. 85)

Primary poverty has not disappeared. A major study by the UK government's Poverty and Social Exclusion unit highlighted problems with heating homes and keeping them free from damp, replacing key electrical goods, buying essential clothing, and mothers doing without meals to feed their children.

It was Peter Townsend's research (1979) that led researchers to strengthen their focus on the inability to meet socially recognized needs and participate in society:

> Individuals, families and groups in the population can be said to be in poverty when they lack the resources to obtain the types of diet, participate in the activities and have the living conditions and amenities which are customary, or are at least widely encouraged or approved, in the societies to which they belong. Their resources are so seriously below those commanded by the average individual or family that they are, in effect, excluded from ordinary living patterns and activities. (p. 31)

Because of the impossibility of making unambiguous judgments about what is customary at particular points in time, criteria were established based on receiving less than 50 percent of average (mean) income, after adjusting for family size and sometimes housing costs. This recognizes that items such as televisions and refrigerators are now standard, and since most young people today wear trainers, it is no use basing poverty measures on the cost of a pair of clogs. Even food is a cultural and not just a physiological issue: people consume "food not nutrients" (Dowler & Leather, 2000, p. 208). Dowler and Leather continue: "Food is an expression of who a person is, what they are worth, and of their ability to provide for basic needs" (p. 200). Indeed, even Adam Smith (2005 [1776]) recognized this in the late eighteenth century:

> By necessaries, I understand not only the commodities which are indispensably necessary for the support of life but whatever the custom of the country renders it indecent for creditable people, even of the lowest order, to be without. A linen shirt, for example, is strictly speaking not a necessity of life . . . But in the present time . . . a creditable day laborer would be ashamed to appear in public without a linen shirt. (p. 691)

Poverty is a material issue but with nonmaterial effects. Increasingly, the case is made by researchers that we need to listen to what people in poverty themselves think are the best measurable indicators (Lister, 2004, p. 5). Living in poverty frequently involves disrespect and humiliation, an assault on human dignity, or a loss of self-esteem (Lister, 2004, p. 7). Amartya Sen's repeated arguments in terms of capabilities and participation—for example, the lack of opportunities to participate, make choices, and achieve well-being—have had substantial influence on United Nations policy (see Lister, pp. 15–20). However, Ruth Lister also warns about the dangers of losing track of material poverty through extended definitions that could apply to other forms of social discrimination or disadvantage; words such as *opportunities* and *capabilities* can allow governments to evade responsible for dealing with poverty (pp. 19–20).

It is also important to recognize that earnings in themselves are not the only material factor in poverty. Townsend (1979) names other types of resource that can affect material prosperity or deprivation: capital assets; welfare benefits provided by employers; the value of public services; and private income in kind (e.g., homegrown vegetables). What has been called the social wage, such as the quality of hospitals and schools or subsidized public housing, clearly makes a big difference.

The Experience of Poverty

Poverty is experienced differently according to the culture we live in, an experience exacerbated when the dominant culture places so much emphasis on buying and owning things. When people are defined by their appearance, wearing the wrong things becomes a source of shame—a disgrace acutely felt by adolescents. As Zygmunt Bauman expresses it, "The poor are re-cast as 'flawed consumers'" (1998, p. 2). He further explains, "The poor of a consumer society are socially defined, and self-defined, first and foremost as blemished, defective, faulty and deficient—in other words, inadequate—consumers" (p. 38). Living in poverty is also immensely stressful, which again affects the well-being and care of children:

A synthesis of thirty such studies by Elaine Kempson (1996) reveals that "life on a low income . . . is a stressful and debilitating experience" especially for those on social assistance who "face a struggle against encroaching debt and social isolation where even the most resilient and resourceful are hard pressed to survive" (Barclay, 1996, p. ix). Generally, the picture painted by qualitative studies is one of: constant restrictions; doing without; running out of money at the end of the week; limited choice; no room for spontaneity; damaged family relationships (Cohen et al., 1992; Kempson et al., 1994). (Lister, 2004, p. 54)

Conditions become even more critical when families who have got into debt are threatened by the debt collector's thugs.

The struggle against poverty can also eat away your time. A lack of transport to work, having nowhere to dry your clothes, working strange hours or juggling two or more part-time jobs, even shifting money between credit card and bank accounts to avoid excess charges, are a waste of time—valuable time that could be spent with children and friends. As Polly Toynbee (2003) discovered, searching for scarce employment is dreadfully time consuming:

As time ticked by the staff disappeared for lunch. By 2pm my name still hadn't been called . . . I sat there thinking how low value permeates everything about the lives of the poor. I had queued in the post office to pay the rent, trekked to the only shop that recharges the electric meter and queued again. Everywhere I was kept waiting and yet my time was precious because, like all the people at the agencies, I needed to get a job quickly. But poor people's time is regarded as valueless. (p. 34)

Paradoxically, when you get work (because it is precarious, especially if it is not unionized), you may find yourself harassed about your use of time despite being paid a pittance. Call center workers are pressurized by flashing messages reminding them that they are exceeding the norm of 65 seconds per call but quickly reprimanded if they do not deal sensitively with clients' difficulties. They may feel guilty that they have not resolved the caller's problems. Caregivers visiting old people and nurses in hospital often find their employers' expectations conflict with the duty of care.

Differences—Race, Gender, Disability

Poverty's effects compound with divisions of gender, race, and physical ability, as well as age. Despite equal opportunities legislation, women's pay is often markedly lower, and women are still normally the ones struggling with feeding the family. The tensions of life in poverty can also lead to domestic violence. Single-parent families are generally single-*mother*, and a high proportion of these live in poverty.

Ethnic minorities are disproportionately affected by poverty. In the UK, for example, three out of five Pakistanis and Bangladeshis have incomes in the bottom quintile (Department for Work and Pensions, 2012). Initially this might be attributed to inadequate English or educational qualifications or low skills levels among first-generation immigrants, but in the second and third generation, racism and discrimination in seeking work are clearly important factors (Craig, 2002). Minority groups are often driven to stay in crowded districts of older housing because of discrimination when applying for accommodation in public housing as well as a fear of isolation and harassment.

There is a two-way link between disability and poverty. Poorer people face a higher risk of becoming disabled, and conversely disability carries a high risk of poverty (Burchardt, 2003). Disability also involves higher costs, beyond the amount compensated for by disability benefits, and disabled people are more likely not to find work or tolerable wages (Burchardt, 2000). This affects not only the individual but also family members: caring often restricts opportunities to take up paid work, and children may have to care for siblings and disabled parents. For various groups, the experience of poverty also compounds with related manifestations of disadvantage. For example, Black and other ethnic minority people suffer worse health; young Black or Muslim men in the UK are many times more likely than whites to be in prison (Howarth, Kenway, Palmer & Morelli, 1999, p. 48).

However, it is important to understand that ethnicity, gender, and disability are not the root causes. Applicants for jobs can be rejected for being too old or too young. You can be turned down for not having the experience, so you never get the chance to gain the experience. Some employers eliminate applicants by postal code because of the stigma attached to living in poor neighborhoods. People who, for whatever reason, have limited school qualifications are not shortlisted for jobs they could do perfectly well; the formal qualifications become an arbitrary gatekeeper unrelated to the skills required for the work. Many young graduates are employed in low-paid irregular work, for example in call centers. Highly skilled manual workers with years of experience in mining, shipbuilding, steelmaking, car manufacture, and other heavy industries have ended up in long-term unemployment or poorly paid service work when their workplaces were closed down or relocated. At the heart of the problem is not the characteristic of the worker, but an economic and political system that fails to utilize people's skills and where the few make vast fortunes from the low pay of the many.

The Geography of Poverty

The past thirty years or so have seen an increased territorial differentiation and separation, though it is dangerous to exaggerate this based on American examples such as portrayed so convincingly in the television series *The Wire* (2002–2008). Loic Wacquant's (2008) comparative studies of Chicago ghettos and Parisian banlieues in *Urban Outcasts* demonstrate serious flaws in equating developments in Europe with North America. The distinction between poor and normal places is not new: poverty is associated with 'deviant' places, contrasted with the 'normal' unproblematic places from which this gaze is directed. (Gough, Eisenschitz & McCulloch, 2006, p. 28).

The stigmatization of poor neighborhoods impacts on entire populations, leading to avoidance of particular housing estates. Parents avoid placing their children in schools associated with the wrong neighborhoods. Areas deemed poor or deviant are often subjected to oppressive policing. However, the situation is also more complex than the simple binary this popular imaginary suggests. Spatial contrasts change as a result of flows of capital and labor, within countries and internationally: "As capital moves, its new absences and fresh presences change places, create new ones, and produce new spatial patterns of inclusion and exclusion" (Gough et al., 2006, p. 28). Earlier attempts to manage capital flows—for example, by moving industries in national ownership into areas of low employment—have been abandoned due to the fatalistic neoliberal belief that the global flows of capital are beyond control.

Other policy efforts are devoted to managing concentrations of poverty, for example by dispersing the poor, which is often also an aspect of neighborhood regeneration projects. Some dispersal efforts have arguably made life worse for the inhabitants, such as the demolition of central Glasgow slums and the removal of populations to the outskirts into high-rise flats with minimal facilities. Such eviction is not new: "The worst 'rookeries' of nineteenth-century London were forcibly cleared and demolished on social-political grounds" (Gough et al., 2006, p. 41).The reemergence of poverty and unemployment in areas which had been renewed (Gough et al.) indicates that geographical division is more a symptom than a cause of economic injustice. As these authors conclude: "Our view, then, is that the conception of poverty needs to focus on oppressive and exploitative social relations." (p. 49) Though concentrations of poverty and deprivation exist, and generalized stress and low self-esteem may also limit social ties (Madanipour, 1998, p. 78), "there is no evidence to suggest that there are 'underclass areas' where social interaction is breaking down (Richardson & Mumford, 2002; Shaw et al., 1999, p. 206)" (Gough et al., 2006, p. 56). Contrary to those such as Putnam (1993), who see the problem as a lack of social capital in poorer neighborhoods:

> The poor generally have strong community ties, reciprocity and social organization, and are closely connected to their own locality, however poor it may be (Carrell and Evans, 1999: Johnston et al., 2000). Indeed, these networks are a key part of coping with poverty. (Gough et al., 2006, p. 56)

Defeats and Demoralization

Poverty does not affect only human interactions, esteem, and self-esteem in the present, it also affects how people see the future. Though not everybody reacts to experiences in the same way, there is an inevitable tendency for defeat and disadvantage to lead to demoralization and sometimes defeatism. People become convinced, often with good reason, that they have few prospects for the future—their own and their children's:

Every day is the same to me. I get up. I get the kids ready. The furthest I go is the shops and I don't see anything else for me. In five years' time, I'd say I'll still be doing that (Daly & Leonard, 2002, p. 117).

It would be wrong to draw the conclusion that poverty leads to a lack of agency—indeed, surviving poverty involves massive initiative and enterprise—but economic and social structure does matter. If your attempts to dig yourself out are repeatedly thwarted, you tend to lose a sense that this is possible. This is why so much of the emphasis on people lacking aspiration is cant.

Coping involves well-honed skills of "resource augmentation, expenditure minimisation and stress management" (Gilliat, 2001, p. 65). It is ironic that politicians and journalists who speak of the fecklessness of the poor have least need to manage their own money with care:

> Many of the poor are very good managers of their poverty. They are resourceful and use their money and time with great expediency. They are precise about planning household accounts and ruthless about expenditure, savagely cutting back to keep out of debt . . . Despite this achievement they understandably describe such work as sacrifice and relentless struggle. (Gilliat, p. 99)

But the energy devoted to such tactical coping may not be available for strategic attempts to escape the poverty trap (Chamberlayne & Rustin, 1999; ATD Fourth World, 2000). Getting *by* can itself block thinking about getting *out*, whether this means acquiring qualifications or collective struggle. There is also a high incidence of depression and mental illness, especially among women in poverty (Davis & Hill, 2001). As Charlesworth (2000) argues, poverty, particularly in the context of long-term unemployment in former industrial regions, has somatic effects: it becomes embodied not only in attitudes but as habitus.

Coping may bring about a habitus of avoiding risk. Even taking paid work can feel too risky (Mumford & Power, 2003), when the limited financial gain is weighed against problems of managing childcare, collecting children from school, and a gap in income due to delays in receiving the first wage. These tensions are especially great for lone mothers. Surprisingly perhaps, even when people are worse off at work than on welfare, the psychological benefits of paid work are an attraction (Farrell & O'Connor 2003, p. 61).

A lack of self-esteem resulting from poverty can limit the possibility of acting together in solidarity. As James (1992) argues, it requires a degree of "self-esteem—a stable sense of one's own separate identity and a confidence that one is worthy to participate in political life" (p. 60). Individual responses such as petty crime, alcohol, or self-blame are understandable responses, yet collective action and organization are not only important to achieve social change but also because they are consciousness changing: they help overcome a sense of powerlessness and fatalism. Other groups such as gay men and physically disabled people have also had to overcome a social stigma to fight for their rights. The slogan of the disability movement "Nothing about us without us" is also pertinent here (Lister, 2004, pp. 158–75).

The people interviewed by Simon Charlesworth (2000), writing from the perspective of a deindustrialized city in Northern England, provide many expressions of impotence and despair:

> I dun't see no point in it. People wi' good grades end up do'in fuck all, what's the point? (p. 96)

> My son, they've made 'im go on these trainin' schemes an' its just cheap labour. They 'ad 'im trainin' to be a welder, an then he were back on' dole; then they 'ad 'im doin' joinery on ET [Employment Training] an' then he were back on' dole again; now they've got 'im doin' fork-lift truck drivin', so I guess next he'll be an unemployed fork-lift truck driver. (p. 96)

> Z: They ought t'leave yer alone if yer studyin'.
> X: Yeh but you 'ave t' show em that yer lookin' for work t' get any money . . .
> Y: Yeh, yer can't just say yer at college. (p. 97) [original dialect markers moderated]

As Charlesworth concludes, our attitudes and aspirations and discourse are conditioned by our circumstances:

> It is within the reference points of this life that their speech circles, often without recognition because recognition involves an act of objectification which their position in the world forecloses upon, because "what else is there?" What kinds of life could there be outside of what is known? Dispossession and brutalization are their own anaesthetic . . .
> It is this sense of a bounded world of practicably realizable practical forms that constitutes the sense of limits that protect working people from the destruction of humanity involved in looking upon the qualities of another life that cannot be lived. (p. 122)

As Lawler (2005) points out, there can be dangers of political defeatism in reading such books as Charlesworth's *The Phenomenology of Working Class Life* or Bourdieu and colleagues' (1999) *The Weight of the World*. This problem is manifest, for example, in the fatalistic political conclusions drawn by Guy Standing (2011) in *The Precariat*. It can itself become a form of othering (Lawler, 2005, p. 431). But we should not underestimate the ways in which past and present shape aspirations for the future.

Stigma and Marginalization

People living in poverty are othered in various ways. They are treated with contempt, regarded as invisible, and treated differently, both by other people and the media:

> The worst thing about living in poverty is the way it gives others permission to treat you—as if you don't matter. (Statement by group of low income parents to the APPGP, Galloway, 2002, p. 13)

As Lister (2004) argues, historically the poor have been constructed as:

> a source of moral contamination, a threat, an "undeserving" economic burden, an object of pity or even as an exotic species. It is a process that takes place at different levels and in different fora: from everyday social relations through interaction with welfare officials and professionals to research, the media, the legal system and policy-making. (p. 101)

Stereotyping can magnify and distort differences (Riggins, 1997); "stereotypes operate as socially exorcistic rituals in maintaining the boundaries of normality and legitimacy" (Pickering, 2001, p. 45) and serve "the interests of order, power and control" (p. 204). There is frequently an intersection with other types of othering around race, gender, and disability.

It is argued that schools, teacher training institutes, and researchers are all "implicated in the framing of poor children as *other*, and in institutionalizing the legitimacy of their *otherness* status" (Polakow, 1993, p. 150). There is also a historical process, at least since the nineteenth century, of seeking to divide the poor into deserving (of charity) and undeserving (i.e., those who have "only got themselves to blame") (see also Lister, 2004, pp. 105–07 for a summary and further references). The undeserving poor were frequently referred to as "the dangerous and criminal classes" (Squires, 1990, p. 54), evoking vice, sexual immorality, disease, and indiscipline. (See chapter 5 for a discussion of Murray's *underclass* concept.)

The process of denigration has been exacerbated by constructs such as the *underclass* (Charles Murray, 1996, ch. 1) and derogatory labels such as "neds" and "chavs." Owen Jones, in *Chavs: The Demonization of the Working Class* (2011), shows how this process relates to attempts by Conservative politicians in Margaret Thatcher's 1980s government in the UK to shift the blame for rocketing unemployment to the victims of deindustrialization and government policies. Entire areas were devastated by the closure of coal mines, steel mills, and shipyards, but those left behind were stigmatized as criminally lazy. In 1979, when Thatcher came to power, more than 7 million people worked in manufacturing, but now there are fewer than 3 million. Over this period, Britain's Gini coefficient, a measure of income inequality, worsened from 29 to 39.

Soon it became respectable to jeer at the poor as a "feckless, feral underclass . . . brainless blobs of lard who spend their days on leatherette sofas in front of plasma TVs" (Patterson, 2009). Lister (2004) presents the discursive symptoms:

It is frequently a language of disease and contamination. Murray (1996) uses the metaphor of "plague"; others, such as Ralf Dahrendorf (1987), of "cancer." Animal imagery is also sometimes deployed to convey a sub-human quality. For instance, the British media have created a new object of fear: "the feral child" running wild in the no-go areas inhabited by the "underclass" (see *The Observer*, 25 April and *Daily Mail*, 26 April 2002). "Brood mares," "breeding mules," "monkeys" and the more generic "animals in the Government barn" are among the animal epithets applied by US legislators to mothers on welfare (Kushnick, 1999, p. 160; Kingfisher, 2002, p. 22). (p. 112)

The aesthetics of disgust can frequently be found even in apparently progressive newspapers, as a form of stylistic exhibitionism indulged in by some journalists:

> There on TV were the mums (no dads) faces studded, shoulders tattooed, too-small pink singlets worn over shell-suit bottoms, pallid faces under peroxided hair telling tales of a diet of hamburgers, cigarettes and pesticides. (Aaronovitch, 2000, cited in Lawler, 2005, p. 431).

This makes it impossible for people afflicted by poverty to speak about their condition without being labeled. Such modes of denigration are bound to impact on children and their education.

Cultures of Poverty: The Roots of Underclass Discourse

Material poverty certainly has cultural effects, but there are serious problems in the construct of a 'culture of poverty', a concept that emerged from anthropological studies in Latin America (e.g., Lewis, 1966) and became a major influence on policy in the United States. The error emerges when observations about the culture turn into the theory that this is the main reason why poverty continues from generation to generation. It is not such a great distance from this culture of poverty argument to more malign concepts such as Murray's underclass.

A powerful analysis can be found in various chapters of *The Culture of Poverty: A Critique*, edited by Eleanor Burke Leacock (1971). Some chapters relate directly to schools, for example, Janet Castro's account of her own naïve missionary zeal as a teacher of "culturally deprived" Black American pupils (p. 82). Murray and Rosalie Wax (1971) illustrate the impact of ridiculous cultural assumptions about Sioux and other Plains Indian children: "meagre experience," "his home is . . . empty!" "we have to teach him everything!" "no home experiences in art or music," and "not told stories by their parents." This "vacuum ideology" involves a belief that these children have empty heads and that their parents suffer from apathy (pp. 130–31).

Charles Valentine (1971) exposes key faults of methodology. Lewis removed his own questions from the interviews; he reorganized materials into "coherent life stories"[Lewis's own words]. Most important of all, Lewis generalized from atypical extreme cases: one particular family, the Rios, are made to stand as a proxy for the rest of the community even though Lewis admits that this family is an extreme case, including its involvement in prostitution, which is atypical. Lewis (1968) later acknowledged, in fact, that only a small proportion of families living in poverty had what he had described as a culture of poverty:

> My rough guess would be that only about 20 per cent of the population below the poverty line in the United States have characteristics which would justify classifying their way of life as that of a culture of poverty. (p. li)

Yet, ignoring such reservations, his concept had enormous public impact, including public policy. It led to two kinds of response: the "benevolent stance toward the dispossessed without granting them any respect" of "welfare-state liberalism" (Valentine, 1971, pp. 216–17); and more militant Conservative responses including removing welfare benefits because they would simply perpetuate the culture of idleness and criminality and undermine the need for the poor to sort out their lives and find work. (The latter stance is certainly characteristic of the UK's current Coalition government.) As Valentine puts it:

> The most immediately apparent reason for the popularity of this doctrine [i.e., culture of poverty] is that it is really an old and satisfying belief in a new guise. Blaming poverty on the poor has long appealed to comfortable and affluent groups. (1971, p. 215)

Anthony Leeds (1971) demonstrates that many of the identifying traits of Lewis's culture of poverty are not cultural but directly economic: the constant struggle for survival, unemployment, low wages, unskilled occupations, child labor, absence of savings, chronic shortage of cash, borrowing from usurers, absence of food reserves in the home, use of secondhand clothing and furniture, living in crowded quarters, low level of education and literacy, higher death rate, lower life expectancy, and so on. As Leeds says: "It seems to me fatuous to call these 'cultural traits'" (p. 252). Others can be described as cultural traits but are actually adaptive and functional responses to material poverty:

> Lack of privacy is entirely a function of crowdedness; gregariousness, among the poor, a function both of crowdedness and of continually mobilized or mobilizable family, ritual kin, friend and neighbor networks. (p. 253)

Another set of headings are concerned more directly with attitudes to life: Strong Feeling of Marginality, Not Belonging, Alienation, That Institutions Do Not Serve Their Interests, Helplessness, Resignation, Fatalism, Dependency, Personal Unworthiness, Inferiority. As Leeds (1971) argues, these are not logically separate but involve a single outlook (p. 254). They amount to *feeling* marginalized, which arises from *being* marginalized!

These feelings are always discovered in the context of the society's failure to meet the vital needs of the poor, because *institutionally* a poor man is *indeed* marginalized, *unserved* by institutions, *made* an alien, *made* helpless, *made* to enter into dependency relations, *told* that he is inferior and personally unworthy (because he is lower-class, he is Black, he is illiterate, or he is "in the culture of poverty" needing psychiatric help). (p. 255)

The culture of poverty argument came to dominate social services, health, psychiatry, and education in the United States (Valentine, 1971, pp. 220 & 217) and beyond (see Leeds, 1971, pp. 255 & 279 on Latin America). It had strong racial overtones (Lewis, 1971) and fed directly into the more militant underclass polemic of Charles Murray. Murray, with Herrnstein, began with an argument about an intellectual underclass who inherited low IQs and whom it was, therefore, futile for the state to spend taxpayers' money trying to educate (for more information see also chapter 4). He then moved on to moralistic arguments concerned with attitudes and lifestyle: young men who preferred crime to hard work and promiscuous young women who supposedly had children in order to accrue welfare benefits. Initially his argument was based on Black ghettoes in the United States, but on the basis of a half day visit to two public housing estates, he felt qualified to announce that Britain, too, had an underclass problem. This ideology fueled Conservative antiwelfare propaganda in the 1980s, as it does today under a Conservative-led Coalition government, but it was also an insidious undercurrent in policy under Blair's New Labour government (Levitas, 2005).

Growing up in Poverty

Children are at greater risk of poverty than the population as a whole. According to the Child Poverty Action Group (2011), the proportion is nearly 30 percent in the UK (2009/10) compared with 20 percent for adults. This is also true of the United States and Canada, for example, but it is not a natural law: the opposite is true for the Nordic countries (Bradshaw, 2000). Households with children are almost twice as likely to face poverty as pensioners. This has a substantial effect on educational achievement: pupils eligible for free school meals in England are half as likely as other pupils to finish compulsory schooling with the target "5 A*–C grades including English and Maths."

This problem is well recognized but response has been dilatory. In 1999, Blair's Labour government gave itself ten years to halve child poverty and twenty to eliminate it—scandalously slow! Progress was made for several years but then stopped, even before the financial crisis and change of government toward the close of the decade. Approximately 3.9 million children are affected (www.poverty.org.uk), with a particularly high concentration in some regions. They include half of all single-parent families. There are high numbers of children living in single-parent families in Sweden and Norway but with lower rates of child poverty, even though single-parent families are still worse off than two-parent families (Bradbury &

Jäntti, 1999). Studies such as that of Gregg, Harkness, and Machin (1999) have shown that where there is no financial hardship in single-parent families, there is no evidence of childhood disadvantage. Similarly PISA studies have shown no impact on achievement in countries with good welfare systems including the Nordic countries, contrasted with very high damage in the United States (probably due in part to its workfare system). Given the emphasis in UK government policy on getting people into paid work, it is important to recognize that more than half of children living in poverty have at least one parent in employment.

In many cases, children still experience absolute poverty. This can take the form of inadequate nutrition, damp housing, clothes that do not fit, or shoes with holes in them. Many also face the trauma of having to move house and school as a result of poverty, but there are also less obvious and more widespread effects, with deep impact on relationships, confidence, and aspirations.

Many of the issues affecting adults also affect children, but it is important to recognize the differences and attend to the limited research designed to hear children's voices. Stigma can be particularly damaging to young people while they are developing identities, and children may need special skills to negotiate the hazards of more troubled neighborhoods. Historically and into the present, there has been too great a tendency to see children in poverty stereotypically, either as victims or as villains (Daniel & Ivatts, 1998) without looking at and listening to their experiences.

Tess Ridge's (2002) study *Childhood Poverty and Social Exclusion: From a Child's Perspective* provides important insights. Among these effects we find that:

- children are unlikely to receive regular pocket money, thus restricting their independence;

- access to affordable transport is a problem, which affects their opportunity to sustain friendships;

- not having the right clothing is a serious concern, again affecting relationships and self-esteem, and can lead to bullying;

- being unable to afford school trips affects curricular progress and can affect relationships with peers and teachers;

- children in poverty are very conscious of having to reject invitations from others to join them in weekend activities.

As Ridge explains:

> Friendships were seen as protective, particularly by boys, because without friends they felt especially vulnerable to bullying and exclusion. Fears of loneliness and social isolation were very real, and some children were clearly isolated. This is an area in which children struggled particularly hard to maintain an acceptable level of social involvement. Lack of financial resources to participate in shared social events with friends, restricted access

to transport, the cost of transport, lack of space and an inability to be reciprocal, are all factors identified as damaging to children and young people from low-income families' social viability. For many children, friendships made at school are valued but harder to sustain beyond the confines of school itself. (2002, p. 133)

This also affects learning. As Ridge points out, school is seen as an opportunity to meet friends, but it is also a source of bullying. Poorer children are unlikely to be able to take advantage of the opportunity schools should provide of meeting a cross-section of children and developing wider social networks (p. 133).

Also important, given what is known about the importance of developing self-esteem for successful learning, is to recognize the ways in which children are "learning to be poor" by restricting their behavior and aspirations (Ridge, 2002, p. 140, cited in Shropshire & Middleton, 1999). It is well established that parents try to protect their children from the worst effects of poverty, but Ridge's research also finds children and young people "struggling to protect their parents from seeing the social and emotional costs of childhood poverty on their lives" (p. 140). For example, they moderate their requests, deny their needs and wants, and self-exclude from school trips:

> I would ask my parents to buy me things and then I realized that my parents couldn't afford things. 'Cos I'd sit down and listen to their conversations and then I stopped asking for things and saved up for them. And that's been ever since I was about D's age, since I was about eight, because I was a quick learner. (Neil, 17 years, two-parent family) (p. 69)

> At that time when we didn't have no money, yeah, because it was real hard to just do anything 'cos all our mates would be doing everything and we'd think—"oh I want to do that." We'd try and ask mum, but then we'd think so, because what if she says, "well look I've only got a bit of money," then we'd feel guilty for asking, so we didn't ask her. (Ridge, 2006, p. 26)

Thus, social exclusion has a particular meaning for children. Ridge is critical of the fact that neoliberal government policies are framed in terms of the longer-term economic impact of child poverty—children as future human capital—and insufficiently concerned with how "children experience the realities of poverty and social exclusion in the immediacy of childhood" (Ridge, 2002, p. 144; see also Prout, 2000).

It appears that government policy connects to economic realities one-sidedly in terms of future contributions as an employee but not in terms of the impact of consumerism and its impact on children's lives. Ridge's (2002) fourth chapter is full of eloquent testimonies by children:

> If you don't wear trendy stuff . . . not so many people will be your friend 'cos of what you wear. (Charlene, 12 years, two-parent family)

If they, like, have clothes that they had for quite a while and they've out of it, and be, like, sort of too short for them and all, then people call them tramps and smelly and all that. (Cally, 14 years, two-parent family)

It's all about my confidence really, if I feel good in what I'm wearing I can talk to people better and stuff. (Amy, 15 years, two-parent family)

I can't go out and look scruffy or anything like that. I won't go out if I look scruffy, I won't do it. (Colleen, 13 years, lone-parent family) (pp. 68–70)

Weekends and school holidays can be a particularly difficult time, as parents can neither buy in to commercially run activity schemes nor afford expensive entertainment venues: "Couldn't do nothing on the weekends, just stayed in, couldn't go out with my friends and go to the shop or anything like that, so . . . bit boring" (Ridge, 2006, p. 26).

Although it is problematic to exaggerate negative descriptions of poorer neighborhoods, we must recognize the risks that children feel and experience and their potential impact on confidence and self-esteem. Malcolm Hill and colleagues (Hill et al., 2006) explore this through interviews with 8–14 year olds, using the findings to confront those who make bland statements about the need for greater resilience without understanding how children learn to deal with their experiences and environments. Children develop a strong sense of dangerous territory:

> Children described the borders between different zones, such as a road separating different housing schemes. . . . If they crossed the border into an area they did not belong to, they risked being attacked. . . . Besides territories of residence, gangs or groups of young people were sometimes seen as controlling certain public spaces at particular times, especially after dark. . . . One focus group described being afraid to attend a youth club dominated by a gang they did not belong to. (Hill et al., 2006, p. 43)

Quoting some of the young people as evidence of the impact on confidence and identity:

> I don't go to scary streets. (10-year-old boy)

> I have learned to keep my head down, so I don't really get picked on 'cause I am just a person walking and I don't dress differently. I just dress in my school uniform. (12-year-old boy)

> You just like walk past them, don't even look at them, you don't look back if they say anything. [Then] usually they leave you alone (11–year-old boy). (pp. 44–46)

Young people learn to move about in a group, to become safer, but this is often seen as threatening by adults—a group perceived as a gang of potential troublemakers. The children interviewed "described adult neighbors who shouted at them for making a noise, walking on the grass, playing games or seeking to retrieve a football" (p. 43). Children and young people are often demonized not only by the media but by adults who take on the roles of gatekeepers of private or public spaces.

Conclusion

This chapter has sought to lay a foundation for the subsequent discussion of competing explanations for the links between poverty and education. It looks forward to explanations relating to material poverty and deprived neighborhoods (chapter 3) in terms of individual abilities (chapter 4) and demands for raised aspirations and increased personal resilience (chapter 6) and to attempts to make families and communities responsible for disengagement and low achievement, whether in terms of patterns of language use or the supposed lack of parental support, often linked to spurious concepts such as culture of poverty and underclass (chapter 5). In examining the range of explanations located outside schools, we undertake to avoid deficit explanations that often result from overgeneralizing negative incidents and encounters.

We also need to reinforce the orientation hinted at in our opening quotation. In its original, it actually derives from a book about the favelas of Rio de Janeiro and referring more generally to inhabitants of favelas—the shanty towns and settlements that surround major cities in Latin America, where people have squatted illegally after leaving the countryside in search of work and established communities with scant or ad hoc infrastructure and resources, and struggled to make a half-decent life for their children. It is equally important as a reminder that children and families in more affluent countries do not generally face poverty because of personal inadequacies or violent tendencies nor from individual or social peculiarity, individual fecklessness, or a collective culture, but because they are the most vulnerable section of an exploited class that is economically and politically under attack due to the limitless greed of the one percent who control the lives of others.

PART TWO

Blaming Individuals, Families and Communities

There is a long history of seeking to place the blame for academic under-achievement outside the school system. This can occur on various spatial scales: the micro or individual level (blame the student); the meso levels of families (blame the parents), and, on a slightly larger scale, whole neighborhoods, as manifested in the culture of poverty. These scales are, of course, interrelated in complex ways, so that parents are somehow held responsible for transmitting the wrong genes, using the wrong kind of language in the home, for failing to stimulate their children, for their supposed indifference to education, a failure to establish discipline in the home, a lack of aspirations, and so on. Young people themselves are also somehow saddled with individual and collective blame, for a poor attitude or lack of discipline and hard work, a failure to progress, or a lack of ambition. All of these are aggregated into the murky waters of neighborhoods where poverty is concentrated, and low achievement is seen as somehow endemic.

What is missing in all these localized explanations is the macro scale—the impact of economic structures and relationships, particularly the determining impact of employment and earnings, but also the impact of life in a consumer society. Rather than acknowledging the overriding downward impact of these macro-level structures on micro- and meso-level experiences and behaviors, the latter are made to stand as a proxy for the former so that genetic make-up, parenting, and patterns of community interaction are seen as working upward, as the prime cause of poverty. It would be unrealistic and undialectical to claim that there is no upward flow of effect, and clearly too such dogmatism would deprive the oppressed of any agency to change things, but we hope to present convincing arguments as to why this is not the main causal direction in class reproduction. All this is the subject of chapters 3–6, which form part 2.

Paradoxically however, in recent decades, politicians have also become adept at blaming individual schools located in areas of poverty, and this is our starting point in part 3. An easy way to deny their own political responsibility for the extent of poverty in the country or, indeed, their poor management of the education system as a whole, is for politicians to blame ineffective or failing schools. We would not wish to deny that some schools are more successful than others in educating disadvantaged children and young people, but it is simply dishonest, as Mortimore and Whitty (1997) point out, to exaggerate the possibility of increasing school 'effectiveness' in an intensely unequal and divided society.

The emerging argument, in what follows, is that micro- and meso-level phenomena have to be understood in ways that recognize the overwhelming impact of macro-level structures, and, within that perspective, we should seek to explore sympathetically the complex interactions between schools and the communities they serve.

CHAPTER THREE

Material Poverty and 'Problem' Neighborhoods

Is it perhaps too inconvenient to entertain the possibility that elites have more social capital than the poor because they've got more money, power and influence, rather than the other way round?
—Ben Fine, 2010, p. 39

In this chapter we explore the complex and contested relationship between poverty and place. It is self-evident that something as material as poverty is also *located*, and from experience we know that there are places where poverty is particularly concentrated. However, this can obscure as well as enrich our understanding. Whoever captures the high ground in defining the 'problem' is also able to construct the supposed 'solution,' and both of these can be miles away from reality.

First in this chapter we re-emphasize ways in which poverty impacts on young people's development materially, relationally, and symbolically, damaging their health, friendships, and morale. We then engage in a multifaceted examination of how the relationship between economic divisions and place is (mis)construed. To provide a solid framework for this, we begin by providing a brief historical overview of how capitalist development led to migration from the countryside to the town, within countries and internationally, leading to concentrations of poverty in particular parts of industrial towns and cities. We look at some of the complexities in our own time, physically and symbolically. We continue by focusing on the interpenetration of different scales, including the futility of area-based initiatives that fail to broach the macro-economic question of providing decent employment. This is followed by a critique of the idea that the problems of the inner city can be solved by an increase of social capital.

We show some of the complexity of young people's occupation of urban spaces marked by poverty. They might be physically present but denied full participation: for example, they might have part-time jobs working in shops and restaurants where they could only dream of being customers. They develop complex tactics of moving around troubled spaces, while struggling not to be stigmatized by the reputation of the places where they live.

We conclude this chapter by scoping out the beginnings of an argument (pursued in later chapters) as to how we might provide young people with the tools with which to speak back to the forces that insist on portraying themselves and their communities in deficit terms.

The Material and Symbolic Effects of Poverty on Human Development

To begin, it is important to stress that poverty itself has a damaging impact on educational development. Poverty works materially as a lack of essential resources, relationally because of the standard expectations of the rest of society and symbolically in terms of stigmatization and low social esteem. All these aspects, separately and together, can have an effect on young people's development and education, as outlined in chapter 2. Even in affluent societies, some children sleep in damp bedrooms, go without meals, or lack waterproof clothing and footwear—poverty is damaging to *health*. Lack of money prevents many from joining school trips or going out with friends, and not having the right clothing can affect self-esteem, especially in a consumer society: poverty damages *relationships*. Children are inevitably affected by the widespread media-driven stigmatization of 'chavs' and 'benefit scroungers': poverty damages *morale*. Poor health, damaged relationships, and low self-esteem and demoralization all have significant impacts on educational development.

The complexity of social inequality and its effects are highlighted by Wilkinson and Pickett (2009) in *The Spirit Level*, which shows the association between countries with wide income differentials and the incidence of poor health, anxieties, addictions, violence, and crime. Therefore, simply lifting people from just below to just above the poverty line is insufficient to remove all the relational and symbolic effects of inequality on young people and their education. The anxiety caused by living in an unequal society damages us all: the better off as a "fear of falling" (Ehrenreich, 1989) but, far more so, the poor as a fear of debt and destitution.

The pervasiveness of discourses of denigration highlighted by Owen Jones's (2011) book *Chavs* implies the need to campaign for a decent living wage, not merely better benefits. In Britain, the minimum wage has been set so low that many low-paid workers can only survive through a variety of benefits, particularly tax credits and housing benefits. In effect, employers paying less than a living wage are being subsidized from the taxation of better-paid workers (particularly since tax avoidance is made so easy for the super-rich). This is often presented in terms of the middle class subsidizing the poor, but more accurately it is a redistribution from one section of workers to another in the interests of the very rich. It becomes very easy in this context for right-wing newspapers and politicians to launch attacks on those who rely on benefits.

The symbolic effects of poverty make it all the more important to involve those most affected in attempts to build an analysis and speak back to those in power: consequently Ruth Lister (2004) argues for "incorporating the perspectives of those with the experience of poverty into the theorization and research into poverty, through participatory methods" (p. 2). As she puts it: "Poverty has to be understood not just as a disadvantaged and insecure economic *condition* but also as a shameful and social *relation*" (p. 7, emphasis in original). The "relational/ symbolic aspects, involving . . . lack of voice, disrespect, humiliation and assault on dignity and self-esteem; shame and stigma; powerlessness; denial of rights and diminished citizenship" (p. 7) impact particularly on adolescents, and these are frequently compounded by school experiences.

Arguments concerning the relational/symbolic effects of poverty are not in opposition to financial explanations. In Lister's (2004) terminology, poverty is both a "material/socio-economic" and a "symbolic/cultural" phenomenon that requires it be tackled through "a combined politics of redistribution and recognition" (p. 10). The error comes when the symbolic/cultural aspect is used to obscure the socioeconomic.

The Geography of Capitalist Development

A historical overview of capitalist development and expansion may help provide a basis for understanding the impact of economics on place. In feudal societies even the poorest were severely exploited while being tied to one particular place. Escape from the village into the town was severely punished, but it provided the opportunity of a better life. It is capitalism that uproots the poor. Workers have the freedom to offer their strength and skills where they may, but this entails the freedom to starve if they cannot. A state-sanctioned process of enclosures, starting in sixteenth-century England, enabled landowners to seize common land. This drove peasants to the cities since they could no longer survive without grazing some livestock. This process was exacerbated by the development of agricultural machinery in the eighteenth and nineteenth centuries. Similarly, in the Scottish Highland Clearances, crofters were driven off the land to make way for cattle. They moved to work in the growing cities or migrated.

This presented a dilemma for the ruling class of what to do with those who could not find work in towns and cities—and in the growing industrial economy—requiring ruthless policies of social control combined with the most basic level of physical sustenance. Those who could not support themselves were either driven on to the next parish in search of work or incarcerated in workhouses: only the most fortunate survived with a modicum of dignity, such as respectable widows who were too old to work.

The rest either concentrated into squalid housing districts surrounding the factories or moved overseas (voluntarily or as convicts). Migration was involved in both cases, whether within a single country or across oceans. The process of dispossession from the land, flight to the cities, and migration began long before the term *globalization* was coined, and it continues to this day across Asia, Africa, and Latin America, creating a *Planet of Slums* (Davis, 2006).

This is the process whereby social class and economic division were/are mapped onto the landscape. It is a process whereby macro- and material forces impact on the meso level, not the reverse. These are places made poor by exploitation and unemployment, not self-generating swamps of inadequacy and moral degeneracy.

The Mapping of Class onto Urban Space

The complex overlay of material, relational, and symbolic effects of poverty is evident when we examine the characteristics of *poor neighborhoods*. Indeed the ambiguity of the phrase with its moral overtones betrays that complexity.

Social geographers such as Lefebvre (1991), Harvey (1996, 2001), Massey (1994, 2005), Soja (1989, 1996), and Sibley (1995) help us view place and space as social and political rather than merely geometric. In Doreen Massey's words, "The social and the spatial are always inextricably entwined" (1995, p. 197). Or as Thomas Gieryn (2000) expresses it, emphasizing the interweaving of physical and cultural aspects:

> Places are endlessly made, not just when the powerful pursue their ambition through brick and mortar, not just when design professionals give form to function, but also when ordinary people extract from continuous and abstract space a bounded, identified, meaningful, named and significant place (de Certeau, 1984, Etlin, 1997). A place is remarkable, and what makes it so is an unwindable spiral of material form and interpretative understandings or experiences. (p. 471)

Just as some neighborhoods are exclusive in both physical and stylistic terms—the word entails rejection as well as desirability (Massey, 1995, p. 196)—others are viewed as settlements of last resort where even the postal code carries a stigma. It is because spaces are intertwined with our narratives and identities and relationships, because they are meaningful, that stigmatization of our home territory is a form of symbolic violence:

> We all live, then, in complex geometries of social power, and our relationship to place may be, and can be used as, an important component of defining our identities. . . . But the crucial point is that we create those places and those geometries of power. We create them via the economics and politics which we vote for or allow to happen; we create them through social and cultural imaginings; we create them in the ordinary business of daily life. (pp. 201–02)

Of course, behind this "we" it is evident that some of "us" are more powerful than others in the creation of places.

Massey's (1995) analysis shows how places in England have long been marked by differences of social status, including "Olde Worlde" villages to which the rich retreat and where the rural English middle class has constructed for itself "a particular kind of white ethnicity . . . in relation to the symbolic meaning of the countryside" (p. 207). In Massey's (1993) view, space is "a complex web of relative domination and subordination, of solidarity and co-operation" (p. 81).

Places act as social controls: while exclusive neighborhoods keep out the poor, others lock them in, whether financially because they cannot afford to live elsewhere or symbolically by damaging reputations and thus restricting opportunities. Charlesworth (2000) quotes from his interviews in a former mining and steel-producing area:

> Rotherham's like a prison without any walls, like people can feel these walls holdin' 'em in but thi' can't just walk out on it. It's like a . . . big desert which nobody 'as energy t'walk out on! (p. 115, dialect markers moderated)

According to Wacquant (2008), neighborhoods can serve as "zones of relegation" in various ways, including as "reservoirs of low-skill labor"; "warehouses for supernumerary populations that no longer have . . . economic utility"; or "spatial containers for the ostracization of undesirable social categories and activities" (p. 11).

But neighborhoods are not simply containers. They are places in which people live out their aspirations, where opportunities are constructed and contested, and where people's worst fears and nightmares become realized. For this reason, Charlesworth (2000) rejects Richard Hoggart's (1957) description of industrial towns as "a landscape with figures" as an aestheticization (Charlesworth, p. 89) that "de-temporalizes the world" and posits it as "spectacle" (p. 90). Industrial towns provide a "background" only in the richer sense of "a field of significance that grounds awareness in meanings disclosed through the forms of concern inscribed in the practices we inherit and the projects available to us" (p. 108):

> Thus, we do not choose this "there," or perspective or context . . . Individuals find themselves cast into a situation, which furnishes the context of plausibility, opportunity and

decision. It is this context that operates as a clearing of sense opening a space of what is possible, what it *makes sense* to do. This practical sense of the realm of plausible possibilities . . . gives sense to what an individual cannot choose to do or, even, what an individual may choose to do, only at the expense of doing something in pure privacy and meaninglessness. The space, or place, exists through realizable projects and availabilities, patterns of use and of users, all of which are practically negotiated daily. . . . An individual knows without much deliberation the range of the possible, and this is the realm of the unreflective sense common to the majority of the town's people. (pp. 90–91)

Here and elsewhere, though at the risk of fatalism and despair, Charlesworth borrows extensively from Bourdieu's emphasis on unconscious habit, applying this to neighborhoods of poverty, and questioning much of the glib talk of choices and aspirations; it is essential to recognize the weightiness of context before working out how we might overcome it.

Such neighborhoods are complex fields, penetrated with hostile state power (benefits offices, the police) that demand clever strategies to survive with a degree of dignity. Another of Charlesworth's (2000) interviewees' remarks on the importance of not appearing too nice, for example at the Job Center, or you'll be taken for a ride. On the other hand, you also need to maintain self-respect, keep the worst features of the neighborhood out of your home, protect your family, and treat others decently (p. 103). Tragically, the destruction of self-respect brought about by deindustrialization has led some young people toward "embracing and even celebrating their alienation as an emblem of what it is: their humanity, a human form that is degraded and stigmatized" (p. 94).

The context of the post-industrial rustbelt impacts on how places are experienced. Writing of South Wales, Valerie Walkerdine (2010) points to industrial structures such as pithead winding gear, docks, and steelworks as a symbolic focus that gives meaning to the space of a community. Once the places of work disappear, the bonds that hold people together are damaged. Drawing on psychoanalytic theory, she speaks of focal buildings in industrial cities as a kind of "skin"; with its loss, we fear "annihilation through spilling" (p. 111). Struggles ensue to find new loci of meaning, for example, places of consumerized leisure. One of Charlesworth's (2000) female interviewees speaks of the town in terms of places to go out at night and shopping: it "is encountered primordially as a medium through which people try to achieve a life" (p. 116).

The Interpenetration of Spatial Scales

Given the tendency to refer, in one-dimensional blanket ways, to disadvantaged neighborhoods, we need to be clear what kind of question we are asking. These need to allow positives as well as negatives to emerge—neighborhoods as resources and not simply as problems. They need to provide a basis for relating the lifeworld of young people to their educational experience.

Neighborhoods are often thought of simplistically in terms of spatial scale, the scale within which we can know each other face-to-face as community. By contrast, some recent theories of globalization have emphasized the interpenetration of scales. The macro, meso and micro levels do not relate

> as a set of Russian dolls which sit inside each other (Swyngedouw, 1997), but as social relations and trajectories that operate at various scales and are tangled together in specific ways in specific locations. . . . It mobilizes a notion of "globalization" (Robertson, 1992)—the ways in which globalized phenomena are enacted in local places—and "vernacularisation" (Appadurai, 1996; 2001)—the ways in which local actors, institutions, narratives, truths, and traditions diffract global-national trajectories to make them distinctive and specific. (Thomson, 2010, p. 124)

It is essential to understand the impact of the macro on local areas, otherwise we slide into deficit conceptions of poor neighborhoods as containers of self-inflicted misery where dysfunctionality circulates in self-reinforcing ways.

Spatial segregation in Britain is now at a high point. As an example, the parliamentary constituency of Bradford West has 75 percent of children in or near poverty, Nottingham East 68 percent, and two areas of Glasgow 98 percent (BBC, 2008). It would be extraordinary if this did not result in significant social dysfunction. This hyper-concentration has led to numerous policies of area-based intervention in the UK, a scale on which government feels it can intervene in the economy. The problems with this tactical response to neoliberalism have become evident.

Ruth Lupton (2003) argues that a failure to discuss how places have been made poor by macro-economic forces has shifted attention to the local concentration of low-income individuals, their characteristics, and interactions:

> In a telling analysis, Power and Gewirtz (2001) found that bids for Education Action Zones were often prefaced by accounts of the changing structure of employment opportunities more generally, but moved to more specific and localized accounts of problems of families as the reason for continued disadvantage. Because ABIs [area-based interventions] start with the problem of local spatial inequity, they tend to "embody an inadequate theorization of the processes through which such disadvantage is generated" (Power et al., 2005, p. 111). (p. 120)

A parallel critique is articulated by Grace (1984) who points to the inadequacy of research literature on urban schools in terms of overemphasis on micro-institutional studies and cultural deficits, and an inadequate sense of power. This is in addition to an exaggerated faith in the efficacy of area-based interventions (Gough & Eisenschitz with McCulloch, 2006; Power, Rees & Taylor, 2005) when unaccompanied by more directly economic policies. This depoliticized mode of analysis leads to social pathologizing, whereby neighborhoods are expressed in relation to the education deficits of people within the area. Places tend to be seen either as containers of people with certain detrimental characteristics, or as sites for the negative effect of family or peer relations, but without any sense that these relations are influenced by spatial characteristics nor the product of wider power geometries. (Lupton, 2010, p. 120)

Lupton points to a long history of such place-based interventions in the UK, dating back to the Plowden Report (1967). She adds, however, that during a period of neoliberal policy, there has been only a token acknowledgment of material issues such as poor housing or macro factors such as the lack of jobs and an increasing tendency to blame schools. She points to the lack of clarity behind many interventions as to how neighborhoods and area-based interventions are supposed to have an effect and how that relates to the educational experience. She argues that area-based initiatives need to examine more closely the relationship between the neighborhood and the experience of education, that critical questions need to be asked about curriculum and pedagogy, and that the impact of a quasi-market system of schools should be reexamined:

> ABIs cannot just concentrate on "fixing" specific areas: they must engage with the dynamic relations between schools and between neighborhoods that drive some to the bottom of the hierarchy and others to the top. (p. 122)

Without this, the general tendency is toward functionalist policymaking, which tends to collapse into

> a conceptualisation of the problems of poor areas as being "residual"—remaining pockets of disadvantage in an otherwise functioning system—and the purpose of education as being to re-fit residents in these areas for their place in the economy. (p. 122)

Implicitly and explicitly, the argument behind area-based initiatives in the UK and Australia is that if we can identify and isolate the risk factors associated with socioeconomic disadvantage, then governments can intervene with the right mix of flexible policy responses to break the cycle. The broad claim is that young people who come from backgrounds of low parental educational attainment, poor health and housing, deficient parenting skills, and diminished employment prospects are vulnerable in contexts of rapidly changing labor markets. These young people are seen as being trapped between dramatically restructuring labor markets and local neighborhood contexts that are hostile to them gaining the necessary human capital with which to navigate the changing contours of the workforce. What is allegedly required is an alternative response to the dual failure of both the state and the market "to resolve [these] social problems" (Milbourne, Macrae & Maguire, 2003, p. 20).

To critique this is not to abandon the notion of area-based interventions altogether but to base them on much clearer principles for the development of community education. As Raffo and Dyson (2007) argue:

1. schools in "disadvantaged" communities working in isolation cannot bring about change on their own—the school needs to be made "the hub of change" (p. 274);

2. people in local communities need to be involved in decision making;

3. learning opportunities preferably of a lifelong kind across age groups through a "Community Learning Center" (p. 274) need to be made available;

4. to kick start the paid employment trajectory, job opportunities need to be provided that are attentive to difficulties being experienced (p. 274); and

5. improvement occurs through raising "confidence, self-esteem and sense of control that would impact on children in local families and hence on learning within the school" (p. 274).

There is widespread agreement in the rhetoric of official policy of the importance of a joined-up or multi-agency partnership approach to tackling social disadvantage and exclusion—frequently given expression in various forms such as the full-service extended school (Raffo & Dyson), or the coordinated HUB approach to supporting learning in contexts of disadvantage. However, this somehow does not appear to include providing cause for optimism through good employment opportunities. Consequently, the sense of futility is reinforced.

A major shortcoming in such approaches, as identified by Milbourne and colleagues (2003), is that "schools, parents and children, as well as [the various] agencies may hold differing views of the roles that project workers entering schools should undertake," not to mention the "inability to embed new strategies within a short time frame" (p. 32). The UK experience has shown the difficulty of support workers fully understanding policy rhetoric or how to meet "the original expectations," and the policy of interagency cooperation being overly ambitious (Webb & Vulliamy, 2001, p. 329).

A further damning indictment of most place-based interventions is that often "neither schools nor the families who are engaged with these projects have been involved in these new constructions of solutions to their problems" (Milbourne, Macrae & Maguire, 2003, p. 32). Even when portrayed otherwise, the reality often is that the real power to identify remedies still resides with mainstream agencies with little apparent space for the young people and their families blighted by social exclusion. The effect is that agencies "fall short of their stated policy aims" (p. 32), the stigma of disadvantage is sustained within a deficit model of disadvantage that locates blame with young people and their families for failing to gain inclusion, and "analysis of social disadvantage based on structural reasons for continued exclusion" is avoided (p. 33).

What we need instead of these confused logics are new ways of thinking about young people's (dis)engagement with education in contexts of disadvantage—one that is much more nuanced and that understands the complexities of the young lives and contexts of those involved. We need approaches that go beyond the "ghetto" or "warehousing effect" (Dillabough, Kennelly & Wang, 2007, p. 137) that portrays these places in pathological, deterministic, and constrained ways. Human geographers (Bauder, 2001) argue that in the context of increasing labor market segmentation—and this applies equally to educational segmentation—we need to engage carefully with "local uniqueness, situatedness and contingency" (p. 47) in order to "understand how place influences life choices" (Nayak, 2003, p. 11).

Doing this necessitates investigating a broad constellation of processes by which young people go beyond localized positioning that portrays them as existing within "demonised schools" (Reay & Lucey, 2003, p. 126) that are vilified and castigated for underachievement and underperformance. Rather, in the spirit of interpretive research, we should "attempt to make sense of their making sense of the events and opportunities confronting them in their everyday life" (Ley, 1988, p. 121). Turning things around in the ways we are suggesting will involve conceiving of everyday lives, families, and neighborhoods as resources rather than depicting them as deficits. It will involve an engagement with notions of place-based education in relation to areas of concentrated deprivation (see chapter 9 on curriculum and pedagogy).

Social Capital

The supposed disconnectedness and lack of social capital of young people growing up in poor urban areas has provided yet another way of blaming people for their own misfortunes. They are seen as

> disconnected from the normal, moral, mainstream life of society . . . "a lost generation". . . . dangerously excluded from the discipline and rewards of working life. (MacDonald & Marsh, 2005, pp. 1–2)

They are said to live in neighborhoods lacking in "social cohesion, community spirit and social capital (e.g., Etzioni, 1993; Putnam, 1995)" (MacDonald & Marsh, 2005, p. 203), so policies are directed at disciplining them back into work to counter their alienation and isolation.

One of the greatest sources of confusion has been the popularization of Coleman's (1966) and Putnam's (2000) versions of social capital, a flawed theory grounded in romanticized and nostalgic evocations of community and that neglects power differences and social conflict (Siisiäinen, 2000; Morrow, 2008; Portes, 1998). Beyond a certain basic sense that networks of support can be helpful, the concept is simplistic and misleading.

The appeal to community in Western social theory has connotations of "paradise lost or paradise still to be found . . . this is definitely not a paradise which we know from our own experience" (Bauman, 2001, p. 3). Coleman and Putnam, the most influential theorists of social capital, both appeal to such nostalgic versions of lost organic community in North America. It is very much tied to the loss of wholesome small-town culture, mythically placed before the days of working mothers, single parents, divorce, and television (Morrow, 2008, p. 747; Siisiäinen, 2000, p. 19). Although Putnam (2000) briefly raises the question of diminishing real incomes in *Bowling Alone*, he sees this as significant only for middle-class parents "because the middle class has traditionally been responsible for the accumulation of social capital in America" (Siisiäinen, p. 19).

These pathologies of social breakdown have been made to carry the burden of responsibility for major structural and economic change in our neoliberal times. Portes and Landolt (2000) identify the macro-economic context in their critique of social capital theory as applied in Latin America:

> The removal of state protections giving way to unrestrained market forces has produced growing income disparities and an atomized social fabric marked by the erosion of normative controls. (530)

In this context, the decontextualized notion of social capital holds out a false promise of "a ground-up alternative" (p. 530) and a "counterweight to the unfettered individualism of the market"—as well as "a means to gain advantages in it" (p. 530, pointing to Putnam, 1993).

Social capital holds an obvious appeal for neoliberal apologists. Tony Blair even formed a dedicated Social Capital Unit within the Cabinet Office: in his Third Way politics of adjustment to globalization, social capital would serve as a substitute, along with raising educational qualifications, for direct state involvement in economic development: "This Third Way . . . will build its prosperity on human and social capital" (Blair, 1998, p. 20). This spurious direction of causality provides ideal cover for damaging macro-level processes, as Ben Fine (2010) demonstrates in a caustic critique:

> Do you sing in a choir? . . . Enjoy regular coffee mornings? Well done. You possess a vitally important commodity. You have social capital . . . (p. 38).
> If we look at America we see that in the last 40 years the share of the top one per cent of earners has gone from well under ten per cent to well over 20 per cent, reversing the previous trend. Surely this has more to do with the decline of US civil society, manufacturing, labour movements and inadequate welfare than the demise of bowling? Is it perhaps too inconvenient to entertain the possibility that elites have more social capital

than the poor because they've got more money, power and influence, rather than the other way round?

Commenting on Prime Minister David Cameron's proposal to develop the "Big Society" in the context of wage and welfare cuts following the banking crisis, Fine adds:

> It is the romantic, part-nostalgic and blinkered belief that each of us could do better if only we would work together, thereby side-stepping systematic unfairness and its impact on those who are now supposed to overcome economic and social disadvantage by networking, volunteering, linking, and bloody well improving themselves. (p. 39)

Social capital is a nebulous concept that "is not adequately contextualized in socio-economic history" (Morrow, 2008, p. 749):

> [It] ignores wider structural factors which create environments of risk which are completely beyond the control of individual actors. . . . As Modell (1994, p. 51) notes, "any meaningful notion of social capital must be situated in a larger set of social and cultural relations that surround the way children grow up in any given society." (Morrow, 2008, p. 758)

Siisiäinen (2000) points out that in Nordic societies, which score high whenever researchers try to quantify social capital, the bedrock for trust is a welfare state that provides a guaranteed minimum income and where state welfare structures are responsive to collective demands from below.

It is significant that Coleman and Putnam have almost totally ignored Bourdieu's very different conceptualization of social capital (Morrow, 2001; Portes, 1998), even though he originated the phrase. As opposed to Coleman and Putnam, who work within traditions of "American pluralism" and "functionalist conceptions of social integration" (Siisiäinen, 2000, p. 1), Bourdieu consistently worked to understand "the contribution that various forms of symbolic violence make to the reproduction of structures of domination" (Bourdieu & Wacquant, 1992, p. 15). For Bourdieu, social capital interrelates closely with economic and cultural capital, serving to multiply their effect (Siisiäinen, p. 11). It is not social networks in themselves that increase prosperity but networking between people who already enjoy prosperity and influence. It follows that one person's inclusion can be another's exclusion: "The same strong ties that bring benefits to members of a group commonly enable it to bar others from access" (Portes, 1998, p. 15).

Whereas Bourdieu deploys social capital as part of an explanation of how wealth and power are retained and reproduced, Putnam's version is unproblematically celebratory (Portes, 1998). It is as if any kind of relationship or network is a good thing, and trust is self-evidently a virtue. In reality, the impact of social networks depends very much on circumstances:

Sociability cuts both ways. While it can be the source of public goods . . . it can also lead to public 'bads.' Mafia families, prostitution and gambling rings, and youth gangs, offer so many examples of how embeddedness in social structures can be turned to less than socially desirable ends. . . . Notice that social capital, in the form of social control, is still present in these situations, but its effects are exactly the opposite of those commonly celebrated in the literature. (Portes, p. 18)

As Portes points out, sociologists have known since the publication of Carol Stack's *All Our Kin* (1974) that everyday survival in poor urban communities depends on close interaction with relatives and friends. The problem is that these ties are often limited to the inner city, "depriving their inhabitants of information about employment opportunities elsewhere and ways to attain them" (Portes, pp. 13–14). Coming a step closer to Bourdieu's view, Putnam refers to this as "bridging capital" as opposed to "bonding capital."

MacDonald and Marsh (2005) also provide strong evidence of the thickness of social networks:

It would be difficult to class our interviewees as excluded. Many felt included. In different ways and degrees, informants were connected to the life of their estates in ways untypical of residents of those apparent paradigms of social order: middle-class, suburban neighborhoods (Baumgartner, 1988). (p. 202)

MacDonald and Marsh point out that networks are not necessarily positive. They may be damaging as well as beneficial, for example, criminal networks or peer groups that "helped hurry young people's departure from school" or "bolstered resistant *learner identities*" (p. 204).

Loyalties and connections are absolutely vital to survival in conditions of poverty, but their absence is not the cause of poverty nor can their enhancement serve as its cure. Enormous creativity and agency are used to establish relationships and rituals for mutual support, yet "connections alone cannot prevent the worst outcomes, but can act to blunt harm" (Goldsmith, 2012, p. 7).

Those who regard social connectedness as unproblematically a 'good thing' find it difficult to recognize alienation and scepticism as legitimate critique and misrecognize resistance to injustice as the sign of a broken society. Cavalcanti and colleagues (2011) reject this argument, pointing to the strong sense of injustice and resentment of a "community announcing its scepticism"; our focus should be on "broken promises" rather than a "broken society"(p. 8). This cuts through the official responses to riots in English cities in 2011 that ascribed the actions of young people to a lack of honesty or morality rather than their loss of hope.

The ideology of social capital and its supposed absence in neighborhoods of deprivation are rampant in the ideology of British politicians: disconnected young people are to be disciplined into becoming connected, as if absence of work were the result of lack of trust rather than lack of jobs. A clear example is the British deputy prime minister Nick Clegg's defence of a new government policy to force unemployed young people into working without wages. He represents this draconian and exploitative policy as an act of therapy:

> Asked if he had any concerns about young people being asked to work, for example, a night-shift stacking shelves in a supermarket for free, Mr Clegg said: "I have absolutely no qualms at all about the idea that rather than have a young person sitting at home, feeling cut off, lonely and getting depressed because they don't know what to do with their lives." (BBC News website, February 21, 2012)

Children's Experiences of Disadvantaged Neighborhoods

Our framing of the issue is through the following questions, some of which will be developed in later chapters:

1. What is the significance of place and locale in the educational lives of young people in contexts regarded as disadvantaged, and how does location affect the value they attach to education?

2. What factors inhibit or enhance the geography of educational opportunities for young people in communities of disadvantage?

3. How do young people's interpretations of educational possibilities around locality and neighborhood interact with or contradict place-based interventions (e.g., extended learning HUBs) aimed at ameliorating disadvantage?

In other words, we need to know how young people from communities regarded as disadvantaged are (1) impacted by the localities and neighborhoods in which they live, and (2) as a consequence, how these young people negotiate learning identities (or not) in these contexts; and (3) the implications of multi-agency responses to disadvantage through joined-up partnership interventions on young people's learning identities and educational pathways.

The impact of such neighborhoods on children's lives has been researched by Hill and colleagues (2006, summarized in chapter 2) and Reay and Lucey (2000). The latter highlight the dangers children have to negotiate on large council estates, and consequent restrictions on their movement imposed by careful parents. However, it also expresses problems caused by stigma:

> They struggle continuously to hold at bay the connotations of deviance, deficit, and failure embedded in prevailing discursive constructions of the urban poor. . . . Press cuttings from the newspaper over the research period variously referred to the estates as "hotbeds of crime," "drug ridden," and "full of problem families." . . . All of the children considered here devised tactics to preserve a sense of themselves as decent and respectable, which was why so many sometimes claimed to be middle-class in spite of living in households where all the adults were both uncredentialled and unemployed. . . . It is increasingly difficult

in the pervasive late 1990s culture of individualism and self-sufficiency to be both decent and poor. As Daniel rationalizes, "Course I'm middle class. I'm not poor no way man. I'm not a dosser." (pp. 415–16)

Younger children point to evidence of dirt, noise, vandalism, alcohol and drug abuse, racism, violence, and other dangers; as the researchers point out, these threats and counter-strategies, along with the struggle to maintain decency and self-respect, "take a heavy toll on the everyday practices of a ten-year-old." The researchers also point, however, to frequent "narratives of belonging and community" (Reay & Lucey, 2000, p. 423) and the desire not to escape so much as to make the place better: "I don't really like it here but I don't want to be anywhere else" (p. 410).

A further sophistication required for understanding the impact of young people's experience of space on their personal development is the realization that a person can be physically present in a place but marginal in participation. For example, you are excluded from leisure facilities that are not affordable; you might not be admitted to more successful schools; you may not feel confident to go to places requiring respectable clothes or trainers with street cred, and you may feel ashamed to take friends back to your flat. Older adolescents encounter the spatial ambiguity of being employed in service roles in cafes and shops where they could never afford the role of customer. The complexity of young people's experience is well captured in this quotation from Doreen Massey (1994):

> The identities of place are always unfixed, contested and multiple. And the particularity of any place is, in these terms, constructed not by placing boundaries around it and defining its identity through counter position to the other which lies beyond, but precisely (in part) through the specificity of the mix of links and interconnections to that "beyond." Places viewed in this way are open and porous. . . . All attempts to institute horizons, to establish boundaries, to secure the identity of places, can in this sense therefore be seen to be attempts to stabilize the meaning of particular envelopes of space-time . . . such attempts . . . are constantly the site of social contest, battles over the power to label space-time, to impose the meaning to be attributed to a space, for however long or short a span of time. (p. 5)

The experience of place is also distinctive in different locations, despite the narrative of globalization. Nordic countries have managed to sustain a greater protection against the unequalizing forces of neoliberalism, and Scotland sustains a stronger belief in the importance of the welfare state and public institutions than England. Some regions symbolically represent upward mobility while others represent decline and consequently lose investment (Allen, Massey & Cochrane, 1998): perceptions have a material effect. Wacquant (2008) insists on a distinction between U.S. ghettoes and the poorer districts of Paris, while Massey (2007) points to London as a modern city where rich and poor live in close proximity but with the rich tending to separate themselves by recourse to private education or healthcare.

Poor Places and Young People's Engagement with Schooling

In this section we want to advance and interrogate the not-altogether novel idea that far from being neutral or irrelevant, context in communities of disadvantage is everything! This is in contrast to the approach of the School Effectiveness paradigm that seeks to separate off (statistically "control for") context as, in a very limited sense, "background." In doing this, we will try to examine how location and geographical and metaphorical positioning act to powerfully shape educational opportunities (or not) for young people deemed to be disadvantaged, and how they and their families become implicated and compliant in the perpetuation of deficit views of themselves and the educational possibilities that flow from those views.

Mills and Gale (2011), in an analysis of a single Australian secondary school in an economically depressed rural town, provide a conceptual way into this through the interactive notions of *positioning* and *stance*. Basically, what teachers argue, with supporting evidence, is that communities, neighborhoods, and schools operate within a broader set of constraints not of their own making, and it is these "broader social and economic influences . . . [that act to] adversely *position* students from low SES backgrounds and the schools they attend" (p. 245, our emphasis).

They found, not surprisingly, that young people are profoundly impacted when they come to school hungry, when they are homeless, if their families experience financial hardship through unemployment or welfare dependency, where there is family dysfunction and breakdown, ill-health, drug dependence, incarceration, mental illness, sexual abuse or domestic violence. But these are not only direct material effects, since all of these out-of-school factors operate to construct a particular image around a range of pathological deficits that collectively add up to a picture of hopelessness. Mills and Gale (2011) portray an array of seemingly insuperable obstacles that together construct a shared image of these young people and their communities as being "without hope or purpose: without a working future" (p. 247).

Regardless of what schools or outside agencies might argue, say, or do—and in circumstances where meaningful paid employment is lacking—these young people are savvy enough to see the scam: they understand the realities of the economic vulnerability within which they live and their degraded employment prospects, despite schooling. As Mills and Gale (2011) put it, their poverty "imposes itself on them with a necessity so total that it allows them no glimpse of a reasonable exit" (p. 249). All of this amounts to the creation of a "narrow imagination," and it matters little what schools promise or attempt to do in these circumstances, because the reality is that they "cannot deliver on . . . promises" (p. 250) over which they have no control—most notably, to provide rewarding employment for young people.

To follow Mills and Gale's argument further, what follows from this disappointment and frustration, whether wittingly or not, is that schools internalize these external constraints and act accordingly. For example, they take the stance, with varying degrees of subtlety (or not), that these students are unable, unwilling, or incapable of engaging in academic pursuits, and furthermore their parents do not value education and see schools as existing to serve children from "good families" (p. 251). Thus, when teachers do not take seriously enough the impact of macro-level economic factors and particularly poor employment opportunities as the root cause of poverty—a reality all too obvious to their students—they may end up working within a professional ideology and mythology that blames students, parents, and communities.

One result—and this also comes through strongly in a hundred interviews with similar young people by Smyth and McInerney (2012)—is the repeated claim that "we are hands-on people." This is really code for their acceptance of the downgraded position they have been allocated and the fact that they see themselves as deserving only insecure jobs that require low-level manual skills. As Mills and Gale (2011) note, aspirations are thus severely downgraded in a way that appears to be natural and uncontested, with schools heavily implicated in perpetuating a vocational scam of economic residualization (Smyth, 2011; Harrison, 2011).

This critical understanding is quite at variance with the dominant policy infatuation with labeling, stigmatizing, and targeting "problem" neighborhoods. In doing so, official policy fails to understand how individuals "in these neighbourhoods . . . recognize their position, status and a sense of belonging—their place-specific identity" (Raffo, 2011, p. 8). Crucially, for young people, this means the networks that "assist [them] in the daily navigations of living in their neighbourhoods" (p. 8).

As Wacquant (2008) argues, we need some tools for rethinking the increasing marginality of young people in contexts of disadvantage. Educators considering how to facilitate young people's understanding of their reality can take an important lead from his detailed conceptual and ethnographic analysis of urban marginality and his five suggested ways of rethinking concentrations of urban poverty:

1. We need to puncture the "*folk concepts* used by state decision-makers . . . to designate neighborhoods of exile" and analyze instead how these neighborhoods arise and their "evolving makeup and position in the sociospatial structure of the metropolis" (p. 8).

2. We need to see neighborhoods of disadvantage historically and politically as the product of larger-scale events and forces. "Thus the brutal implo-

sion of the black American ghetto in the wake of the urban uprisings of the 1960s was propelled from the outside, by [factors including] the restructuring of urban capitalism" (p. 9). Otherwise we will mistake as "neighborhood effects" what are "nothing more than the spatial retranslation of economic and social differences" (p. 9).

3. Methodologically, we need ethnographic observations to "pierce the screen of discourses whirling around these territories" so as "to capture the lived relations and meanings that are constitutive of the everyday reality of the marginal city-dweller" (p. 9). Of necessity, this will involve the integration of "field observation, structural analysis and theoretical construction . . . [that will] advance in unison and mutually reinforce each other" (p. 10).

4. We need to distinguish between the social condition characteristic of an area and the "conditions it entails (which can, over time, crystallize into a local culture and panoply of typical strategies)" (p. 11); its positioning within a hierarchy of places, both in material and symbolic terms; and the function the neighborhood serves for the broader metropolitan system. Possible functions may include "reservoirs of low-skill labor," "warehouses for supernumerary populations that no longer have any identifiable political or economic utility in the new polarized capitalism," or "spatial containers for the ostracization of undesirable social categories and activities" (p. 11). Wacquant argues that neighborhoods can "fulfill one or other of these functions in succession" (p. 11).

5. Finally, we need to examine the "degree and form of state penetration" (p. 11), while recognizing the gap between government policies "on paper" and the actions of "street-level bureaucrats" (Lipsky, 1980). Particular attention needs to be given to the activities of police as a "frontline agency" directed toward "precarious and marginal categories" (Wacquant, p. 12), but also to schools and hospitals, housing and social welfare, firefighting and transportation. This study of "state penetration" must also take onboard the agency of local populations: "even when poor city-dwellers fail to overturn the 'rituals of marginality' that bind them to the governing elite, their collective action continually engenders new meanings and multistranded exchanges that open up a possible space for collective demands and social critique (Velez-Ibanez, 1983)" (Wacquant, pp. 11–12).

Learning to Speak Back

Sound epistemologies and perspectives are important in order to help communities, including their young people, to speak back and develop agency. Neighborhoods are not simply benign dormitory spaces in which people reside, and from which they commute to and from if they have work, or points from which they access services if they are not part of the paid workforce. Nor are they places to be homogenized, categorized, castigated, and used as compliant sites for government social experimentation. On the contrary, neighborhoods are places in which people live out their aspirations, where opportunities are constructed and contested, but also places in which peoples' worst fears and nightmares become realized and crystallized, and where neoliberalism has produced what Bauman (2011) calls "collateral damage" through the ways in which distant forces of globalization, deindustrialization, and economic restructuring do their ugly, deforming work.

Lupton (2010) argues the need to "use space in more social, historical, relative, contingent, and dynamic ways to examine the educational experiences of economically disadvantaged young people" (p. 121). Such accounts, she argues, would

> demonstrate that both the meaning of poverty and the meaning of education are constructed in space, and that relations between places, as well as the characteristics of particular places, are instrumental in creating educational successes for some groups of young people and educational failure for others. (p. 121)

At the most elementary level, schools located in areas of poverty suffer from guilt by association. Even people living close by tend to assume that a school situated on their public housing estate cannot be up to much. In such circumstances, the way the school presents itself can take on a different and greater significance than the standard PR work of schools operating within marketized systems. For example, an early encounter (TW) with a school that dramatically raised both its pupil numbers and their level of achievement made clear how this helped to overcome a sense of fatalism:

- the ugly brick chimney by the entrance was painted with icons of aspiration, such as the Statue of Liberty

- the new head took charge of the school's annual show *Oliver* and relocated it into the main theater of the town

- the head and management team moved out of their offices into an open-plan area to give easier access to parents and students

- the weekly school assembly was transformed to get masses of students up on stage under whatever pretext they could devise (talent shows, quizzes, dance performances, etc.)—soon even the rugby team were up on stage singing Christmas carols

- the staff began to think and speak about the students as "first generation academics," a discourse which was quickly taken up by the students themselves.

Successful reengagement of students with school education cannot, however, avoid a rethinking of curriculum and pedagogy along with the development of community agency. This can occur through "curricular and critical pedagogies that encourage students to understand their social and material place in the world and how it came to be the way that it is" (Thomson, 2010, p. 125). Pat Thomson admits that this is "not easy" to do because it "runs counter to a system which continues to demonize children living in poverty," but such approaches are crucial because of the way this kind of thinking "resists homogenization, celebrates difference, and refuses the equation of poverty plus education equals failure" (p. 134).

Clearly, young people need to learn to 'speak back' to the wider social and political forces that have put them in the deficit situations ascribed to them. This involves constructing viable alternative learning identities that are radically different to ones traditionally assigned to them (see chapter 9; Smyth & McInerney 2013; and many practical examples in Wrigley, Thomson & Lingard, 2012).

Along similar lines, Meg Maguire (2010) identifies the need for a collective dislodging of deeply entrenched and stigmatized conceptions and stereotypes of underachieving students—school-level ideologies that reflect those circulating in the wider society:

- that lack of success is their own fault and the result of low aspirations;

- that intergenerational failure is to be expected;

- that the reason for their discontent with school is that they are simply persistent troublemakers who are insolent and talk back;

- that they are uneducable and incapable of academic abstract learning and suited only for unskilled, menial, insecure, and poorly paid work (p. 137).

These deficit stereotypes operate within a context in which neoliberal capitalism simultaneously (1) seeks to limit the purpose of schooling to preparation for work (Ball, 2008) and (2) fails to provide this work. This can only lead to disillusionment and demoralization, or (one hopes) revolt.

According to Maguire (2010), the way these young people typically respond to the academic and social challenges of education is to choose from a well-known repertoire of:

- selectively or totally giving up on school (i.e., "I do not do school") (p. 141);

- constructing more viable identities for themselves outside of schools (p. 140) around youth and possibly drug and criminal cultures;

- engaging in a sharp critique of school as being "boring" and "irrelevant" to their lives and just wanting to "get on with their lives" (p. 140); and

- tending to "stay local" in the sense of regarding local networks and relationships as working for them and "staying in and around the immediate area where they lived" (p. 143).

Such trajectories are common in communities and neighborhoods that have been dealt devastating blows as a result of globalization. However, simply to dwell on typical responses and tendencies can result in reinforcing deficit views, including the notion of a culture of poverty (see chapter 5). We need to encourage students and teachers alike to speak back against these one-dimensional "underclass" renditions, constructed around notions of "dysfunctional families" with "domestic violence," absence of "male role models," and supposed climates of "indiscipline" (Power & Gewirtz, 2001, p. 46). This can only be done by enabling young people and parents to articulate both strengths and weaknesses of their situation and alternative explanations of how it has come about. This necessarily involves a focus on macro-level economic forces as well as their internalization as neighborhood issues.

As Carlo Raffo (2011) points out, this also requires an understanding of youth cultures and identities that includes a sense of agency as well as habitus.

> Young people can and do operate at the boundaries of any particular symbolic system, opening themselves to new and different experiences that go beyond the immediate locale (Raffo, 2000; Raffo & Reeves, 2000) and that provide different ways of thinking about self and in demonstrating autonomy. (p. 9)

We need to look at external (including macro-level) factors that impact on young people to make them the way they are, but also to examine more positively what resources people in contexts of deprivation have, how they use these resources, and to what effect. Shifting outside of the area-based frame of reference allows us to jettison simplistic conceptions and pursue approaches that are much more embedded in the lives and aspirations of people and the way they theorize about them.

CHAPTER FOUR

Blaming Individuals and Blaming Their Genes

We pass through this world but once. Few tragedies can be more extensive than the stunting of life, few injustices deeper than the denial of an opportunity to strive or even to hope, by a limit imposed from without, but falsely identified as lying within.
—Stephen Jay Gould, 1996, pp. 60–61

The intelligence of an individual is not a fixed quantity, a quantity that one cannot augment. . . . We must protest and react against this brutal pessimism.
—Alfred Binet, 1909, p. 101

A chapter about genes might seem out of place in a book about poverty, class, and schooling, but it is crucial to our argument. We first confront the myths of fixed, singular, and inherited intelligence that have been used to tilt the education system in favor of some young people to the considerable detriment of many others. We reveal how these false views of intelligence were bolstered by attempts to measure intellectual ability—some of them resulting in infamous scientific scams. We show close relationships between these concepts of innate intelligence and the class-based and racially targeted eugenics movement that was perpetuated under the guise of legitimate science. Even though the science on which this was based is discredited, rigid assumptions about ability continue to inform class-based processes of social stratification in schools. This has been exacerbated in the context of highly competitive and regulated education systems. Our conclusion is that rethinking what is meant by intelligence is crucial to the way marginalized young people and their families are treated educationally.

Explanations of social and intellectual difference based on the notion of fixed and inherited mental characteristics extend back through time. The argument dates back to Ancient Greece and is attributed to the elitist philosopher Plato who, in his justification of aristocratic rule, spoke of people having different and fixed natures that fitted them to their assigned social roles. To be more exact, he described this story as a "useful falsehood," a lie, a myth with which to keep people in their place:

> "You are all brothers," our story will tell them, "all of you in the city. But when God made you, he used a mixture of gold in the creation of those of you who were fit to be rulers, which is why they are the most valuable. He used silver for those who were to be auxiliaries, and iron and bronze for the farmers and the rest of the skilled workers." (Plato, 2000 [c380 BCE] *The Republic*, book 3, § 415)

In modern times, too, the notion of fixed and inherited intelligence has served as a convenient myth with which to justify unjust social and educational systems. It has served not only to block access to educational opportunities but also to divert attention from the failure of the political system as a whole to tackle inequalities of wealth and income.

How one conceptualizes ability or intelligence is fundamental to discussions of school improvement. If you believe that achievement is mainly predetermined by a student's gene pool, there is little point putting a lot of effort and resources into trying to educate those born with lower-class brains. More sensible, then, to concentrate on those with higher ability, writing off the rest as more or less uneducable. A common strategy, then, is to invent a way of segregating students with different amounts of intelligence into different kinds of school, tracks, or streams.

Other Concepts of Ability

There is a further source of difficulties. Conceiving of intelligence as a single entity, rather than specific abilities to do different things or solve different kinds of problems, can lead us to underestimate the complexity of learning. Traditionally, because the people who debate and define these matters tend to be those with high levels of competence in abstract modes of writing and in mathematical logic, there has been a tendency to see intelligence only in terms of these more abstract activities. Terman (1921), who adapted Binet's original test for the United States, explicitly defined intelligence as "the ability to carry on abstract thinking" (p. 128). Musicians might have talents and the electrician who fixes your lights has skills, but intelligence is an inner quality reserved only for abstract thinkers like . . . academics and teachers! This is not, of course, true of all cultures and societies: Polynesian sailors, Bedouin nomads, or military commanders might hold different priorities and values.

In recent years, thinkers such as Howard Gardner (1983) have challenged the concept of generic innate intelligence through models of multiple intelligences. (Unfortunately, a new form of genetic essentialism has arisen, which Gardner strongly condemns, namely writing off Black or working-class pupils, and especially boys, as 'kinesthetic learners'.) This debate is not entirely new: nineteenth-century thinking divided into two distinct traditions, craniometry, which sought to measure a generic mental capacity by the volume of the skull, and phrenology, which linked different parts of the head with different activities. Craniometry was the metaphorical foundation of concepts of a unified innate intelligence measured by IQ tests, and twentieth-century psychologists such as Burt continued to speak of a fixed *capacity* to learn. The other tradition, though no more scientific in itself, fed into notions of abilities being specific to different fields of activity and learning.

In the early twentieth century, Louis Thurstone (1938) spoke of distinct "primary mental abilities" (p. 1) that relate to different types of activity, for example, numerical ability, verbal comprehension, and spatial visualization. More recently, Robert Sternberg (1977) has made distinctions between three fundamental aspects of intelligence, which he called "cognitive styles": analytic, creative, and practical. Most intelligence tests relate only to the first of these.

In addition, in recent decades we have seen the development of theories of distributed or situated cognition (Salomon, 1993; Robbins & Aydede, 2009). These theories understand mind or problem-solving ability as something that is not simply contained within the skull but is stretched between our brains and senses, the languages and technologies we derive from our cultures, and the tasks and contexts where the problem is located. This is a radically different way of thinking from the cognitive model that underpins notions of an innate generic intelligence possessed separately by each individual.

The Social History of IQ

For most of the twentieth century, however, the notion of individuals possessing a quantity of generic inherited intelligence was the dominant one. It is important to grasp the context in which this idea became established.

Earlier explanations of intellectual ability were crude but also quite blatant in terms of social class and race. Attempts were made to justify slavery and later the British Empire in terms of spurious differences in skull capacity (Gould, 1996, pp. 105–41) as well as exaggerated and deliberately distorted comparisons with cranial shapes of apes.

Such scientific argument was located in a society that sought to keep the working class in its place. In terms of educational policy, at least in England, it was unthinkable or intolerable to educate working-class children above their station in life, so schooling for the working class, when it eventually became statutory, was restricted to poorly funded *elementary* schools. Children learned the 3

Rs (reading, writing, arithmetic), obedience, and pride in the British Empire. As late as 1902, school boards were forbidden to introduce higher-grade classes, such as science or art, and an academic secondary education was only for those whose parents could afford to pay (Chitty, 2009, p. 19; Simon, 1965, pp. 208–46). Even in the UK this pattern varied between countries; in Scotland universal primary education was a premise of the Protestant Reformation, and although the school experience was basic and often brutal in its discipline, a minority of poorer children received bursaries to go to university.

The first attempt to test intelligence occurred in France in 1904, when Alfred Binet was asked by the education authorities to identify children who needed extra tuition to succeed in school. He devised a test consisting of a broad range of quite random items that children of different ages might be expected to know or understand, while trying to avoid anything that might result from rote learning at school. Results of the test were recorded in terms of how many years the mental age was below the physical age:

In fact Binet (1905) was sceptical about the use of the term "measurement":

> The scale, properly speaking, does not permit the measure of intelligence, because intellectual qualities are not superposable, and therefore cannot be measured as linear surfaces are measured. (p. 40, cited in Gould, 1996, p. 181)

Binet could recognize the dangers of testing and was forthright about the conclusions that should not be drawn. He did not appear to regard intelligence as a quantity or unitary entity; the score was simply an aggregate of many performances. He worried that teachers might use low scores as an excuse "for getting rid of all the children who trouble us" (p. 169, cited in Gould, p. 181) or that they could become a self-fulfilling prophecy. The tests could not distinguish the causes of a child's backwardness but were "to study his condition at the time and that only. We have nothing to do either with his past history or with his future" (p. 37, cited in Gould, p. 182).

Binet was interested in ensuring that children received appropriate remedial education, and the possibility of teachers writing off children as irredeemably stupid made him angry (Gould, 1996, p. 180–84, including original sources) As David Perkins (1995) puts it:

> What most amazes me about Alfred Binet . . . was the conclusion he did not jump to, the theory he did not assert . . . He figured out a way to measure intelligence. However, he held back from the obvious conclusion—intelligence as a pure essence measured out more to some people and less to others. He left the door open for learnable intelligence. He focused simply on how one could put a number to a phenomenon—the phenomenon of intelligent behavior. (pp. 23–24)

Unfortunately, as the idea of testing for intelligence was adopted in the United States and England, in their particular ideological environments, Binet's principles were ignored and his aims turned upside down. The process was aided when the German psychologist Stern in 1912 recalculated a difference (chronological age minus "mental age") into a quotient (mental age divided by actual age), laying the foundation for regarding IQ as stable (Gould, 1996, p. 180).

The leading U.S. proponents were firmly convinced that people were poor as a result of stupidity: "The people who are doing the drudgery are, as a rule, in their proper places" (Goddard, 1919, p. 246). Speaking to Princeton undergraduates in 1919, Goddard justified gaps of wealth and income as the result of different levels of intelligence:

> Now the fact is, that workmen may have a ten year intelligence while you have a twenty. To demand for him such a home as you enjoy is as absurd as it would be to insist that every laborer should receive a graduate fellowship. How can there be such a thing as social equality with this wide range of mental capacity? (cited in Gould, 1996, p. 191)

Similarly, Terman (1916) believed that people generally worked in, and should be directed toward, particular types of occupation as a result of different levels of innate intelligence:

> Common observation would itself suggest that the social class to which the family belongs depends less on chance than on the parents' native qualities of intellect and character. . . . The children of successful and cultured parents test higher than children from wretched and ignorant homes for the simple reason that their heredity is better. (p. 115, cited in Gould, 1996, p. 213)

On both sides of the Atlantic, the pioneers of intelligence testing regarded it as axiomatic that intelligence was mainly inherited. In England, a major forerunner was Darwin's cousin Francis Galton (1869), who had published a genealogical study of families of famous scientists to assert the claim that genius was genetically transmitted. Cyril Burt, who was to become the most influential educational psychologist in England, tested the sons of Oxford University academics and the sons of skilled manual workers in the town. He regarded the higher scores of the university children as proof that intelligence was genetic, disregarding any possible effects of upbringing, family culture, or the different schools they attended. Moreover, even in this early study, Burt openly acknowledged that he had adjusted the test scores to accord with their teachers' opinions of the pupil's intelligence (Gould, 1996, p. 305).

The assumption that the higher scores of the sons of richer and better-educated parents were due to genetic rather than environmental reasons (i.e., early upbringing) exemplifies an elite's ideological attempt to justify its own wealth and privilege. In reality, as Bowles and Nelson (1974) point out, parental wealth is always far more influential. They demonstrated, for the United States at that time, that, even when both children have average IQ, a child whose family is in the top 10 percent economically had a 25 times greater chance of reaching the top 10 percent as an adult, compared with a child from the poorest 10 percent.

Furthermore, this ideological position was entangled with *eugenics*, the belief that the British "race" (or white Western Europeans, in the case of the United States) would degenerate unless the poor were prevented from breeding (Chitty, 2009, p. 45).

Eugenics

The eugenics movement, originating with Galton, was hegemonic in Britain from the start of the twentieth century until the mid-1940s when the Nazi extermination programs revealed just where it led. It also had major impact across Northern Europe, North America, and beyond. To illustrate the extent of this, nearly 63,000 sterilizations were carried out between 1935 and 1975 in Sweden, including gypsies who were targeted as racially inferior, and in the state of Virginia alone in the United States, more than 7,500 sterilizations were carried out in mental health facilities "primarily upon white men and women considered feeble-minded and antisocial, including 'unwed mothers, prostitutes, petty criminals and children with disciplinary problems'" (Gould, 1996, p. 365). In 1908, the novelist D. H. Lawrence confided in a letter to a friend:

> If I had my way, I would build a lethal chamber as big as the Crystal Palace, with a military band playing softly, and a Cinematograph working brightly; then I'd go out into the back streets and main streets and bring them in, all the sick, the halt and the maimed. (Boulton, 1979, p. 81)

For the most part, however, members of the Eugenics Society restricted themselves to persuasion, birth control, and enforced sterilization. Marie Stopes, the great pioneer of birth control, was a eugenicist well before she became interested in birth control. She believed that too many children were being born to "immigrants such as Irish Catholics and Polish, Russian and German Jews, along with casual laborers, the thriftless poor and the feeble-minded—a trend which must result in national deterioration" (summarised by Chitty, 2009, p. 60).

Burt did not derive his theories of innate generic intelligence from pure theory or objective scientific research: he was thoroughly saturated with class prejudice and the eugenics ideology:

> However much we try to educate the ignorant, train the imbecile, cure the lunatic and reform the criminal, their offspring will inherit, not the results of such education, but the original ignorance; not the acquired training, but the original imbecility; not the acquired sanity, but the original predisposition to lunacy; not the moral reform, but the original

tendency to crime. All our work will have to be done afresh with each generation. (1913, p. 172, cited in Chitty, 2009, p. 70)

While still a student at Oxford, Burt had written in his undergraduate notebook:

The problem of the very poor—chronic poverty: little prospect of the solution of the problem without the forcible detention of the wreckage of society or otherwise preventing them from propagating their own species. (Rose, Lewontin, & Kamin, 1984, p. 87)

Intelligence Testing and Social Selection

In the United States, prejudice took a directly racial tone, for example, Terman's (1916) belief that low intelligence

is very common among Spanish-Indian and Mexican families of the South-west and also among negroes. Their dullness seems to be racial, or at least inherent in the family stocks from which they come. . . . Children of this group should be segregated in special classes. . . . They cannot master abstractions, but they can often be made efficient workers. (pp. 91–92)

Modified versions of Binet's tests were used in the United States to control immigration, in order to keep out refugees and migrants from southern and eastern as opposed to northwest Europe. Though the tests were supposedly a reflection of innate intelligence and ostensibly culture free, they included questions about famous baseball players, tennis nets, and how to hold a bowling ball (Gould, 1996; Rose et al., 1984). In the United States in particular, the application of intelligence testing connected, from 1907, to the passing of

compulsory sterilization laws aimed at genetically inferior "degenerates." The categories detailed included, in different states, criminals, idiots, imbeciles, epileptics, rapists, lunatics, drunkards, drug fiends, syphilitics, moral and sexual perverts, and "diseased and degenerate persons." (Rose et al., 1984, p. 88)

Intelligence testing was adopted for a variety of reasons in different societies. Bisseret (1979, pp. 6–32) shows a different chronology in France but the logic is fundamentally similar. In Britain, Will Cowburn (1986) argues, the growing strength of the labor movement (trade unions and the recently founded Labour Party) made it impossible for the ruling class to continue speaking openly in terms of educating working-class children "for their station in life," or referring explicitly to the general intellectual inferiority of the "lower orders." Indeed, Cowburn locates the last official use of such language in the Consultative Committee on Higher Elementary Schools of 1906, when employers' representatives called for schooling that would make working-class children "efficient members of the class to which they belong":

> Faced with such increasing radical activity, the language of class arrogance was hardly appropriate. It was becoming no longer possible to dismiss the vast majority of working class children as being unfit to receive a secondary education because of their class alone. (Cowburn, 1986, pp. 122–25)

The situation was compounded by the anger of demobbed soldiers in Britain at the end of the First World War and by serious shortages of skilled labor. While most working-class children were still restricted to a cheap elementary education, a small minority were given access to grammar schools as preparation for clerical or professional employment. Intelligence testing provided the perfect sifting mechanism. Pupils were tested at the age of ten and those with the highest scores were granted a scholarship to follow an academic secondary curriculum at grammar schools, though many were still excluded simply because their families could not afford expensive school uniforms and equipment. (More affluent parents continued to pay tuition fees to guarantee their children's secondary education.) This pattern remained fundamentally the same for the next fifty years. In effect, it represented a continuation of class-based reproduction, justified on the assumption that intelligence is hereditary apart from a few whose gene pool was somehow out of line with their parents' occupational level.

Such use of intelligence testing relied strongly on Burt's professional reputation, which appeared beyond challenge. He was the first Educational Psychologist for London County Council and subsequently a professor at London University. His advice was accepted as authoritative by government policymaking committees.

The Identical Twins Studies

Burt's scientific procedure had often been cavalier, including asking headteachers for estimates that would override the test results (Gould, 1996, p. 305), but that scarcely mattered since his conclusions were ideologically convenient. As Rose, Lewontin, and Kamin (1984) point out:

> Burt never provided even the most elementary description of how, when, or where his "data" had been collected. The normal canons of scientific reporting were ignored entirely by Burt, and by the editors of the journals that published his papers. He never even identified the "IQ test" he supposedly administered. . . . Within many of his papers, even the sizes of his supposed samples of relatives were not reported. The correlations were given without any supporting details. (p. 102)

Burt's fixation with hereditary explanations led him to seek the ultimate proof, namely that identical twins separated from their natural mother would retain her IQ rather than that of the adoptive parents. He published three separate studies that were eventually discovered to be fraudulent—they had simply never happened! Around the time of Burt's death, Professor Leon Kamin pointed out the implausibility of this repeated correlation, presented to three decimal points .771, which remained absolutely stable while the number of pairs of twins increased from 21 to 53 (Kamin, 1972 and 1974, in Rose et al., 1984, p. 103). Burt's friend and biographer Leslie Hearnshaw set out to clear the great man's name but could find no evidence of any records of research having taken place; the twins themselves and their parents had disappeared without a trace, and Burt's two researchers appeared to be a fiction (Rose et al., p. 104). Somebody should have smelled a rat many years earlier when reading the studies, but Burt's conception of intelligence was so hegemonic that no one asked questions.

As Rose and colleagues (1984, p. 106) point out, the few later studies of separated identical twins by other researchers are also seriously flawed. Many pairs of twins were only temporarily 'separated'; they were cared for by relatives or close friends, went to the same school, and remained in close contact. It is actually very difficult to find twins separated soon after birth and adopted by unrelated and dissimilar families. A more viable investigation consisted of comparing the IQ scores of adopted children who were not twins to their natural and adoptive parents. The general tendency is for adoptive parents' scores to be higher, largely because of the adoption agencies' selection processes. These studies show a substantial rise in the child's IQ score from that of the natural parents to the adoptive parents, with IQ correlating as strongly between adoptive mother and adopted child as between the adoptive mother and her natural children (Rose et al., pp. 110–14).

Declining Trust in Intelligence Testing

The intellectual struggle against the idea that intelligence is inherited, innate, and relatively fixed was essential to the political struggle to extend educational opportunities. It was a process that took more than two decades to accomplish across Britain following World War II.

In 1952, the Bournemouth Education Committee allowed a number of pupils who had failed the 11+ test to be given the school-leaving examinations at age sixteen that were intended only for those who passed. Most scored very high (Simon, 1953, pp. 82–83, also for other historic examples). In 1954, it emerged that girls were having to score considerably higher marks than boys in the test to gain access to grammar schools (Chitty, 2009) though this did not become widespread knowledge until much later. The proportion of pupils gaining grammar school places ranged from 8 percent in some areas to more than 60 percent in others, making a mockery of claims that the test distinguished those naturally capable of a grammar school education from those who were not. There was also major irony in the official claim that intelligence tests reflected innate intelligence while pupils in their final year of primary school were spending an hour a day practising the tests in order to raise their scores. Eventually, across most of England and all of Scotland and Wales, comprehensive schools replaced a divided system.

Other doubts have arisen concerning the idea that we have a fixed quantity of inherited intelligence, in other words a genetic limit on our intellectual development. Tests applied on a mass scale and over a long period show scores rising by about 15 percentage points every thirty years—a major upward shift causing tests to be regularly recalibrated. For example, the average IQ of U.S. recruits in World War II was a standard deviation higher than in World War I. All young men beginning compulsory military service in the Netherlands took a nonverbal mental ability test: in 1981 82 percent scored over 24 out of 40, compared with 31 percent in 1952. This phenomenon has become known as the Flynn effect (Flynn, 1999), and it remains a stumbling block for those who continue to believe that intelligence tests measure hereditary intelligence.

This is not to suggest that our genes make no difference, but there are a number of reasons for rejecting the idea that we have a fixed amount of ability:

1. Psychologists are unable to relate IQ tests to real-life problem solving in any convincing way; as Boring put it (1923), intelligence is "what intelligence tests measure" (pp. 35–36).

2. The concept involves a reification of cognitive activities, so that our skill in carrying them out is perceived as a *substance*, with the illusion that it can be measured and quantified.

3. There is confusion around the term *hereditary*; as Gould (1996) explains, the fact that something is inherited does not mean that it is unchanging.

4. Mathematical processes alone cannot establish whether intelligence is unitary or consists of multiple capacities that partly overlap. Spearman invented one correlation procedure specifically to demonstrate the existence of a generic, inherited intelligence; whereas Thurstone's vector-based method is designed to identify distinct "primary mental abilities" (Gould, 1996, p. 326).

5. The distribution curves produced by test results do not prove the reality of IQ, since the tests are themselves calibrated in order to produce a "normal distribution curve. . . . Tests are judged to be good if they produce results such that two-thirds of the population fall within 15 percent of the mean" (Rose et al., 1984, p. 92).

Biological understanding has also moved on, so that it becomes much more difficult to sustain a determinist position. It is no longer possible to think of specific genes producing intelligence in any direct way; simple mechanisms such as Mendel's explanation of the transmission of yellow or green color in peas are now known to be atypical, as most genetic processes are vastly more complicated than a pair of chromosomes underpinning a discrete characteristic. Steven Rose (1998) summarizes it as follows:

The ultra-Darwinists' metaphysical concept of genes as hard, impenetrable and isolated units cannot be correct. Any individual gene can be expressed only against the background of the whole of the rest of the genome. Genes produce gene products which in turn influence other genes, switching them on and off, modulating their activity and function. (p. 215)

And that is before we even consider the effects of environment. The scientific specialism of epigenetics has established how gene expression can change without changes in the underlying DNA sequence and how environmental factors such as nutrition or pollutants can switch genes on and off.

We also know that the size and shape of a brain are influenced by early experience, and even by intellectual activity in later life; for example, an increase in size of part of the brain has been discovered when new taxi drivers in London study the location of city streets. This is radically different from mechanistic unidirectional models whereby we begin with a quantity of something called intelligence that limits our capacity to learn for the rest of our lives.

The Zombie Influence of IQ Measurement

Despite clear refutations and disproof, notions of inherited generic intelligence continue to impact on educational practice, and in particular on the children of manual workers and those living in poverty. This is due to a combination of unexamined and residual common sense beliefs, tacit assumptions, and lay and professional pseudoscience, along with the continuation of habitual practices of testing and classroom organization. This is not surprising, given the hegemony of IQ and associated school selection for most of the twentieth century.

In Britain, many schools use a form of intelligence test, the cognitive ability test (CAT), to predict future examination results in order to determine the pupils' curriculum; although the producers of these tests make no claim for innateness or heritability, it seems likely that many teachers make that assumption. Test results are intended to raise expectations when they reveal a higher than expected potential masked by poor behavior or effort. However, while such tests are better than simple prejudice (is the child clean and well-behaved?) and can raise signals that some pupils are underachieving, they can also limit expectations. It is easy to forget that the tests indicate levels achieved as a result of earlier life experiences rather than some fixed capacity, and that the test designers admit a wide margin for error.

In Northern Ireland and some parts of England, children are still segregated into grammar schools and secondary modern schools at age eleven, despite many of the secondary moderns being renamed comprehensive or high school. Almost all English secondary schools are now entitled to select 10 percent of their pupils according to a particular aptitude for the school's specialism (e.g., mathematics, science, business, languages, or creative arts), though most do not exercise this power. (No one has been able to explain how a ten-year-old's aptitude for business can be identified, and nor can potential in music or languages be easily demonstrated by children who have never had the opportunity to learn.)

Similarly, every English school is expected to identify and list which pupils are "gifted and talented." The first word relates to core academic studies, and the second to other activities such as creative arts. This is intrinsically discriminatory, since it is impossible to identify a pupil's potential as a violinist if she has never had the opportunity to play. On this basis the identified pupils can attend weekend or summer schools. Such opportunities should be extended to disadvantaged pupils in order to discover gifts and talents that have never had the chance to develop.

In many parts of Britain, it is common for teachers to place children onto different tables as ability groups for reading, writing and maths within weeks of entering primary school. Although the grouping is, in theory, subject-specific, in practice the same children tend to find themselves on the triangle table for maths, the blue table for writing, and the donkey table for reading. Despite the euphemisms the children know that they are grouped together because they are "not very clever." It would be revealing to investigate:

- What do the teachers mean by judging them able or less able?

- How do they form this judgment?

- Do they consider whether this is the result of early experiences?

- Do they seek to provide experiences the "less able" pupils have missed out on?

- Do they really believe these children can catch up?

- Why are the activities assigned to the "less able" group always so boring?!

A belief in some children's inability to learn results in providing them with a curriculum that makes it impossible for them to learn—a self-fulfilling prophecy.

We need to consider the residual influence of a belief in fixed intelligence and the notion of meritocracy that it underpins. Justification of income differences and social status on the grounds of intelligence has been an issue since the start of the twentieth century and constantly recurs, often linked to race. The most significant reemergence was Herrnstein and Murray's (1994) *The Bell Curve*, a book that resurrected the old myth that Black Americans' lower scores on IQ tests reflect a genetically carried inferiority, which in its turn was used to justify their low social position. Again, contrary evidence was ignored, including the gap between IQ scores of African Americans who had grown up and gone to school in the northern and southern states. (See detailed critique in Gould, 1996, p. 367.) In fact, the test used is one that clearly depends on school learning for success rather than any innate intelligence unaffected by schooling. Racial differences that show up on IQ tests simply cannot be separated from differences in the quality of schooling and in life experience overall.

This book included a claim to have identified an intellectual underclass. One of the authors, Charles Murray, went on to develop that idea in cultural and political terms, in an argument seeking to push the blame for poverty onto the victims. He claimed that poverty is caused not by low wages or unemployment but by the fixed attitudes and lifestyles of poor urban neighborhoods.

There is of course a blatant contradiction between the two explanations of inherited genetic intelligence and cultural inadequacy, but they have in common a deficit perspective on people subjected to poverty and a belief that the state should not waste money derived from (higher earners') taxes on early intervention or welfare benefits. Although *The Bell Curve* became notorious because of its racism, the authors also sought to justify differences in wealth. Challenging this, Fischer and colleagues (1996), in *Inequality by Design*, demonstrate that only a tenth of the growing income differentials in the United States can be explained by differences in measured intelligence (see also McNamee & Miller, 2004).

New Thinking, New Practice

The notion of a generic intelligence at least in the cognitive domain, operating across a range of different activities, cannot be written off, but there remains the danger of marginalizing thoughtful activity that is creative, emotional, or practical. Some fruitful attempts have been made to follow Binet's trail and intervene educationally to raise the cognitive abilities of less successful pupils, for example, Feuerstein and colleagues' (1980) instrumental enrichment programs.

A strong example of more specific approaches to improving ability is Philip Adey and Michael Shayer's cognitive acceleration projects (Adey & Shayer, 1994; Shayer & Adey, 2002). This began in the fields of science and mathematics, focusing on key concepts of those disciplines but has been extended to other parts of the curriculum. Another very important initiative is represented by Susan Hart and colleagues (2004) in *Learning without Limits* (see also their sequel, Swann et al., 2012). Rejecting the notion of different capacities to learn and the associated differentiation by segregation and tracking, they demonstrate in theory and practice the vast untapped potential of children within the present education system.

Educational theorists have only recently begun to think through the significance of a radical reconceptualization of mind and cognition. Using Vygotsky's work as a starting point, a new psychology is emerging that rejects the idea that mind is somehow contained within the skull and sees it as spread between an individual, other people, the physical context, artifacts, including those that assist thinking (calculators, telescopes, etc.), and cultural tools such as language and other symbolic systems. (For examples, see Perkins, 1995; Salomon, 1993; and the international network of scholars building on Vygotsky's cultural-historical paradigm such as Yrjö Engeström, Michael Cole, and James Wertsch.) Clearly such non-Cartesian views of cognition are incompatible with reified notions of fixed intellectual capacity.

The tacit common sense of residual ideologies of fixed intelligence will not die out of its own accord. A deep and thorough rethinking of what we mean by intelligence or ability is vitally necessary as part of the project of overcoming the limitations suffered by marginalized and impoverished families. Unless they have available some more coherent and helpful theories, operable amid rapid classroom decision making, teachers will continue to make ad hoc but lasting decisions that some children are bright and others are 'low ability'.

CHAPTER FIVE

Speaking the Wrong Language

Linguists have known for years that all children—including poor children—have impressive language ability. The vast majority of children enter school with vocabularies fully fit for everyday life, with complex grammar and with deep understandings of experiences and stories.
—James Gee, 2004, p. 17

W e continue our discussion of the alleged deficits of young people from working-class (i.e., manual worker) backgrounds by looking at theories concerning deficiencies in language use. According to these theories, the language registers they have acquired at home handicap working-class children and even render many of them ineducable. Although the focus has shifted from 'working class' to 'poor', these arguments constantly re-emerge. The discussion is also often racialized, particularly in the United States.

We dig down into the foundational research on language and educability to show the pervasiveness of stereotypes. Despite very thin evidence, we will examine how findings from flawed research became hegemonic. Indeed language deficit theories quickly displaced a tarnished IQ theory as the dominant explanation for underachievement.

The claim that working-class children have restricted language registers, as we show, seems to have more to do with the differences between language use in home and school; those who emphasize the supposed deficiencies of the former have, unfortunately, little to say about the way the most common classroom discourses restrict children's learning. We go on to show how these myths became insinuated into teachers' thinking and the professional development they were subjected to. We also point to the link with a discredited anthropological belief that primitive peoples are linguistically and intellectually inferior.

Lest we be lulled into believing that these arguments are no longer relevant, we point to the contemporary revival of linguistic deficit views, particularly the widespread influence of American Ruby Payne. Payne (2005), whose continuing professional development business consists of peddling snakeoil solutions to teachers about how to remedy the so-called culture of poverty problem, eschews the need for solid evidence through an amalgam of damaging stereotypes and bizarre connections made between language styles, behavior, and criminality.

In the final part of the chapter, we look at research concerning more general aspects of parenting. We show that, here too, despite the good intentions and professionalism of research teams, there remains a tendency to construct comparisons in terms of a comparative deficit including overgeneralizing from the most damaging situations.

We conclude by asking the obvious question: how did this explanation of the link between class and home-school learning environments become so popular? From what we uncover in this chapter, it becomes clear that this is what happens when research is not read critically, when research nuances are not picked up, when contradictions are covered up, and particularly when 'common sense' prejudices enable poorly conceived theories and practices to be popularized.

The Emergence of Language Deficit Theories

The chronology of the language deficit argument and its popularization is in itself significant. One of its early critics, Harold Rosen (1972), explains its timeliness in replacing the discredited theory of inherited intelligence (see chapter 4):

> It was just when this theory [i.e., innate intelligence] was looking sadly tattered and when the high-priest of the psychometric ideology himself, Professor Vernon, felt obliged to publish a self-critical restatement of his position, that the theories of Bernstein began to be available. These early papers, which he himself now says "were conceptually weak and . . . horrifyingly coarse" (Bernstein, 1971, p. 11) . . . were readily seized upon . . . because they seemed to offer theoretical respectability to the widespread notion among teachers and others that an intrinsic feature of working-class language, rooted in their way of life, disqualified working-class children educationally and, by the same token, justified the notion of the superior educational potential of the middle class . . .
>
> No serious writer could go on asserting that working-class speech was ungrammatical, lazy, debased and so forth. Bernstein's theories made it possible to bypass all that and to suggest a much more profound and intractable deficiency. The theories pointed to a basic cognitive defect. (p. 3)

Significantly, Bernstein (1986) later referred to his codes as the "genes of social class" (p. 472).

As with IQ, language deficit arguments, which in Britain focused on class, were largely connected with race in the United States—with African Americans often serving as proxy for poor or working class. In the context of the growing struggle to desegregate schools and resource them adequately, the supposed defects of African American children served as a convenient scapegoat and a diversion from the real deficits of their schools.

The stigmatization of working-class language became part of a wider deficit perspective on how children were brought up within a 'culture of poverty', which later found new expression in the even more negative notion of an underclass. In its extreme form, a stereotype was created of homes that were so chaotic and neglectful that children arrived at school with virtually no language at all. Bereiter and Engelmann (1966) argue:

> For purposes of getting along socially and of self-expression, language is a convenience but not a necessity for the young child [i.e., in poor families, and predominantly black]. It is quite possible to make one's wants known, to enter actively into play and other social relationships, and to give vent to one's feelings without language. . . . People who work with disadvantaged preschool children report a considerable number of children who are four years of age hardly speak at all. Language is apparently dispensable enough in the life of the lower-class child for an occasional child to get along without it altogether. (p. 31).

Similar positions were espoused by Jensen (1968), who oscillated between genetic intelligence and verbal deficit theory at different points in his career:

> Language in the lower class . . . consists more of a relatively small repertoire of stereotyped phrases and expressions which are used rather loosely without much effort to achieve a subtle correspondence between perception and verbal expression. Much of lower-class language consists of a kind of incidental "emotional" accompaniment to action here and now. (p. 116)

Such myths acquired academic respectability and become part of the professional folklore of teachers. Bereiter and Engelmann (1966) claimed that disadvantaged children do not recognize single words but chunk together sounds to make "giant words; thus, 'He bihdaw' (He's a big dog) or 'Uai-ga-na-ju' (I ain't got no juice)" (pp. 34–35). These are, as Gordon (1981) points out, fictitious examples made up by the authors, and an indication of the researchers' unfamiliarity with the children's pronunciation and intonation. Speech does not, in fact, segment neatly into separate words with spaces between.

Elsewhere, Bereiter and Engelmann (1966) argue, with a crude and stereotyped link between social circumstances and linguistic expression that is close to Bernstein's position, that in "lower-class homes . . . language is primarily used to control behavior, to express sentiments and emotions, to permit the vicarious sharing of experiences, and to keep the social machinery of the home running smoothly" but not "to explain, to describe, to instruct, to inquiry, to hypothesize, to analyze, to compare, to deduce, and to test" (p. 31). These powerful assertions were based on negligible evidence.

As Gordon (1981) points out, these authors "seem reluctant to accord the speech that they so dislike the status of language at all and propose nothing less than its systematic eradication at least in school settings" (p. 55). We illustrate this by adding italics to the following quotation from Bereiter and colleagues (1966):

> It seems to have been taken for granted by other educators that one must begin by encouraging the child to make the fullest possible use of the language he already possesses before one may set about improving it. Our estimation of the language of culturally deprived children agrees, however, with that of Bernstein, who maintains that this language is not merely an underdeveloped version of standard English, but is a basically *non-logical mode of expressive behavior which lacks the formal properties necessary for the organization of thought.* From this point of view, the goal of language training for the culturally deprived could be seen as not that of improving the child's language but rather that of *teaching him a different language* which would hopefully *replace the first one*, at least in school settings. The two languages share lexical elements and these we made use of, but apart from this we *proceeded much as if the children had no language at all.* (pp. 112–13, our italics)

This line of thinking was no mere aberration on the part of a few out-of-touch academics: the authors designed a particularly restrictive version of compensatory preschooling dependent on rote learning and disengagement with children's home lives, which became a major strand within the massive Head Start project in the United States.

This was the most extreme version of language deficit theory, but its more widespread, sophisticated, and plausible versions concerned (1) the ineducability of children who speak nonstandard varieties of English, particularly Black Americans; (2) the argument that working-class children, in the main, only learn to speak about what is right in front of their noses.

The following two sections will deal with these versions of language deficit theory in the United States and in Britain, respectively, and include critiques of them by Labov and Rosen.

The Logic of Nonstandard English

Local dialects have long been stigmatized in Britain, and pupils derided for speaking them inside school. As George Bernard Shaw (2009 [1912]) once said, "It is impossible for an Englishman to open his mouth, without making some other Englishman despise him" (p. 5). Riessman (1962), in *The Culturally Deprived Child*, displays such snobbery when he derides the use of words such as *telly* and *pub* as indicators of lower social class and inferior language. The prejudice against Black American versions of English are probably even stronger, as indeed with

Caribbean dialects following migration to Britain. Out of the baseline assertions about children without language, more specific explanations developed that the syntax used by African Americans was illogical and, if uncorrected, would hinder cognitive development.

William Labov (1969), in "The Logic of Nonstandard English," provides a forceful critique that still resonates. His arguments concern the flawed conditions in which data was being gathered as well as the faulty linguistic understanding of the researchers. To those who claimed that African American children "receive little verbal stimulation . . . hear very little well-formed language . . . cannot speak complete sentences, do not know the names of common objects, cannot form concepts or convey logical thoughts" (p. 179), Labov replies that they clearly have never seen these children on their own ground:

> The concept of verbal deprivation has no basis in social reality: in fact, Negro children in the urban ghettos receive a great deal of verbal stimulation, hear more well-formed sentences than middle-class children, and participate fully in a highly verbal culture; they have the same basic vocabulary, possess the same capacity for conceptual learning, and use the same logic as anyone else who learns to speak and understand English. (p. 179)

His critique highlights the flawed research procedures used to support deficit accounts:

> In the literature we find very little direct observation . . . most typically, the investigators ask the child if he has dinner with his parents, and if he engages in dinner-table conversation with them. He is also asked whether his family takes him on trips to museums and other cultural activities. This slender thread of evidence is used to explain and interpret the large body of tests carried out in the laboratory and in the school. (p. 183)

Labov points out the intimidating effect of white middle-class academics taking young children from the ghetto into alien environments: it is no surprise that these four-year-olds become silent. By contrast, Labov produces transcripts of street debates that demonstrate articulate young people using language powerfully to debate religious and political ideas.

Restricted Codes and Limited Horizons

The most sophisticated version of language deficit theory was developed by Basil Bernstein (1971) in England. Essentially this was based on the notion that working-class families' use of language is overwhelmingly directed toward the here-and-now, and consequently the children are handicapped when required to speak of more remote or complex matters in school. Bernstein (1971) spoke of a restricted code derived from the whole way of life (work and domestic) of these families, a pattern of family life that somehow determined the language structures they used. Bernstein concedes that middle-class families also use restricted code language patterns when the context is fairly local and routine, but he claims that, unlike working-class families, they also habitually use a more formal language regulated by an elaborated code to speak about more distant things. He clearly struggled to explain what he meant by codes and how these inner regulators (a reification) formed a bridge between social conditions and relations and characteristic speech forms (Edwards, 1976, p. 94).

According to Anthony Edwards (1976, p. 88; see also Bernstein, 1971, p. 6), Bernstein was particularly inspired by a paper by Schatzman and Strauss (1955) "Social Class and Modes of Communication" that analyzed different observers' reports of a hurricane in Arkansas. As Edwards rightly says:

> Linguistically, their article is infuriating. No transcript material is given, nor is there any clear evidence for the striking differences they claim to have found. These have to be taken on trust. (p. 83)

The analysis in Schatzman and Strauss (1955) is based on two groups of ten in-terviewees, "selected by *extreme* position on educational and income continuums" (p. 330, our italics), and contrasts their responses to an interviewer's questions about what they have seen. Toward the end, the researchers acknowledge that the lower-class interviewees may feel intimidated by the "well-spoken, educated" interviewer, and that the higher-class interviewees will be more familiar with mak-ing this type of report because of their occupations; it is, they admit, a "conversa-tion between the classes . . . it is not surprising that the interviewer is often baffled and that the respondent frequently misinterprets what is wanted" (p. 337).

However, these dynamics are not adequately considered in the analysis. For example, we are told that the lower-class interviewees provide a description as seen through their own eyes—which is presumably what they thought was expected of them as eye-witnesses; after all, the interviewer's opening question was, "Tell me your story of the tornado." By contrast, some of the higher-class respondents present a more elaborately structured, almost literary narrative that "qualifies, summarizes, and sets the stage with rich introductory material, expands themes, frequently illustrates, anticipates disbelief" (Schatzman & Strauss, 1955, p. 332) and so on.

The evaluation by Schatzman and Strauss (1955) is full of false expectations. For example, the lower-class interviewees are criticized for a lack of knowledge about how organizations such as the Red Cross are structured, so they tend to personalize its actions, for instance, when talking vaguely about "the Red Cross helping people." Despite the framing of the interview, they are condemned for providing the account from their own perspective; for example, "We run over there to see about them, and they was alright" (p. 331). Even their efficiency and honesty in marking the end of their report with "That's all I know" are criticized as a failure to recapitulate the events.

The crucial point that impressed Bernstein was the confusion that arose when some of the lower-class interviewees made too many assumptions about what the interviewer knows: "There is much surnaming of persons without genuine identification, and often terms like 'we' and 'they' are used without clear referents" (p. 331). This is clearly a problem that can lead to confusion and misunderstanding, and we are told that

> the most unintelligible speakers thoroughly confound the interviewer who tries to follow images, acts, persons, and events which seem to come out of nowhere and disappear without warning. (p. 331)

However, there is a real danger of overgeneralization, since we learn that in the best cases among the lower-class interviewees: "The respondent . . . became aware that his listener was not present at the scene and so located objects and events for him" (p. 331). It is worth emphasizing a number of features of this research report that ring true of many later studies of working-class 'language deficit', including, as we will see, Bernstein's own.

1. Its cosmology is based on a polarization between unskilled working class and well-qualified professional middle class. Furthermore, judgments are made about the general competency of the working-class group as a whole on the basis of its least articulate representatives.

2. Precious little direct evidence is provided, so we are expected to take the findings on trust.

3. The impact of the context, including power imbalance between investigator and investigated, is not adequately considered.

4. The frame provided by the interviewers' questions is left out of account.

5. There is a tendency to make judgments according to literary criteria rather than those appropriate to an oral report, and elaboration beyond what is called for by the task and situation is expected. Working-class respondents are then criticized for their failure to provide an oral report in literate genres.

6. There is an underemphasis on economic factors in the reproduction process, along with an overemphasis on family relations.

A Flawed Research Methodology

Despite an extended research program, Bernstein's (1971) project is supported by very little secure evidence. Moreover, as Rosen (1972) points out, his ideas had already become extremely popular on the basis of some early papers that Bernstein later condemned as "horrifyingly coarse":

It would be difficult to exaggerate the extent to which his ideas have received acceptance throughout the educational world and well beyond it, so much so that they are always referred to with deference at the level of professorial debate and the terms "restricted" and "elaborated" codes have entered the folk-lore of classroom teachers . . .

The way in which Bernstein's theories have permeated contemporary educational thinking and have been used to justify educational practices is a rare phenomenon in English education and calls for some explanation. Educational academics can weave theories and publish researches to their heart's content, and these can accumulate over decades, without affecting practice one iota or causing a ripple in staff room discussion. (1972, p. 2)

Bernstein's early papers are concerned with developing an opposition between context-dependent and context-independent uses of language. He refers to these first as public and formal language but later refers to restricted and elaborated codes. Because the context supplies part of the sense, the former can involve grammatically incomplete sentences, pronouns rather than nouns, and more limited qualification by adjectives and adverbs; the latter has to be much more explicit and tends to use more elaborate syntax, a wider and more precise vocabulary, and so on (Bernstein, 1971, pp. 42–44 & 55).

The discussion of these different kinds of language use, as broad types, is basically sound, though we should recognize that all genres of texts and oral speech assume some kind of shared knowledge. The problem comes when Bernstein connects these to a binary of social classes and, mapped onto this, a binary of two different kinds of family. He divides society into working class (more precisely, unskilled and semi-skilled manual workers) and middle class (in fact, well-educated professionals); the former are said to have *positional* families, the latter *personal* ones. His claim is that only middle-class (i.e., personal) families make regular use of a formal language or elaborated code.

The evidence Bernstein provides is extremely limited. First, there is no good evidence to support his claim that the lives of semi-skilled or unskilled manual workers tend to restrict them to language use that relates only to the immediate context. Second, his claim about two radically different family types is spurious. Finally, his assumption that one binary (family type) maps onto the other (occupationally based social class) is dubious and lacking in evidence.

His initial empirical study compares young men who attended secondary modern schools and left school at age fifteen with others who are still in full-time education at fee-paying independent schools. The former, he discovers, include some with high scores on nonverbal tests but only average on verbal. Rather than relating this to their different school education, Bernstein (1971) assumes a relationship to social class and later to supposed family type (p. 152).

The most telling evidence he eventually deployed took the form of a sketchy account of an experiment by one of Bernstein's research officers, in which five-year-olds from different socioeconomic backgrounds were shown picture stories and asked to explain what was happening. This is worth quoting verbatim:

> The children were given a series of four pictures which told a story and they were invited to tell the story. Here are the stories:
>
> 1. Three boys are playing football and one boy kicks the ball and it goes through the window the ball breaks the window and the boys are looking at it and a man comes out and shouts at them because they've broken the window so they run away and then that lady looks out of her window and she tells the boys off.
>
> 2. They're playing football and he kicks it and it goes through there it breaks the window and they're looking at it and he comes out and shouts at them because they've broken it so they run away and then she looks out and she tells them off.
>
> With the first story the reader does not have to have the four pictures which were used as the basis for the story, whereas in the case of the second story the reader would require the initial pictures in order to make sense of the story. (Bernstein, 1971, p. 178)

What is remarkable about this—as critics soon pointed out and we can also infer directly from the final paragraph—is that the boys and the researcher actually *did* have the pictures in front of them. Consequently, the second version of the story is actually more appropriate than the first! Furthermore, as Rosen comments:

> These are not stories told by actual children, but are constructed by Hawkins who, in his own research report, calls them "slightly exaggerated" (Hawkins, 1969) and who nevertheless had several hundreds of the original stories to choose from. (p. 12)

Certainly the genuine transcripts contained in Turner (1973) of children role-playing what the man and the woman said show a much richer range than suggested in either of these two exemplars.

The two boys' accounts, as presented, appear to be more than slightly exaggerated. Bernstein's argument critically depends on the notion of exophoric pronouns, in other words pronouns that refer outside the text rather than to an earlier word within it. Hawkins's extract (2) seems to include 12–15 exophoric pronouns, whereas there are none in extract (1) (an exact count is difficult as some are hard to classify). However, his summative table 4.3 compares an average of 4.12 exophoric pronouns per working-class child with 2.84 for each middle-class child, a much smaller contrast. We might also question whether only pronouns can be exophoric: "a man" and "that lady" in extract 1 are scarcely explicit or, in Bernstein's terms, manifestations of elaborated code.

Everything hinges on the children's choice between nouns and pronouns. Notwithstanding the question of appropriateness, the frequent use of exophoric pronouns is taken as an indication that the working-class children are only capable of speaking about what is actually present or at least familiar or perhaps only accustomed to context-dependent speech (restricted code). This in its turn is assumed to result from living in a closed and static community of people whose occupations require compliance and routine rather than planning, initiative, and problem solving.

A Faulty Class Analysis

Harold Rosen's (1972) critique in *Language and Class* is extremely powerful. He questions Bernstein's binary of working class and middle class and points out that the ruling class has completely disappeared. Bernstein himself had once clarified that he actually meant *unskilled or semi-skilled* manual workers. As for the middle class, the examples Bernstein provides of their conversations are clearly typical of a cultivated metropolitan group, even though the elaborated code is supposedly characteristic of the whole middle class. Rosen says pointedly that this is "Hampstead man, not Orpington man" (p. 11). (Hampstead is a fashionable inner suburb of London, and Orpington a commuter outer suburb occupied typically by lower-grade clerical workers and civil servants.):

> Imagine a husband and wife have just come out of the cinema, and are talking about the film: "What do you think?" "It had a lot to say." "Yes, I thought so too—let's go to the Millers, there may be something going on there." They arrive at the Millers, who ask about the film. An hour is spent in the complex, moral, political, aesthetic subtleties of the film and its place in the contemporary scene. (Bernstein, 1971, p. 177)

How, Rosen asks, can the language of this much smaller group be the explanation for why middle-class (i.e., white-collar workers) children in general do better at school than working-class children in general?

Rosen develops his argument that this distorted view of class structure serves to construct a deficit view of working-class speech and consciousness:

> No further attempt is made at differentiation, whether in terms of history, traditions, job experience, ethnic origins, residential patterns, level of organization or class-consciousness. (p. 6)

> All attention is directed towards the home. No attention is paid to that vast area of critical working-class experience, the encounter with exploitation at the place of work and the response to it; nor to the ways which take workers beyond the "particularistic" circumstances of day-to-day work experience and move them on to explore the theory and practice of how to change society. (p. 7)

> We must distinguish between those who are quiescent and defeated and those who are articulate, highly verbal, between those who are submerged in what Freire (1971) calls "the culture of silence" and others who are capable of being quite explicit about principles and operations in those areas of experience which have been their universities. (p. 8)

When Bernstein (1971) claims that "assertion is a collective rather than an individual act" (p. 143) for the working class, Rosen (1972) argues that this

> is to conflate the concept of solidarity with mindless conformity and a sheep-like response to undercurrents in the herd. It implies that since the outcome of the experience of a group is the decision to act together, it has not been preceded either by what Bernstein calls "the exploration of individual differences" or, we can add, by prolonged formal and informal debate about alternative courses of action. These activities can occur only if language is available which is adequate to the task. What kind of people imagine that the 1972 miners' strike, for example, was made possible merely by the incantation of a few rabble-rousing slogans? (p. 9)

Bernstein constantly protested that he had not presented a deficit account of working-class language. However Tony Edwards (1976) paraphrases Bernstein's position as follows:

> Lower working-class children were confidently described as less sensitive to words as mediators of feelings and ideas, less curious about their environment, and more "rigid" in their thinking. They were less able to communicate exact logical distinctions, or relationships needing to be precisely formulated. They were progressively pointed towards description rather than analysis. Simply, they were less equipped to learn. (p. 145)

Furthermore, Edwards argues that the failure to produce a particular type of language in a poorly constructed experiment should not imply an inability to do so at other times. His own experiments were constructed so as to place particular demands on the children:

> The lower working-class children made no less use of nouns relative to pronouns, of complex verb forms, or of dependent clauses. Their vocabulary was not obviously more limited, nor their grammar "simpler," nor their style more "concrete" . . . There was no evidence of "coding principles" over-riding the demands of the immediate communicative tasks. (p. 101)

Alternative Explanations

Joan Tough's (1976) deficit argument was somewhat different in nature. Tough argued that working-class children only experienced language used for a limited set of purposes, namely controlling others, expressing needs and wants, self-protection, and labeling. According to Tough, these children have little experience of having their questions answered, hearing explanations, reasoning, predictions, or projections into the experience of others.

Tizard and Hughes (2002[1984]) scrutinized these claims in detail. They examined the frequency of these more complex uses, as well as, for example, the use of conditionals associated with hypothetical events (if . . .), making generalizations, forming future plans, or describing the purpose of objects. They concluded that there is a greater frequency of more complex syntax and purposes in the conversations of middle-class mothers but the difference is quite modest. They also pointed out that these averages conceal wide variations and overlap between the social classes:

The middle-class mothers did, however, seem to talk more often about

> people who were not present, and about past and future events. Further, a larger proportion of their talk was concerned with conveying information to the children, and they gave their children more of the kind of information we classified as "general knowledge" (science, history, geography, etc.).
>
> Perhaps related to this, the vocabulary they used in talking to their children was larger. Even in a very small sample of 200 words each, beginning with the first and the tenth page of each transcript, middle-class mothers and their daughters used a significantly larger number of different words than did working-class mothers and daughters. . . . We had the impression that middle-class mothers were more concerned with deliberately extending their child's vocabulary, and encouraging them to use words correctly. (Tizard & Hughes, 2002 [1984], pp. 120–21)

Wells' study (1987) similarly pointed to relatively little difference between different parts of a socioeconomic continuum. Dividing the population into four groups, based on a sliding scale of scores derived from both parents' occupations and qualifications, he found little difference between the groups, and differences within the groups "were much greater than the relatively small differences between the averages for each group" (p. 134). Although the half dozen or so most advanced children tended to come from the better-educated professional homes, and vice versa, this amounted to only 10 percent of the sample.

Wells (1987) found a similar distribution of circumstances that might be expected to produce a language difference: "Differences *between* groups . . . pale by comparison with the variety of individual circumstances found *within* each of the same groups" (p. 134). The quality and amount of conversation varied enormously, but "the differences were not significantly associated with family background" (p. 142).

When these children were assessed at school, the researchers were surprised to find a greater link between parental background and achievement. The difference was partly linked to "the ease with which they adjusted to the linguistic demands of the classroom" (p. 144). However, to a great extent it was because school-based assessments tended to overlook speech and concentrate on literacy. Wells (1987) and his team tracked this back to different experiences of books and stories in early childhood, which did correlate with family background. Again, the relationship is only partial:

> If some lower-class children did suffer from linguistic disadvantage, therefore, it was not in relation to their command or experience of oral language, but in the relatively low value placed on literacy by their parents, as shown by their own very limited use of these

skills, by the absence of books—either children's or parents'—in the home, and by the infrequency with which they read to their children, if they ever did so at all. (p. 144)

Both these studies point to a more modest and differently weighted conclusion than the language deficit theorists. They suggest (1) a relatively modest difference between working-class and middle-class averages; (2) that there is substantial overlap, and the different averages are brought about by a minority within the wider group; (3) that rather than a working-class deficit that makes these children difficult to educate, there is a middle-class advantage.

This relative advantage, in school terms, probably results from a combination of the parents' higher education, the language they use at work, a deliberate effort to develop their children's vocabulary and experience to the full, and a greater closeness to school discourses and subject matter. It does not suggest that most working-class or indeed most children growing up in poverty are inadequately equipped for school.

This is an important distinction since it suggests the importance of providing a language- and experience-rich environment in nurseries and the early primary years in particular, rather than the restricted pedagogies frequently used with lower-achieving groups in schools. It reinforces the importance of well-educated and well-paid staff in nurseries and the ongoing problems of regarding this as a menial and low-paid job.

Professional Impact

The various strands of linguistic deficit thinking were not entirely separate even in the hands of their proponents and became entirely confused as they circulated within the teaching profession, forming a complex of myths about working-class children and their learning difficulties. They were circulated, at the level of professional development and informal teacher conversation, accompanied by casual anecdotes about working-class mothers smacking their children rather than giving them reasons. There is considerable irony in such examples since the one place where most children were guaranteed to suffer physical punishment at that time was in school!

The hybridization of these versions is unsurprising, especially given the presence of more extreme versions of deprivation theory in Bernstein's earlier published papers. Moreover, Bereiter and Engelmann, who articulated cruder deficit views, relied on Bernstein's name to increase their credibility. In both academic research and school staffrooms, encounters with a few mothers in poverty who did barely talk to their children and some children who suffered from more extreme forms of social deprivation became generalized into arguments about working-class life as a whole (Edwards, 1976, p. 85).

The belief that African American children in particular were unable to form sentences led Bereiter and Engelmann to develop a compensatory preschool program that really did involve a debased form of language use and a highly didactic and decontextualized style, counter to the best principles of early years' education. Bereiter and Engelmann (1966) provide the following script to exemplify how early years teachers should imprint on children the most basic and artificial forms of correct Standard English syntax:

1.   Adopt a stereotyped procedure.

a.   Present an object and give the appropriate identity statement, "This is a ball."

b.   Follow the statement with a yes-no question. "Is this a ball?"

c.   Answer the question. "Yes, this is a ball."

d.   Repeat the question and encourage the children to answer it.

e.   Introduce *what* questions after the children have begun to respond adequately to the yes-no questions. (p. 140)

These authors argue that it is illogical to answer the question, "Where is the squirrel?" with "In the tree," and children must be made to say, "The squirrel is in the tree" (p. 140). There is clearly linguistic confusion between the requirements of written and spoken English. In most dialogue, the spoken word works with features of the environment—or the speakers' shared experience—to produce the message, whereas written language often needs to compensate for the absence of these environmental components, particularly when it relates to contexts not physically present. (See Wertsch, 1990, for some of the implications.)

Similarly, as Stubbs (1980) points out, Bernstein's notion of elaborated code is actually just conventional literacy practices:

Bernstein has put his finger on a useful distinction, but has put the distinction in the wrong place. . . . He suggests that schools are predicated upon elaborated code: but one might equally say that they are predicated upon written language. (p. 285).

The error is in judging spoken language by the standards of written language and then concluding that the former is deficient.

The assumption that the vernacular, as spoken by lower-status social groups, is defective as a vehicle for rational argument links back to older assumptions about the difference between modern and primitive peoples. As Drucker (1971) points out, the stereotype that preliterate peoples are inferior in terms of language and rationality continues to circulate, and even extremes of practical intelligence, such as the Eskimo who sketched a map of 6,000 miles of coastline from memory, were interpreted by comparative psychologists such as Werner as deficits because they were *too* close to physical reality! (This was the anthropological paradigm that Boas fought hard to counter.)

Rather than working with children on the interface between experience and symbolic representation, and developing in them a flexibility of movement between vernacular and literate versions of a language, the deficit view seeks to replace the former by the latter; rather than enrichment, the end result is a silencing of the vernacular voice within school and a stultified version of the standard written language. The crassness of such didactic approaches is exemplified in the advice and description contained in Bereiter and colleagues (1966). To his credit, Bernstein (1972) entirely disowned such approaches and the philosophy behind them.

Fortunately, more enlightened reformers continued to insist on a positive engagement with families. For example, Lady Plowden, who chaired a key working party on primary schooling in Britain, noted:

> We are in danger of thinking that overnight we must make the whole population think the same way as we do ourselves . . . education for the deprived child [should be] complementary to his home . . . rather than compensatory which really means that the home has no merit. (cited in Edwards, 1970, p. 48)

This attitude, built on respect for the language of the home and street, as well as the other languages brought in by migration, characterized the influential work of Harold Rosen, Douglas Barnes, and many other teachers and academics in England in the 1960s to 1980s.

The Revival of Linguistic Deficit

Various intensive observational studies have since been undertaken in the United States to explain the growing achievement gap between rich and poor, black and white, though without relating this to the destructive impact of neoliberal social and economic policies. Hart and Risley (1995), in *Meaningful Differences*, recorded that three-year-olds with professional parents had vocabularies of 1,100 words, whereas children whose parents were on welfare had vocabularies of about 525 words. This work has attracted enormous attention in policy circles, resulting in some simplistic policy demands for decontextualized instruction based on vocabulary lists from preschool onward, though there is little justification in their book for such a response. Once again, the comparison was made between opposite ends of the social spectrum, with more extreme cases standing proxy for a wider section of society.

Even so it would be a mistake to read this as a language deficit account, in any straightforward way. The authors emphasize that all of the families played and talked with their children, taught them good manners, and provided them with the same toys. They explain that the far greater incidence of reprimands than encouragements in the poorer families, which affects self-image and confidence, results from their struggle to bring up their children to survive in a divided society and to make it possible for them to gain employment in low-status jobs requiring obedience:

> Parents seemed to be preparing their children for the jobs likely to be open to them, jobs in which success and advancement would be determined by attitude [and] how well the children presented themselves. (Hart & Risley, 1995, pp. 133–34)

Unfortunately, Hart and Risley popularized their findings with a sound bite that the welfare-family child has heard 30,000,000 fewer words by the age of three than the professional-family child (Hart and Risley 2003). Such headline comparisons are crude, since they leave out of account how many of these words are actually meaningful to the child, and indeed most are simply repetition. However, the original study was meticulously prepared and conducted, and it is important to examine the detail in their report. They compare the average of 487 utterances an hour in the professional families with the average of 178 in the welfare families. The authors conclude that the extent of vocabulary at age three correlates well with language attainment at age ten. (In fact, the correlations are less than perfect, lying between 0.5 and 0.75 on various tests.) They examine in detail quality features within the variety of vocabulary, range of tenses, and sentences with two or more clauses. Hart and Risley produce two sets of figures: the occurrence of each indicator per hour of observation and the "richness" in terms of frequency per utterance (p. 120). This distinction is crucial and relates to the fact that some parents spend much more time per hour in verbal interaction with their children than do others.

The crucial finding in this analysis, contrary to hypotheses of verbal deficit, is that, on these various quality indicators, there is no difference in richness between parents of different socioeconomic groups. The difference appears only on the first statistic, that is, occurrences per hour of observation. In other words, although the welfare children do not hear as many longer sentences or past tenses, for example, as the children of professional parents, this is not due to any difference in linguistic complexity. There remains, of course, a possibility that the differences in exposure will affect children's progress when they reach school.

Thus, professional parents used 0.12 multiclause sentences per utterance, compared with 0.11 for welfare parents—hardly any difference. However, per hour the first group of children heard sixty multiclause sentences and the second group only sixteen. We are not provided with reasons why welfare parents spend less time per hour in verbal interaction, for example, the pressure of other domestic tasks in a single-parent household perhaps, although the authors do point out that the welfare parents do not appear to sustain exchanges as long.

We can conclude from this that Hart and Risley are not so much arguing a verbal deficit theory based on transmission of cultural deprivation but that the children of professional parents are able to give their children some advantage in terms of school learning and academic literacies by maximizing the quantity and quality of talk. A reasonable inference appears to be that the material pressures and conflicting demands of parents bringing up children in poverty is the substantial cause rather than any difference in linguistic style or competence.

The other significant feature of the findings, which Hart and Risley (1995) do not highlight, is the very wide range within any of their groups of parents—a recurrent problem in research comparing different social groups. We are informed of the gap between the average for the extreme groups, in this case professional and welfare, but not the range within each group. Fortunately Hart and Risley provide the reader with tables, on a case-by-case basis, ranked according to a socioeconomic index. On average, the professional parents use 380 different words per hour, and the welfare parents 156. However, the gap between the highest and lowest score among the welfare parents is 114, and within the professional parents' group there is a range of 209. The highest welfare parent score is not far below the lowest professional parent. These differences, as pointed out earlier, largely reflect the amount of time spent in verbal interaction per hour of observation: the average for different words per utterance is 4.43 for professional parents and 3.76 for welfare parents.

As Gee (2004) points out:

> Linguists have known for years that all children—including poor children—have impressive language ability. The vast majority of children enter school with vocabularies fully fit for everyday life, with complex grammar and with deep understandings of experiences and stories. (p. 17)

Researchers working with anthropologist Annette Lareau (2003) in *Unequal Childhoods* also engaged in intensive observation, moving in to each home for three weeks. They identified a pattern of "concerted cultivation" (p. 2) in the middle-class families: these parents engaged their children in conversation as equals, treated them like apprentice adults, and encouraged them to ask questions, challenge assumptions, and negotiate rules. They planned countless cultural activities to encourage their development. The poorer parents gave their children much more freedom in the afternoon but less freedom to question authority or talk back. (This is, of course, a very different picture from underclass accounts of chaotic family life.) The researchers recognize the connection between these patterns and family circumstances: concerted cultivation "places intense labor demands on busy parents" (p. 13), including sorting out disputes about parental decisions. They also recognize the greater independence and socialization of the working-class and poor children. However, they conclude that the middle-class children do better at school because they are more used to adults taking their concerns seriously and have a stronger sense of entitlement. (This may be a rather idealized view of relations in large primary classes.)

Selling Snake Oil

Both Hart and Risley (1995), and Lareau (2003), present analyses that are basically empathetic. They are a far cry from Ruby Payne's (2005) highly popular training program, ostensibly designed to inform teachers about poverty. Her pejorative stereotype of people living in poverty includes knowing how to get guns, raiding supermarket garbage bins for outdated food, having common-law marriages, viewing jail as an ordinary part of life, and living in homes that are disorganized, noisy, violent and nonverbal. Men are fighters, lovers, and absent fathers, while single mothers (and their teenage children) have multiple sexual relations (summary by Dudley-Marling, 2007, p. 3).

According to Payne's (2005) stereotypes, presented without any sign of evidence, "The noise level is high (the TV is always on and everyone may talk at once), the most important information is *non-verbal*" (p. 9). Drawing on a hotchpotch of language deficit stereotypes, Payne highlights:

- a limited vocabulary and reliance on nonverbal signs

- circumlocution and indirection

- more audience involvement

- a casual register that is not valued in school or work (pp. 28–31).

She describes all of these as deficits that schools need to help students overcome. She sees nonverbal cues as replacing language and limiting the explicitness of poor people's speech, so "to be asked to communicate in writing without the nonverbal assists is an overwhelming and formidable task, which most of them try to avoid" (p. 28).

Payne (2005) regards audience involvement (common in non-European performances) as interruptive of a continuous narrative stream; she believes it results in a failure to develop logical thinking. She links the lack of a formal register with a tendency "to meander almost endlessly through a topic" (p. 28). There are clearly contradictions here: language in poor families is marred by both nonverbal assists and circumlocutions—it uses too few words and too many! This set of parents is clearly in a no-win situation.

It is remarkable how positives are turned into negatives. Payne (2005) describes the oral storytelling of people in poverty (which particular ethnic groups?) as composed of disorganized episodes interspersed with audience participation, including overlaps, interjections, and interruptions. Interaction with others is clearly seen as a negative here rather than a manifestation of social capital. She claims that there are just two registers of English, two distinct varieties, *formal* and *informal*, and that poor students "cannot use formal register" (p. 29). Indeed, she claims that they are trapped within a barely verbal casual register—clearly a contradiction with her account of storytelling.

In their powerful critique, Bomer and colleagues (2008) point out, "Everyone uses varied registers in appropriate social situations, and the variation among language groups that might live in poverty is much greater than the similarities" (pp. 2516–17). In addition to the abusive stereotypes, Payne prescribes direct teaching of supposedly middle-class language patterns as the cure. As Bomer and colleagues put it, she "positions teachers to look for errors and to correct them." This contradicts established good practice and linguistic expertise whereby language is "learned through meaning, shared attention, and through building on the competence of the learner, rather than aiming for the remediation of deficiencies" (p. 2517).

The supposed language deficits of the poor are then concatenated into claims about their illogicality and potential criminality, in a bizarre chain of cause and effect. The implication is that particular language patterns and an underclass lifestyle create poverty, rather than the reverse:

> If an individual depends upon a random, episodic story structure for memory patterns, lives in an unpredictable environment, and **has not developed the ability to plan**, then...
>
> If an individual cannot plan, he/she **cannot predict**.
>
> If an individual cannot predict, he/she **cannot identify cause and effect**.
>
> If an individual cannot identify cause and effect, he/she **cannot identify consequence**.
>
> If an individual cannot identify consequence, he/she **cannot control impulsivity**.
>
> If an individual cannot control impulsivity, he/she **has an inclination toward criminal behavior**. (bold in original, Payne, 2005, p. 90, cited in Bomer et al., 2008, pp. 2518–19)

The scandalous levels of incarceration of poor and particularly Black and Hispanic Americans is evidently a consequence of their narrative style!

As Bomer and colleagues (2008) point out:

> Payne makes her way from a narrative style (which she has incorrectly described as random among people in poverty) all the way to criminality. The initial assumptions are incorrect, about the chaotic lives, random narrative style, and inability to plan among low-income citizens. The studies cited earlier demonstrate that lives at the edge of economic stability are often carefully ordered and planned, even if they do not mesh well with the structures of some social institutions. Moreover, the notion that people "cannot plan" is an indefensible assertion of a cognitive deficit. Economic hardship does not make planning impossible as a mental act; it makes the realization of plans difficult, as a

material outcome. . . . Payne's assertions again characterize the poor, without evidence, as deeply flawed human beings, whose personal failings make continued poverty—or worse conditions—inevitable. (p. 2519)

Though ostensibly intended to improve teachers' understanding of the neighborhoods where they work, all of this inevitably serves to intensify prejudice, lower expectations, and encourage routine and unchallenging teaching methods.

Poverty and Parenting

Fortunately there is a more responsible tradition of research on the impact of parenting on children's intellectual development and particularly their language acquisition. This research produces valuable data to press for improved nursery provision. At the same time, we must be wary that it can be misread as another deficit account of working-class parents, particularly when it is cited and recycled crudely without attention to the details.

The research typically makes comparisons between family background and vocabulary acquisition at the age of three or five, before making connections to subsequent school achievement. There are several dangers that compound one another:

1. The poorest group is compared with the richest, rather than with the average, thus developing an exaggerated narrative of 'poor parenting';

2. averages are given for each group, which fails to show how much they overlap;

3. the focus is generally on the *backwardness* of the lowest group—in other words, a deficit perspective—rather than on the extent to which better positioned parents are able to create an educational *advantage*.

It would be surprising if degree-level education, high income, and occupations that involve high levels of literacy and a more sophisticated vocabulary did not create educational advantage; and conversely, if limited education, financial insecurity, and tedious work (especially where they coincide) did not impact on the quality, or at least the educational orientation, of early upbringing. The dilemma is how to moderate this *comparative* disadvantage without engaging in unsupportive and negative family and childcare policies.

The executive summaries and sound bites used to gain attention for the research understandably highlight the degree of disadvantage. What is most surprising, however, on scrutinizing some of the data, is the relatively small difference and the degree of overlap. Though the gap is significant, it does not add up to a language deficit of a broad social group. Let us look briefly at some examples from England, Scotland, and the United States.

1. Gutman and Feinstein's (2008) report "Parenting Behaviors and Children's Development from Infancy to Early Childhood" shows a higher number of mother-child interactions from graduates than from mothers with low-level qualifications at age sixteen. However, the average score for these groups, on a 5 point scale, varies only from 4.2 to below 4.7 at six months, and diminishes to 0.1 difference at 42 months (p. 543). There is almost no difference for outside activities at any age, nor, in terms of outcomes, for either social development or fine motor development preschool (p. 544).

2. Bradley and colleagues' (2001) report "The Home Environments of Children in the United States" (p. 1850) includes observation data on different groups of mothers. We learn that the mother spontaneously spoke to the child twice or more, excluding scolding, in 92 percent of cases for nonpoor European Americans, and at the opposite extreme 86 percent of cases for poor African Americans (p. 1850). The most extreme difference is for answering the child's questions or requests verbally: 92 percent nonpoor European Americans compared with 77 percent poor African Americans (p. 1852). This suggests that *some* parents, from various causes, provide an upbringing involving more limited verbal interaction, but it does not suggest any kind of parenting underclass.

3. The extended research project by Kathy Sylva and colleagues (2007) shows some correlation between various parental status groups (occupational, qualification, and income) and childcare patterns, and then between these and formal academic development, including reading and mathematics at age ten. There is a link between parental status and the home learning environment (HLE, scored 0–45, p. 64), which influences school achievement. The surprise is a correlation between either SES or mother's qualification and HLE of only 0.32 (p. 65), and also that HLE has around twice the impact of socioeconomic status or income (p. 66).

Among white British families, the data show the mean HLE of professional parents as 26.8 compared with 20.3 for low socioeconomic groups. According to their background data (P. Sammons, 2012, personal correspondence), 41 percent of parents without any qualifications score 20–45 on HLE, compared with 83 percent of degree-educated parents. These differences, between groups at opposite ends of the range, are significant; they show that some children of unskilled or minimally educated parents may not be well stimulated, at least in terms of the researchers' chosen indicators, whereas there is greater consistency at the other end of the social spectrum. This should not be exaggerated or lead to stereotypes: indeed, of the potentially most disadvantaged group (parents who have never worked) only a quarter score 0–13.

4. Recent Scottish research (Bromley, 2009) shows, not surprisingly, that degree-educated mothers are more likely to read books or look at stories with their children every day. The differences are remarkably small between the two extremes: 51 percent for mothers with no qualifications at all, compared with 78 percent for university graduates (p. 16). On a range of other indicators, such as playing games, singing, painting, physical exercise, visits to places such as cinemas, farms or swimming pools, there are substantial differences (pp. 20–24), but it is clear that they arise from lack of financial means rather than indifference: the poorest parents express dissatisfaction at what they can provide their children (p. 31).

5. Other research from Scotland (Bradshaw, 2011) shows differences in vocabulary acquisition according to parental income, occupational level, and education. The comparison is likely to have considerable impact at school: at the extremes, the children of degree-educated parents are around eighteen months ahead on vocabulary at the age of five when compared with those whose parents left school with no qualifications (p. 11). However, further data from the researchers show the extent of overlap:

- a third of the highest quintile by income are below average for the age cohort, and a third of the lowest quintile are above average

- the most advanced quarter of children in the lowest of five categories for either parental income or education have a bigger vocabulary than the average for the top-level group.

The data from this study contradict underclass stereotypes: of the poorest fifth, only one in five has no qualifications and a third have some Highers (i.e., the qualification for university entrance in Scotland) or a university degree. The statistics show that even this latter group's children are damaged by poverty (conceivably through its impact on health, housing, morale, or disconnection from more interesting work environments) though their education gives them a better chance to protect their children's development.

Close scrutiny of the data (correspondence with lead researcher Paul Bradshaw, October 2012) identifies a particular problem for the less educated parents within the poorest fifth: 28 percent of this group's children are more than one standard deviation (SD) below the average for the age cohort as a whole. (This compares with 16 percent for the whole cohort, and 8 percent of the top quintile.) This is a serious situation, calling for much improved support. However, the data do not back those who would write off these children; poverty damages children's development from an early age, but the situation deteriorates as children proceed through school.

Even for this group, 8 percent of the children are more than 1 SD above average (cf 16 percent of the age cohort as a whole). However, the data also indicate that other children benefit from an early age from a combination of high family income and well-educated parents. Of these children 24 percent are more than one standard deviation above average in vocabulary acquisition. It supports Lareau's (2003) contention that more advantaged and better educated parents tend to engage in "concerted cultivation" (p. 2) from an early age.

A Way Forward

All this data flatly contradict the notion still perpetrated by hardline deficit propagandists of an educational underclass whose lives are irremediably damaged at an early age. The situation is far more complex. A smaller number of children are being seriously handicapped by their home environment and need intensive help as a result of a complex mix of conditions (perilous financial situation, limited parental education, housing, demoralization, drug abuse, etc.).

The dominant tradition of early intervention for poorer families seems premised on the notion of removing children from parents for a large part of the day and compensating for poor parenting. It is time to rethink this in favor of more participatory models that involve parents for at least part of the time in order to facilitate the sharing of ideas and practices between parents with respectful encouragement and modeling from professionals and including resources like libraries of toys and books for children to take home.

The situation also suggests the need for improved opportunities for adult education for qualified parents as well as affordable and accessible cultural and leisure opportunities. This enrichment would quickly impact on children and, in some cases, help parents gain better paid and more satisfying employment. This is quite a different notion, we should note, than the assumption that simply getting parents into work would lift them out of poverty.

Furthermore, nursery education is of variable quality and delivered, in some countries, by low-paid staff who are seen as caregivers rather than educators. The situation demands a dramatic improvement in the pay, status, and qualifications of early years' staff, as well as professional development to ensure the richest possible linguistic interaction in nurseries and primary schools.

We do, however, need to recognize that early education is not a stand-alone. At every stage thereafter, differences of income and education have an effect: for example, the least advanced children from more advantaged families overtake the most advanced from poorer families by the end of primary school. Language enrichment remains a challenge beyond the nursery stage.

This returns us to the important pedagogical project of Rosen, along with his collaborators Douglas Barnes and James Britton (Barnes et al., 1969), who had a major influence on teachers in English-speaking countries in the 1970s and beyond. First, these educators insisted on the need to extend children's stylistic range by building on vernacular speech, not undermining it. Second, their research highlighted the restricted nature of traditional classroom discourse—dominated by the teacher's voice, with pupils' contributions limited by a succession of closed questions permitting only two- or three-word answers. They believed that working-class pupils were trapped in a culture of silence not by their home environment and early upbringing but rather by the discursive patterns they regularly encountered in schools.

These educators showed the importance to cognitive and linguistic development of small-group discussion uninterrupted by the teacher, in which pupils could hypothesize and debate alternative ideas. They pointed to the need to link the abstract theoretical discourses of academic learning to the experiences of the learner. This was applied as much to monolingual indigenous children as to the growing number of bilingual and multidialectal children in inner-city schools.

CHAPTER SIX

Aspirations and 'Cultures of Poverty'

What might look like "low aspirations" may often be high aspirations that have been eroded by negative experience.
—Carter-Wall and Whitfield, 2012, p. 4

In this chapter we examine another ideology of blame, the failure to aspire. We seek to dislodge the notion that young working-class people from areas designated as 'disadvantaged' are the way they are because they are simply unambitious. This psychologizing of disengagement is cut loose from economic contexts and the enabling conditions necessary to fulfill aspiration. We debunk the misleading idea that opportunities are simply there for the taking.

What we show instead is that whether young people succeed—or not—has much to do with the availability of networks of support. We discuss how positions, stances, and aspirational maps are formed as a consequence of the social and economic contexts in which people are embedded and of how schools ascribe diminished aspirations to poorer children.

There is a process of family culture and school culture working in harmony for more advantaged young people. Working-class families, on the other hand, have to guess their way through unknown territory for their children to go on to higher education and risk the tensions and turbulence it involves. Some young people, unfortunately, see no alternative but to develop their own negative oppositional identities and cultures.

Connecting all this, we argue that, in order to develop a sense of agency among students, we need to show them real possibilities and provide genuine pathways and opportunities.

Policies of Aspiration

The notion of *aspirations* has been extremely prominent in recent debate and policy formation. In England, as elsewhere, a number of high-profile initiatives have focused on improving the aspirations of young people and their parents. Government policy seems dominated by a feeling that working-class areas are characterized by low aspirations and that this is the cause of underachievement and future poverty. (See, for example, Department for Education, 2010; DCSF, 2007; HM Treasury and DCSF, 2007.)

However, a number of recent research projects sponsored by the Joseph Rowntree Foundation conclude that the problem is not, in fact, a lack of aspirations by either young people or their parents, nor is it a need to make them more aspirational, but rather there is insufficient knowledge and means to make goals achievable (Goodman & Gregg, 2010; St. Clair, Kintrea, & Houston, 2011; Carter-Wall & Whitfield, 2012).

There is no doubt that attitudes affect actions, and indeed individuals vary in their responses to the circumstances and experiences: some see the glass as half-full and others as half-empty. However there is a danger that simplistic notions of low aspirations can become a new way to blame the victim. The problem is that an exaggerated and decontextualized rhetoric about aspirations, as cause or cure, tends to essentialize and reify, rather than looking at the dialectic relations between young people and their circumstances. It individualizes and psychologizes a complex social interaction.

Aspirations, like other attitudes, operate within a field of opportunities; they grow or shrink partly in response to the perceived possibilities of a successful outcome. As Carter-Wall and Whitfield (2012) express it in their summary of research by Goodman and Gregg (2010): "What might look like 'low aspirations' may often be high aspirations that have been eroded by negative experience" (p. 4). Similarly:

> What looks like "parental disengagement" may actually be the result of a high level of commitment to their child's education, which is not matched by the capacity to provide effective support or by the ability of schools to work effectively with parents. (Carter-Wall & Whitfield, 2012, p. 4).

This is true not just on an individual scale but collectively: young people living in areas of chronic unemployment and poor work learn that aspirations can be futile and lead only to disappointment. This sense of futility runs through the interviews conducted by Simon Charlesworth (2000), but the following quotation is especially pertinent and worth repeating:

> My son they've med 'im go on these trainin' schemes an' it's just cheap labor. They 'ad 'im trainin' t' be a welder, and then he were back on' dole; then they 'ad 'im doin' joinery on ET [Employment Training] an' then he were back on' dole again; now they've got 'im doin' fork-lift truck drivin', so I guess next he'll be an unemployed fork-lift truck driver. (p. 96, dialect markers moderated)

An analysis of three case study schools in contrasting areas, though all seriously disadvantaged, showed little sense of fatalism or despair in pupils generally. There was no evidence to support arguments that young people in areas of disadvantage were lacking in aspirations; indeed,

> most aspire to go to university, and young people aspire to professional and managerial jobs in far greater numbers than the proportions of those posts in the labour market. (St Clair, Kintrea, & Houston, 2011, p. 7)

However, it found much higher aspirations toward professional jobs in the London school among a "diverse, ethnically rich population" but much lower in Nottingham in a predominantly white working-class community:

> While many in Nottingham aspired to go to university and have professional jobs . . . a large number of young people were interested in traditional roles, with boys aspiring to trades and girls to care occupations. (p. 6)

Between ages 13 and 15 the Nottingham aspirations for university attendance fell while they increased slightly in London, where they were already the highest.

Psychologizing Disengagement

An emphasis on aspirations separated from any sense of economic context sits within a meritocratic ideology, with its illusions that opportunities are simply there for the taking, and what holds young people back is a negative attitude and a failure to work hard enough. There is a continuity here from the attitudes satirized in Charles Dickens' (1989 [1849]) *Hard Times*:

> This, again, was among the fictions of Coketown. Any capitalist there who had made sixty thousand pounds out of sixpence always professed to wonder why the sixty thousand nearest Hands didn't each make sixty thousand out of sixpence. . . . What I did, you can do. Why don't you go out and do it? (pp. 155–56)

Similar fallacies have centered on the use of the term *resilience*, particularly favored in the United States; although in the UK it tends to be used more cautiously, simply to refer to the fact of overcoming obstacles rather than as an explanation (e.g.,

Sylva et al., 2007). Rosa Aronson (2001, p. 18) argues that resilience must be seen as a "process rather than a trait," and "any attempt to measure it in individuals may be futile." There are enabling conditions such as supportive parents or teachers, coping strategies such as perseverance or creating distance, and barriers such as isolation and conflict between school and home, with a different pattern in each individual case. Her writing shows the emotional struggle involved, including experiences of fear, resentment, internalization, and shame, as well as, in some cases, the burden of early responsibility. Often young people choose to "create a wall around them to protect themselves from further hardship." Aronson (p. 15) argues that resilience is a process that requires more than just one individual, that social institutions such as school and church play an important role, but that policymakers can make or break resilience by creating or destroying opportunities for advancement.

A very common explanation for the disaffection and low achievement of Black Americans is the "burden of acting White" argument deriving from Ogbu (1991; Fordham & Ogbu, 1986). The argument is basically that academic success is so strongly associated with the white population that many potentially high achieving Black students intentionally underachieve for fear of being stigmatized and isolated by their Black peers. They prefer to develop identities and behaviors that hinder academic success, those associated with a Black 'underclass.' This argument, known as the *oppositional culture* thesis, underpins countless after school and mentoring programs in the United States designed to help close the achievement gap but with little apparent success.

Questioning this analysis, Mocombe (2011) contends that it fails to analyze the social and economic context, namely the loss of job possibilities resulting from deindustrialization or the shift of industrial production overseas. His argument is that African American youths are opting to follow apparently more profitable careers and role models such as

> gangsters, rappers, athletes and entertainers, because other means not associated with education, such as sports, hip-hop culture, drug dealing and other illegal activities appear to be more viable means to economic gains, status, and upward mobility. (p. 166)

These alternative careers and identities are, however, themselves strongly commodified and driven by a postindustrial capitalism that is increasingly focused on the media and consumerism. He argues that we need to develop a more social (structural) analysis rather than a discretely cultural or psychological one.

In the UK, Chris Creegan (2008), of the National Centre for Social Research in the UK, presents a different but equally powerful critique of the aspirations discourse favored by politicians. Based on multiple open-ended interviews with "people we do not usually hear" but for whom "we design interventions," he argues that the key issue is not a lack of aspirations but the truncation of opportunity that prevents aspirations from being realized:

> The stories of loss, waste and limiting of opportunities were threaded through people's lives and had been triggered at different life stages, by events or circumstances over which they had varying degrees of control. (p. 4)

Furthermore, he argues, rather than focusing on the attitudes of the disadvantaged, we need to look to the structure and culture of the whole society, with its failure to provide affordable housing or jobs while others exercise limitless aspirations for property accumulation and luxury lifestyles:

> We must remain alert to the pernicious effect of poverty of aspiration, whether caused or perpetuated by lack of opportunity. But we must also reframe the meaning of aspiration which has become impoverished by contemporary excesses. And when we talk about poverty of aspiration, we need to think not merely about enriching the aspirations of individuals, but also our collective aspirations as a society. . . . Without a shared aspiration for equality, individual opportunities will continue to be truncated. That means facing up to the consequences of excessive individualism, consumerism and greed individually and collectively. (Creegan, 2008, p. 10)

Positions and Stances within a Field

The importance of context has always been part of Bourdieu's sociocultural theorization of inequality and its reproduction:

> Bourdieu refers to the social contexts in which individuals act as "fields," "markets" and "games": that is, "structured space[s] of positions in which the positions and their interrelations are determined by the distribution of different kinds of resources of *capital*"(Thompson 1991, pp. 13–14). The volume and structure of capital (economic, cultural and social) possessed by individuals determines their position in a field, and these positions "interact with habitus to produce different postures (prises de position)" (Mahar, Harker & Wilkes, 1990, p. 8), or stances. (Mills & Gale, 2011, p. 245)

Drawing on Bourdieu's framework, Carmen Mills and Trevor Gale argue that we should not examine *stance* (position *taking*) without looking at *position*. They use each of these concepts to speak of both students and their schools: stance to refer to the attitudes students take to school and schools take to students, and position to refer to how the broader social and economic situation adversely positions students as well as how the schools that poorer children attend are positioned within an education system.

For Mills and Gale (2011) the economic situation is fundamental. Analyzing one particular Australian school, they state:

> Context . . . positions students in this community without hope or purpose, without a working future. The students are very conscious of their town's economic vulnerability

and know that it will be difficult to obtain employment in the town after they graduate. (p. 247).

Despite opportunities within national labor markets, disillusionment can develop because of the lack of employment opportunities in the local community. The problem is exacerbated by the current overemphasis on human capital functions of schooling, and many young people "reject school culture because they see through the myth of meritocracy" (p. 250).

Aspirational Maps

A number of writers have argued that what many families need is not to have their aspirations raised but a sense of what is required in order to fulfill them. Commenting on their three-city study St. Clair notes:

> There were kids who wanted to become lawyers who were going to take three GCSEs, and there were those who wanted to become hairdressers who were going to take ten. (Kintrea, St. Clair, & Houston, 2011, cited in Stewart, 2011)

The problem was one of understanding what was required. However, it was not the case that young people spend their time fantasizing about becoming pop stars or premiership footballers.

Many young people have little idea of what university might be like. According to Moogan (2011) they think it will involve attendance from 9 to 4 as in schools, fear they will be kicked out if they fail a module, and are worried about debt but lack the data to make careful cost-benefit calculations. Many would, therefore, prefer shorter courses or a predictable part-time schedule that will combine with work. Supplying this knowledge, enabling them to spend some time at a university, arranging for them to meet with students to gain a better knowledge, would, Moogan argues, serve more good than the pressure to "be more aspirational."

Pollard and Filer (2007) speak against the stereotype of nonsupportive working-class parents, arguing that what is missing is the knowledge and confidence to deal with key choices or crises in schooling:

> Perhaps they lacked sufficient social capital or confidence when dealing with formal organisations. Certainly, compared with middle-class parents, working-class parents were more trusting of teachers and school systems even when, in some cases, these were badly failing their children. (p. 450)

This is a world away from the anecdotes in Richard Riddell's (2010) study of elite families whose sons attend prestigious English private schools, and who can call on a carefully cultivated network of acquaintances as well as relatives and friends for advice, especially if they feel the school is giving inadequate guidance:

My godfather is Professor . . . at Cambridge. So for instance last night . . . they came back with this Cambridge form and the teacher said "if you haven't got anything positive to say on the square . . . don't put anything in it." So I thought "that's a bit odd, if they don't put anything . . . it doesn't look very keen if you don't put anything else," so I rang up my godfather and said "what do you think here, should we put something in this space? And if so, what should I put?"

So I do, you know, [use contacts]. And then his teacher here said "don't apply to Y [College] because um, that's really difficult to get into, it's very popular, go for one of the rubbish ones" or something. . . . So I said "what does he think one of the rubbish colleges at Cambridge is?"

Well, I said to my godfather "what have you got to say on this as well? You know, is St John's too ambitious, should we try somewhere else, does it make any difference?". . . And he said, "No, just tell him to apply for St John's; if they want him at Cambridge they will offer . . . or put him in the pool. Do that." (Riddell, 2010, p. 22)

Jessica Bok (2010) builds on Appadurai's (2004) metaphor of aspiration as the ability to read "a map of a journey into the future":

Aspirations are complex understandings of the future pathways available to people. Students can access these pathways if they are provided with knowledge and experiences that enable them to make powerful choices . . . or to take risks discovering for themselves what lies ahead. In other words, students' capacity to aspire is influenced by past experiences with reading and successfully following their map of aspirations, in combination with their confidence to explore unmapped possibilities. People from more affluent and powerful groups often have more experience reading such maps and Appadurai (2004) argues that they "share this knowledge with one another more routinely" (p. 69). (p. 164)

Bok explores the role of parents and others who, in more affluent or educated families, can use their navigation experience and skills to help the young. This involves "hot" knowledge as well as "cold" (Ball & Vincent, 1998). In less advantaged families, where nobody previously has gone to university or embarked on a professional career, this is like "a play without a script" (Bok, p. 175):

A map or a script provides the actor with direction that can help them produce the desired outcome. From this perspective, the capacity of low SES students to navigate their aspirations may be like performing a play with no rehearsal—experiments and experiences—to prepare them and a minimal script that requires much improvisation. (pp. 175–76)

Bok is by no means deterministic, looking for various ways in which some (extended) families or teachers can assist the navigation. However, she clearly presents the different sense of aspirations that are frequently to be found in poorer families: less defined wishes for their children to "succeed in life," be happy, find work, a "good job," even just to stay out of trouble:

Student 3: Well . . . to me, a good life is like, um . . . having a great job. Having like, if you want a family, having a family. Not going to gaol, not doing drugs, not drinking a lot, and stuff like that. Um . . . Like not being rich but not being poor, or like average and stuff . . . And not like . . . umm . . . doing stupid stuff, and all of that, going to gaol and all of that stuff. (p. 167)

Riddell (2010) demonstrates very clearly how elite private schools make progression to high-status universities appear natural, almost inevitable. Their pupils do not actually need to aspire, in the sense of making a deliberate decision, because the school and its corporate habitus provide a kind of distributed aspirational framework. One teacher describes the process as a "drip feed that just builds and builds" (p. 33), including a schedule of talks by former pupils who attend particular universities or are successful professionals, career and university conferences, the role of sixth form tutors, academic staff who maintain strong links with their former universities and often serve as role models in terms of subject choice and a relentless focus in school events on achievement in various fields (p. 31). The family culture and school culture work in harmony, constantly reinforcing each other and making failure to reach university seem unthinkable.

The Complexity of Aspiring against the Odds

It is much more complex and contradictory to steer young people in poverty, or more generally from manual-worker families, toward university and high-level professions. This is particularly the case if the school is unable to support and compensate for a lack of aspirational roadmaps within the family.

In contrast to the coherence of ambition among elite families attending private, fee-paying schools in Riddell's (2010) study, we find serious tensions and turbulence. As argued above, less privileged families may be ambitious for their children but have a more modest, generalized, and realizable desire for a good life; they may not understand the route or the steps to be taken to achieve unfamiliar destinations or have the knowledge or confidence to intervene when things are going wrong at school. They are wary of seeing their children as in any way different or *special*, since that label usually has negative connotations, whereas privileged families are often determined to make their children *special* by acquiring markers of talent and academic potential.

Adapting and downscaling Appadurai's (1996) concept of -scapes (ethnoscape, mediascape, etc.; pp. 33–36), we might consider the experiential, conceptual, and emotional landscapes of young people growing up in disadvantaged circumstances. Appadurai points out that terms ending –*scape*:

point to the fluid, irregular shapes of these landscapes . . . these are not objectively given relations that look the same from every angle of vision but, rather, that they are deeply perspectival constructs. (p. 33)

In terms of art history, eighteenth-century landscape painting sought to fix and harmonize this vision, showing the owned land from the landowner's perspective.

Landscape, as a genre, was in harmony with family *portraits*, and indeed the two genres sometimes merged: the aristocratic family in the land it owned. Following land acquisition by Enclosure, the land itself had been reshaped from woods and farmland into private parkland, and the habitations of farm laborers removed from view. The art reflected this. We find another strong example of the cleansing of the landscape in the way farm labor and those who carry it out are made completely invisible in Jane Austen's novels (see Williams, 1985, p. 166). This is not dissimilar to the harmonization and shaping of prospects in elite schools and families described by Riddell (2010).

Young people, their families, and teachers in areas of poverty and disadvantage constantly struggle to deal with all kinds of counterflows; unlike those in Riddell's book they cannot simply shut out other perspectives. In terms of *ethnoscape* and *mediascape* (Appadurai, 1996, p. 33), they are deeply affected by discourses of denigration against the communities they belong to (see Jones' *Chavs*, 2011). In terms of *ideoscape*, contradictory discourses are at play: not just the call to "raise your aspirations" but residual ideologies about inherited lack of intelligence or concepts such as underclass. The *financescapes* are certainly parlous: alongside English politicians' imposition of £9,000 per year tuition fees on university students, and despite their argument that higher earnings will easily allow the graduates to pay off the consequent debts, young people from poorer families and neighborhoods have a sharper sense of what serious debt can entail, including repossession, eviction, extortionate interest rates, and violence from debt collectors. Certainly the prospect of extended periods of studentship conflicts with immediate needs to earn money and, frequently, other family responsibilities (see McGregor, Mills & Thomson, 2012).

There are disjunctions and conflicts, too, in terms of identity, with more prestigious schools and universities (for those lucky enough to get into them) tacitly expecting a cultural dis-identification with the student's family and surroundings. (This is not new—see, for example, the chapter "Scholarship Boy" in Richard Hoggart's *The Uses of Literacy*, 1957.) Conformity to school behavioral norms often involves acceptance of a much more passive set of behaviors than required by life outside: surviving school involves accepting reduced possibilities of agency for both boys and girls, albeit in gendered ways (Connell, 1989; Keddie, 2007; Jackson, 2006). Resolving this turbulence of social expectations requires considerable identity work (Kenway, Kraack, & Hickey-Moody, 2006). As Jackson (2006) argues, reconciling the need to "act cool" with study requirements comes easier to those with greater financial resources (books and Internet access at home; no need for part-time jobs; the money to dress stylishly). There is, moreover, a greater danger that students with no family history of academic success over-read the school's expectation of the good student and come to believe that being docile and well organized is the road to success without also learning to think critically and creatively—a difficult contradiction to negotiate for those without a "map" (Thomson, 2010; also Ingram, 2009).

All of this requires a different kind of discursive and pedagogic work in order to give any coherence to aspiring and producing beneficial outcomes, including more assertive and oppositional challenges to hegemonic assumptions (see, for example, Sarra, 2012). All of this ultimately depends on economics rather than attitude.

The core problem is the absence of real opportunities for mobility and the presence of real barriers:

> Simply directing resources into raising their aspirations in order to raise outcomes is unlikely to be successful. Indeed, given that poorer children (and their parents) generally have high aspirations and positive attitudes to education already, attempting to raise these further misses the point that high aspirations alone are not enough. (Carter-Wall & Whitfield, 2012, p. 6).

PART THREE

The Role of the School

The four chapters of part 2 concerned attempts to blame young people, their parents, and local communities for poor school engagement and achievement and ultimately for their own poverty and class position. They showed how the center of gravity had shifted from innate intelligence to language deficit to the lack of aspirations, though even when arguments had been won at an academic level, these explanations continued to have an effect as residual ideologies among policymakers, in the teaching profession and in the public at large. We have shown how none of these ideas provides a substantial account of the link between poverty and underachievement.

We have shown some of the ways in which generalizations from particularly desperate cases are converted into 'truths' to explain the wider picture, and how activity and interaction are reified, essentialized, and psychologized. The impact of macro-economic forces is concealed by theories that claim poverty is caused by deficits in students, parents, and neighborhoods, and dubious solutions are pursued that assume that a change of heart and attitude can substitute for a transformation of economic power structures.

In part 3, the focus shifts to the school and begins, in chapter 7, with a new ideology of blame. Particularly in the past two decades, the argument that some schools appear less *effective* than others has been used by politicians as yet another excuse for not facing up to the massive economic divisions in society: the implication is that it is not poverty but poor teaching that is damaging young people.

Though we argue that much School Effectiveness research is flawed, we also recognize that politicians have proved adept at making selective use of its findings to support their own interests.

Ironically, both discourses of blame are overlapped in the most hypocritical way. Politicians, government agencies, and the media seem not to notice the contradiction between stigmatizing the most marginalized sections of society and castigating those whose job it is to educate them.

We then move, in chapter 8, to a discussion of school change, to highlight the inadequacies of dominant models of School Improvement. We examine some critical issues concerning school structure and culture, including patterns of differentiation involving segregation and hierarchy.

In chapter 9, we take a more positive stance and attempt to develop some key principles for a socially just curriculum and pedagogy. We draw attention to curricula and pedagogies that can help break the cycle whereby poverty and low class position are reproduced through the school process. Whereas traditionally schools have tended to reinforce the sense of humiliation and futility resulting from living in poverty, we point to teaching and learning that strengthen self-esteem and give the satisfaction of success. We show the importance of the school curriculum connecting up with young people's lives as well as opening up new horizons.

Throughout this, we hold to our central position that we cannot hope to understand the relationship among class, poverty, and schooling by localizing responsibility and blame, but only through an empathetic interpretive stance that is aware of the complexity of interactions between schools and communities. Moreover, we maintain the need to understand the concentration of power at the macro level and the way it flows down through the system in order to influence micro-level symbolic interactions between teachers and pupils in the classroom.

CHAPTER SEVEN

Neoliberal School Reform

Blaming Teachers, Blaming Schools

Education might be thought of as the pursuit of politics "by other means."
—Stuart Hall (1974, p. 49)

W e begin this chapter by confronting the elephant in the room—the class-based contradiction that underpins education. Capitalism requires *skilled but compliant workers*, or as one of us expressed it in an earlier book, "workers who are clever enough to be profitable but not wise enough to know what's really going on" (Wrigley, 2006, p. 8). This irresolvable contradiction has had profound effects on the history of school provision, internal and external relationships, and the development of curriculum and pedagogy. Here we relate it particularly to intensified demands for more effective schools in the wider neoliberal politics whereby the role of the state is reassessed along with the relationship of service provision to the economy.

We hope to show how this contradiction has been allowed to work its way through a series of contemporary policy relays. First, we show how schools are being spot-welded onto the economy through hegemonic notions of neoliberalism and accountability. Second, by drawing on a problematic research paradigm based on the notion of differential 'school effectiveness', a litany of ameliorative solutions is generated that pays no heed to context. We reveal how this has given rise to a new deficit ideology, this time applied to the schools and teachers who serve the most disadvantaged neighborhoods, and underpins practices of naming, shaming, and blaming schools for poverty-related underachievement. We then show how this translates into new models of management and governance, including eventually the privatization of state-funded schools. Indeed, both the English and the U.S. contexts show how identifying more and more schools as failures is used to feed the insatiable hunger of the privatization lobby.

The Slow Development of State Education

Patterns of educational opportunity, participation, and achievement cannot be divorced from divisions in the wider society. This is not just the case for more disadvantaged or marginalized young people but is true more generally. It is important to begin by establishing a general understanding before moving on to look at the particular issue of education of children from working-class families—though we must be careful about how we deploy that phrase—and especially those growing up in poverty. Crucially, we aim to use class in its Marxist sense to distinguish those who own and control the means of production and those who sell their labor power: capitalists versus employees.

Capitalism has always had a problem with education. Since the Industrial Revolution, and the early days of mass schooling, the ruling class has been caught between the need to increase the skills of future workers and the fear that they could become more articulate, knowledgeable, and rebellious. The precise form and impact of this contradiction have varied through different stages of technical and political development, and partly indeed in response to the power and influence of teachers. The fundamental nature of the contradiction has, however, remained largely the same.

In the early nineteenth century in England, Hannah Moore set about founding Sunday schools for children who were forced to work the rest of the week. Faced with opposition from landowners who thought that any form of education for their laborers would be dangerous, she explained the restricted nature of what she aimed to provide:

> They learn, on weekdays, such coarse works as may fit them for servants. I allow of no writing for the poor. My object is . . . to train up the lower classes in habits of industry and piety. . . . Beautiful is the order of society when each, according to his place, pays willing honour to his superiors. (cited in Simon, 1960, p. 133)

Perhaps that is why reactionaries still prefer children completing tedious exercises rather than expressing their feelings and ideas.

Throughout the nineteenth century, English policy documents bluntly stated that working-class children (the masses, the working classes) should not be educated beyond their station in life. (The situation was somewhat different in Scotland, where the Calvinist version of Protestant Reformation demanded universal literacy.) When eventually, worried by industrial competition from Germany, the government made elementary schooling compulsory, its curriculum and ethos were designed to teach basic literacy and numeracy, discipline children into the rhythms of factory life, and instill pride in the Empire. From the start, though, there were always teachers who opposed this limited view and struggled to overcome it within their own classrooms.

Often the British ruling class's fear of overeducating workers, and its determination to keep the education of different social classes separate, endangered its international competitiveness. At the start of the twentieth century, local school boards were forbidden by law from funding anything that might be deemed secondary education, including science and technical education. In Marxist terms, this is a good example of the *relations* of production (class structure) putting the brake on the development of *forces* of production (the technology). For most of the twentieth century, technical courses in schools were of low status and restricted to woodwork and metalwork for boys, needlework and housecraft for girls, even though the economy had moved on. The pedagogy was about following instructions and designs provided by others. Such craft teaching served a disciplinary socializing function, but it clearly had limited relevance to current modes of industrial production. It was only near the end of the twentieth century that this was superseded by the design and technology paradigm, which included designing as well as making and involved students evaluating the result of their own creativity (Eggleston, 1996).

Times have changed, but the basic principle remains: capitalism needs workers who are "clever enough to be profitable but not wise enough to know what's really going on" (Wrigley, 2006, p. 8). This appears stark but is fundamental to understanding the dynamics. There are two main factors that complicate the basic contradiction, however, so that we cannot simply map schooling and curriculum onto socioeconomic analysis. First, employers have different views of what they need: some insist on back to basics—spelling practice and multiplication tables—whereas others, more forward looking, point to the need for communication skills and initiative—but within limits! Second, there have always been many teachers, individually and organized in curriculum associations and trade unions, who persist in believing that schools should do more than prepare young people for work and for subordinate roles in the social hierarchy.

Neoliberalism and Accountability

The last few decades have seen a deep ideological struggle over the relationship between state functions such as education and the priorities of capitalist economy. Neoliberalism was conceived as an attempt to turn the clock back by curtailing the role of the state. This was hypocritical since it involved no attempt to reduce military spending or policing. The neoliberal decision to deregulate the banks eventually led to a multinational financial crisis, whereupon states immediately stepped in using taxation intended for welfare provision to bail out the banks, thus illustrating the highly selective application of anti-statist principles (see Harvey, 2005, for a more comprehensive account).

Meanwhile school reforms in England, while reducing the influence of local government, subjected nominally self-governing schools to increased regulation by central government. This contrary movement—an apparent shift toward greater school autonomy combined with increasing centralization and standardization—was facilitated through a rhetoric of raising standards and ensuring greater equality of provision and opportunity. Neither of these aims has been accomplished, as we show below. The establishment of quasi-market relations between schools was also justified in terms of increasing parents' rights. In reality, the main effect of these reforms has been to align schools with economic demands, though employers' organizations continue to complain.

Stephen Ball's (2003) studies of the intrusion of big business into public education, including direct involvement in its governance and management, have also demonstrated the extent to which the aims of the capitalist class have become dominant. He argues:

> The social and economic purposes of education have been collapsed into a single, overriding emphasis on policy making for economic competitiveness and an increasing neglect or sidelining (other than in rhetoric) of the social purposes of education. (pp. 11–12)

Quoting a key speech from Tony Blair:

> Education is our best economic policy. . . . This country will succeed or fail on the basis of how it changes itself and gears up to this new economy, based on knowledge. Education therefore is now the centre of economic policy making for the future. (cited in Ball, 2008, p. 12)

As with the moral panic in the United States when the USSR launched its Sputnik satellite in the 1950s, the fear of economic and technical competition has been a key driver in seeking to make education more efficient. This is at the center of the high-stakes accountability drive. It should also be recognized that right-wing governments have sheltered behind declining or only average scores in international tests to introduce reactionary policies.

It is into this hegemonic configuration that policies concerned with inequalities of educational outcome have had to fit. The needs of lower-status social groups, including less skilled manual workers, the unemployed and migrants, and particularly families affected by poverty, have been recognized only within the broader class-determined policy framework. The need to reduce attainment differences has been accepted only grudgingly, within the wider neoliberal drive for greater effectiveness.

One of the most corrosive features has been the construction in England and elsewhere of a "high surveillance, low trust" regime (Mahoney & Hextall, 2000,

p. 102), which is certainly not an ecology of sustainable development. It affects all pupils educated in publicly funded schools—more than 90 percent of the population—but arguably impacts on the most vulnerable young people most of all. Numerous committed researchers have commented on its corrosive effects. It is demotivating, and most of all it demoralizes teachers in more challenging schools. The standardized curriculum it depends upon fails to connect with the majority of pupils but is probably most disconnected from the lifeworlds of young people growing up in poverty. The 'name and shame' approach of publicly identifying low-attaining schools also names and shames the students and their teachers, particularly targeting schools in poorer areas. The climate of fear it engenders undermines the formation of supportive relationships with young people whose lives have been made fragile.

As Fred Inglis (2000) points out in relation to this regime:

> "Accountability" is, after all, not the same thing as responsibility, still less duty. It is a pistol loaded with blame to be fired at the heads of those who cannot answer charges. . . . The preposterous edifice of auditing . . . blinds vision and stifles thought. Their most certain consequence is to make enquiry service, knowledge instrumental and, above all, to make all of us, teachers at whatever level, boring, exhausted and hating the job. (pp. 424–28)

Michael Fielding (1999), concerned as always with the quality of interpersonal relationships, asks:

> How many teachers . . . are now able to listen openly, attentively, and in a non-instrumental, exploratory way to their children/students without feeling guilty, stressed or vaguely uncomfortable about the absence of criteria or the insistence of a target tugging at their sleeves? (p. 280)

Elsewhere Fielding (2001a) speaks of researchers encountering

> students expressing doubts about the genuineness of their school's interest in their progress and well-being as persons, as distinct from their contribution to their school's league table position (Ball, 1999; Fielding, 1999; Reay & William, 1999). The overriding instrumentality of conversations makes listening difficult: attentiveness is overdirected; clues to meaning are trodden underfoot in the scramble for performance; dialogue disappears as reciprocity retreats under the sheer weight of external expectation; contract replaces community as the bond of human association. (p. 152)

School Effectiveness Research

The body of statistical research known as School Effectiveness has served to underpin these policies. Of particular interest here is the question of the 'school effect', or more precisely the extent to which individual differences in attainment can be explained by differences between schools.

School Effectiveness research has consistently told its own story in opposition to James Coleman's (1966) conclusion that, in the United States at least, there was little difference between schools that could not be ascribed to social background:

> One implication stands out above all: That schools bring little influence to bear on a child's achievement that is independent of his background and general social context; and that this very lack of independent effect means that the inequalities imposed on children by their home, neighborhood and peer environment are carried along to become the inequalities with which they confront adult life at the end of school. For equality of educational opportunity through the schools must imply a strong effect of schools that is independent of the child's immediate social environment, and that strong independent effect is not present in American schools. (p. 325)

Coleman is clearly arguing against meritocratic myths that schools are the great equalizers, the place where the poorest can excel, and that Huckleberry Finn can become president of the United States. We should note, however, that the Coleman Report, and others that followed soon after, was commenting on schools as they currently exist, it is not talking about future possibilities. There were also many limitations in the research, including reliance on easily measurable variables: school quality was measured in terms of the cost and quantity of material and human resources (number, salary, and years of experience of teachers; size of school library; etc.). These points are forcefully made by the editors of the *Harvard Educational Review* following the publication of Jencks and colleagues' (1973) *Inequality*:

> It is important to recognize that Inequality is a description of our past, rather than a delimitation of our nation's educational future. . . . Surely educational success will be very difficult to achieve. . . . But given the infancy of systematic attempts to improve the schools, it is too early to assume that the schools cannot be developed so that they do succeed in reducing overall social inequality in America. (Editors, 1973, pp. 49–50)

They point out that "new paradigms for educational research" are needed, without which "we are destined to repeat ourselves again and again in concluding that nothing makes any difference" (p. 49). In the same issue, Coleman (1973) himself argues for research that will show what might improve pupils' cognitive skills and encourage them to stay at school but also how to improve social and entrepreneurial skills and so on. In the same issue, a group of Black scholars (Edmonds et al., 1973) points to the racism in schools and in assessment tools and methods used by researchers. They highlight the fallacy of Jencks's assumption that schools have done everything that can be done to help poor and Black children:

> We hasten to point out to Jencks that public schools are not now, nor have they ever been, committed to the radical notion that they are obliged to teach certain minimal school skills (reading, writing and computation) to all pupils who are free of certifiable handicap. (p. 83)

Furthermore, we should recognize that if a very small number of schools provide much better opportunities, this is unlikely to show up by number crunching the data from vast numbers of schools. Jencks's team (1973), revisiting Coleman's data, found that the gap between rich and poor lay as much within schools. This suggests the need to tackle this problem directly rather than setting up a spurious competition between schools. Much more recently, UK researchers Cassen and Kingdon (2007) conclude that, although pupils with free school meal (FSM) entitlement tend to be placed in weaker schools

> only about 6 per cent of the net association between FSM and low achievement, other things being equal, is due to FSM students attending worse quality schools. The bulk of the effect of FSM is the disadvantage that FSM status reflects. (p. 25)

Despite this, school effectiveness research has been used by politicians to claim that schools and teachers are primarily responsible for low levels of achievement and particularly in disadvantaged populations. The data provide a more mixed picture. As Bangs, MacBeath, and Galton (2011) point out: "Hundreds of studies later [i.e., since Jencks' 1971 reassessment of the Coleman Report's data] the school effect remains stubbornly in the 8 to 15 per cent region" (p. 35).

Despite the small percentage generally attributed to school effect, research studies that focus on atypical schools (outliers) show some dramatic differences between a few very successful schools and the bulk of schools in areas of poverty. Rutter and colleagues (1979) detailed comparison of twelve London secondary schools shows:

> After adjusting for intake characteristics, children at the most successful secondary school got four times as many exam passes on average as children at the least successful school. Or expressed another way, children in the bottom 25 per cent of verbal ability in the most successful school on average obtained as many exam passes as children in the top 25 per cent of verbal ability at the least successful school. (p. 19)

Rutter explains that statistical results show a very small school effect in terms of the small variation among the majority of schools when compared with a larger variation in terms of families:

> Other things being equal, a predictor with a wide range will always account for a higher proportion of the variance than a predictor with a narrow range. Because it is likely that schools tend to be more homogeneous than are families and because the differences between the 'best' and the 'worse' schools is likely to be far less than that between the 'best' and 'worst' homes, it necessarily means that . . . family variables will usually have a greater 'effect' than school variables. But this does not necessarily mean that schools have a lesser influence than families on achievement. (1983, p. 3–4)

Effective Engagement with Students and Families

Finally, as Angus (1993) has argued, there is a deep problem in attempting to separate out school effect from background factors. What we should be doing is looking at the interactions as they affect students in their daily movement between school and their diverse lifeworlds. One of the most revealing studies (Brookover et al., 1978) examined school climate from the student perspective. The most important school effect factor by far was the student sense of *academic futility*:

> Students feel they have no control over their success or failure in the school social system, the teachers do not care if they succeed or not, and their fellow students punish them if they do succeed . . . High futility indicates a high degree of hopelessness in the school situation. (p. 314)

Brookover and colleagues point out that this sense is more typical in "majority Black schools than majority white ones" and "somewhat more characteristic of low SES [socioeconomic status] white schools than high SES white ones." Because of this correlation with composition of the student body:

> The students' sense of futility is thus an alternate explanation for much of the between-school difference in achievement which is explained by racial and socio-economic composition of the school or the racial and SES family background. (p. 315).

We are clearly in territory here where the nature of teacher-student interaction, teachers' perceptions and judgment of students, and students' experience of their movement between home, neighborhood and school, are the real issue, rather than a simplistic apportionment of responsibility or blame that invariably turns into one or other form of deficit theory. Reading between the lines of Brookover's account, we might infer that negative emotions associated with racism and class prejudice affect the symbolic interactions of teachers and students.

School Effectiveness: A New Form of Deficit Theory

As argued earlier, concerns about social justice and poverty-linked underachievement have been reconfigured within a wider accountability movement related to neoliberal policy and economics. Valencia (2010) shows how this developed in the United States, where viewing the nation as 'at risk' from foreign competition set the parameters for discussing the at-riskness of students. Then, as now, the argument was based on a false premise: that a skills shortage was to blame for economic stagnation and that an increase in the number of well-qualified young people would lead to the emergence of new jobs. This displaces a problem of the economic system onto education. Even before the current financial crisis it was abundantly clear from the high level of graduate unemployment in many countries that capitalism had no way of utilizing the existing qualifications of young people, let alone needing more. An emphasis on 'knowledge economy' employment, requiring that education maximized its output of higher qualified employees, led to an emphasis on quantity (specifying number of years and hours of study of core subjects, leadership for maximizing school efficiency) that was insufficiently focused to assist more marginalized students.

By contrast with *A Nation at Risk* (National Commission on Excellence in Education, 1983), *Barriers to Excellence: Our Children at Risk* (National Coalition of Advocates for Students, 1985) pointed to the significant barriers of discrimination and differential treatment faced by more disadvantaged young people: "inflexibility of school structure, abuses of ability grouping and tracking, misuses of testing, narrowness of curriculum and teaching practices, lack of democratic governance, and lack of early childhood education programs" (Valencia, 2010, p. 108; see also Ainscow, 2010, for England).

Furthermore, when specific programs were introduced relating to 'at-risk' students, there was a failure to address "system bases of academic failure such as schools with inferior resources and unqualified teachers" and a "strong tendency to stereotype" (Valencia, 2010, p. 112):

> As Levin (1992) notes, we must be cognizant that at-risk factors "are only indicators of at-risk populations rather than definitions.". . . many students from these groups are not at risk for school failure, "and we must take care not to stereotype children from these populations in a mindless way that precludes their educational success" (p. 285). (Valencia, p. 112)

Blaming Schools for Poverty: "If They Can Do It, Why Can't You?"

The importance of controlling for SES or prior attainment is well established in school effectiveness research for all its other problems. This was sometimes reflected in England's accountability statistics, though in a crude form and at whole-school level; in its usual form, the proportion of pupils achieving higher levels of qualification was matched against the proportion with free meal entitlement (FSM). This was convenient since the data were readily available, but it took no account of other factors such as parents' occupations or education levels.

This method has a serious logical flaw: most of a school's higher qualifications tend to come from non-FSM pupils, and whether a school has 10 percent or 30 percent of pupils on free meals tells us nothing about the backgrounds of the rest of its population. Of two schools that both have 25 percent of pupils with free meal entitlement, one might also have 25 percent with graduate parents, whereas the other has none. The former case has been referred to as *bipolar distribution*, and is rarely considered in evaluations of school effect.

Politicians in various countries conveniently ignore SES when it suits. In England, despite the highly sophisticated statistical analysis provided to school inspectors, it is well known that they are far more likely to fail schools located in areas of disadvantage. In 2007 Prime Minister Gordon Brown announced a floor target of 30 percent of pupils achieving five or more higher grade GCSEs) including English and Maths. (The GCSE or General Certificate of Secondary Education is the examination for 16-year-olds.) A fifth of state secondary schools (overwhelmingly in poorer areas) did not meet this target and were targeted for closure and privatization. No regard was paid to the levels of disadvantage in the schools. In June 2011 Conservative Education Minister Michael Gove escalated by raising the floor target to 50 percent by 2015 (Department of Education, 2011).

In January 2012, Gove's Schools Minister Nick Gibb launched an attack on schools in disadvantaged areas by blaming teachers for the low attainment of disadvantaged pupils. (The official criterion is either free meal eligibility or children in public care, though numerically it is almost entirely the former.) He expressed dismay that only 33.9 percent of disadvantaged pupils were achieving five or more higher grade (A*-C) GCSEs with English and Maths, against a national average for all pupils of 58.2 percent. This gap had remained almost unchanged for five years:

> These tables show which schools are letting children down. We will not hesitate to tackle underperformance in any school. . . . We will not let schools coast with mediocre performance. (Gibb, 2012)

To support his case that the blame lay with teachers, he pointed to twenty-one schools where more than 80 percent of disadvantaged pupils gained five higher grades with English and maths. "If they can get it right, then so can all schools." On closer analysis, it turned out that half these schools were selective grammar schools that admitted hardly any disadvantaged pupils, only those excelling at age ten. A quarter were successful comprehensive schools in affluent areas, with a very small proportion of disadvantaged pupils. Of the remaining six schools, three were very small and with religious admissions criteria.

A further attack was based on data showing more than 200 schools (nearly 9 percent) where disadvantaged pupils did better than the national average for all pupils. Again, a closer analysis shows that the vast majority either had few disadvantaged pupils, selected their pupils by prior attainment, exploited spurious alternative qualifications, or were girls-only schools (which generally attain higher grades).

The Distribution of Material Resources

Inequitable distribution of resources (including staffing) continues to be a major source of contention, although the Coleman Report unexpectedly found that this was less significant a factor than family background. In the UK, schools in poorer areas generally receive higher budgets, whereas in the United States they get less.

However, in neither situation is staffing sufficient to meet the cumulative and complex needs of their population.

Arguments are frequently made by those reluctant to increase spending on public schools that class size makes little difference. This fails to recognize research that shows that class size and teacher quality have a greater impact on minority ethnic and poorer families (Wolfe, 1975, cited by Gamoran & Long, 2006, p. 9). Extra teachers can bring particular benefits at certain stages, for example, the Tennessee class size experiment in the early elementary grades (Finn & Achilles, 1999, cited by Gamoran & Long, 2006, p. 8). In the American context, too, internal divisions within large schools are an important issue; students are divided into 'tracks' that predetermine their educational careers (see Gamoran & Long, 2006, p. 9 for further references).

In other socially divided countries, such as Latin America, there are huge differences between schools, and a lower budget can mean a severe lack of resources (Gamoran & Long, 2006, p. 14). For example, while elite private schools in Brazil are well equipped, public schools in poorer urban areas have to operate on a shift system—in effect three different schools each occupy the same building for just four hours a day, with teachers working up to eight hours a day in two of these sessions to earn a living wage.

In Germany, there are big differences between types of public school. Children are assigned to one of three school types as early as ten years old, based on parental preference or teacher recommendation, which has the effect of strongly segregating by family background. The German PISA team pointed out that working-class children needed to achieve higher grades to get into grammar schools, and that children from class I were three times as likely as class V or VI to attend grammar schools (Gymnasium) rather than the middle-ranking Realschule—*even with the same level of literacy* (Baumert & Schümer, 2002). All of this points to the dangers of transferring conclusions from the United States, where school effectiveness research is strongest, to other countries with different social structures, cultures, and education systems and transferring findings from one social or school context to another.

In state schools in Britain, the pupil-teacher ratio and school budgets are actually higher in areas of disadvantage than elsewhere but nowhere near enough to deal with the extreme problems teachers are confronted with in some areas, particularly those where deindustrialization in the 1980s and 1990s led to chronic intergenerational unemployment or where "problem families" have been concentrated in particular public housing estates or blocks of flats. Teachers' energies can become entirely exhausted in dealing with social welfare and behavior issues, and senior staff have little time left to improve the quality of teaching and learning after dealing with multiple crises.

By contrast, around 7 percent of the UK population (4 percent in Scotland) attend fee-paying private schools with generous per-capita budgets, smaller classes, and superior material resources. These schools are able to apply remedial support to learning problems that would appear minor in most urban schools. They are able to develop an esprit de corps through an extensive sport and cultural program. All of this combines with the corporate aspirational work outlined in chapter 6.

Wellington College, for example, set in 400 acres of countryside, charges annual fees approaching £30,000 (US$45,000) per pupil. Its thousand students not only enjoy small classes and exceptionally well-qualified teachers, but also

> an astonishing array of sporting and extra-curricular opportunities. The school has sixteen rugby pitches, two floodlit AstroTurf pitches, a state-of-the-art sports hall, twenty-two hard tennis courts, twelve cricket pitches, an athletics track, two lacrosse pitches and six netball courts, a shooting range, a nationally acclaimed nine-hole golf course, six art studios, its own section on the Saatchi website (Wellington@Saatchi), its own theatre . . . its own TV crew . . . a professional recording studio for aspiring musicians, and a number of concert venues. (Benn, 2011, p. 136)

Independent schools are not subject to the draconian regulation imposed by the state on public schools, and, as Melissa Benn comments with some irony, are able to engage in their own form of privileged progressivism:

> Later I am shown an airy classroom dominated by an oval table, part of a school experiment in pioneering the Harkness approach in which the teacher guides learning rather than lecturing to students. Wellington also emphasizes what Seldon [the headteacher] calls "roundedness," or what the press liked to call "happiness lessons" when first introduced, to much media fanfare, in 2006. Students are taught "well-being" as part of the development of "multiple intelligences," learning about the importance of deferred gratification, physical good health, empathy and flourishing and so on—although given the school's general sumptuousness, one suspects little gratification need be deferred here, nor flourishing become an overly onerous task. (pp. 137–38)

Markets and Privatization

The reform of school governance in England and the United States provides an eloquent example of the workings of class on schooling. Aspects of it have been imitated in other countries, but nowhere so strongly or over such a long period.

The original thinking of Margaret Thatcher's Conservative government in its reform of school governance was that a free market system would drive quality in a survival of the fittest: schools that attracted few customers would simply close and be replaced by newly founded schools. Subsequently, they invented mechanisms to accelerate this competition between schools, including league tables of results and an inspectorate that could publicly "place a school in special measures." (The press have had no difficulty translating this phrase to "failing school.")

What actually happened was that parents gravitated toward schools located in more affluent areas and away from those located in poorer neighborhoods. Parents higher up the social scale were cleverer at operating systems of choice to their children's advantage, but also ambitious parents in poorer areas moved their children away from the local school. Rather than driving up standards, the quasi-market proved to be a mechanism for promoting social segregation. Consequently, schools in poorer locations with vacant places were compelled to take in pupils that other schools had thrown out. This was a downward spiral, which within ten years led to large numbers of seriously troubled schools.

Here we see at work a neoliberal view that seeks to remodel public services on private business lines; we should also recognize that this has not involved an abandonment of the state but its cooption to a new purpose. Though school closure has been in the hands of national and local officials rather than a simple commercial event, the new system did in fact establish a quasi-market driven by competition. Whether this resulted in school improvement is a different question.

Examination results went up, but research by Tymms (2004) has demonstrated that some assessments were becoming easier over time, so that only part of the apparent improvement was real. This particularly affected the national tests for 11–year-olds, for which the criteria for achieving the target grade in reading were lowered. At the upper secondary stage, competition led schools to steer students toward subjects that appeared easier; the reduced numbers entered for maths and sciences then triggered a reduction in the required standard for these subjects at university entrance level (age 18).

There is currently an investigation into whether competition between commercially run examination boards has gradually led to a lowering of standards. A new Conservative-led government is seeking to create a moral panic about falling standards in England to suit its own purposes, indeed exaggerating the data, so it is important to be critical of official claims; however, it remains the case that PISA results for England have fallen dramatically. Given the nature of the PISA assessments, this suggests that pupils are being crammed to *remember more* while preparing for tests and exams but that such methods are leading them to *think less*. In other words, the system was not aiding cognitive development.

The most damning indictment of the effects of a school system run on commercial lines has come from Diane Ravitch (2010), and is all the more telling because she is a veteran scholar of unimpeachable conservative values. She even served as assistant secretary for education in the administration of President George H. W. Bush, and for nearly two decades she was a fervent advocate of the very reforms she is now denouncing. Ravitch says quite openly that she has changed her mind now that she can see the damage done by a system built on choice, competition, and threat. She explains how both parties, from right-wing Republicans to Obama's progressive wing of Democrats, fell in behind calls for "accountability, high-stakes testing, data-driven decision making, choice, charter schools, privatization, deregulation, merit pay, and competition between schools. Whatever could not be measured did not count" (p. 21).

Her account of city-wide reforms in New York and San Diego is a tale of lawyers and entrepreneurs taking over education departments, of bullying management styles, of intimidation leading to disaffection and high teacher turnover, of consultants functioning as spies, of mass sackings and flight of school principals, to be replaced by novices with leadership diplomas but precious little experience of education.

The new system even led entire states to cheat in order to win more federal government funding. The apparent rise in attainment on the basis of state tests did not tally with the more stable standards of the federal test. For example, Mississippi claimed that 89 percent of its fourth graders were at or above proficiency in reading, but according to NAEP only 18 percent were. Chicago claimed that the proportion passing maths had risen from 33 percent to 70 percent, but NAEP scores were flat (Ravitch, 2010, p. 106).

Ravitch (2010) concludes her book with a dire warning for the future of U.S. education:

> At the present time, public education is in peril. Efforts to reform public education are, ironically, diminishing its quality and endangering its very survival. We must turn our attention to improving the schools, infusing them with the substance of genuine learning and reviving the conditions that make learning possible. (p. 242)

These problems affect everybody reliant on the public education system, that is, those who are not wealthy enough to pay private school fees. The damage is particularly great (1) for those whose parents do not have a sufficient education themselves to compensate; and (2) those made vulnerable by poverty. Andy Hargreaves (2003) warned some years ago of an apartheid model of school development in countries like England and the United States. While schools in more advantaged areas are granted flexibility to develop as learning communities that prepare their students for the knowledge society, others are constrained to instruct their students for short-term attainment gains in preparation for low-level service jobs.

One of the most potent ways in which interschool competition affects schools in disadvantaged areas is through appraisal systems which have financial consequences for teachers, and where judgments are often made on a simplistic and narrow basis of test results. Schools in more challenging areas have always been unattractive to teachers who are not already committed to principles of social justice, but such appraisal systems linked to payment by results turn high-poverty urban schools into places to be avoided if a future career is valued. The loss of teachers and the difficulty of recruiting heads are serious problems in these schools in

England. In the United States, Darling-Hammond's research shows a correlation between underqualified teachers and low-SES schools but also demonstrates the impact on student achievement:

> Students who score in the lowest decile of the API (Academic Performance Index), compared to those scoring in the highest decile, are six times more probable to be taught by unqualified teachers. Darling-Hammond (2004) states: "The presence of underqualified teachers is strongly related to student socioeconomic status and to student achievement" (p. 1939). (Valencia, 2010, p. 119)

School Privatization

The 1980s and 1990s saw an international movement toward delegating decision making from regional or local authorities to individual schools. The significance of this varied country by country, and in some countries provided space for teacher empowerment and community involvement. It was perhaps most contradictory in England, where the delegation of financial and organizational powers to schools was accompanied by the centralization and standardization of control over curriculum through a national curriculum policed by national tests and a privatized inspectorate. Results and judgments were publicized to drive parental choice.

Many of the early critics of this new regime read local management as a form of privatization or recognized that it could lead that way (Smyth, 1993, 2011). What eventually occurred was beyond imagining. In 2000 a Labour education minister announced that a few low-achieving urban schools would be placed under the control of business 'sponsors'. Three 'city academies' were opened in 2002 and a dozen by 2004. Before any examination results or evaluations were available, Prime Minister Blair announced the rapid expansion of the program, though still with the pretext of improving opportunities for pupils in areas of deprivation.

A new Conservative-led coalition government in 2010 abandoned the link to urban underachievement, and, largely as a consequence of financial incentives, by 2012 more than half of England's secondary schools had become academies. The government's ambition in England is to privatize the other half and also a large number of primary and special schools.

Like the war on Iraq, this was a case of policy-based evidence rather than evidence-based policy. Government-funded research has consistently overlooked vital data, including the impact on examination results of the early academies changing the balance of their pupil population to include fewer pupils with free meal entitlement and recruiting the children of more ambitious parents from a wider area. Furthermore, they ignored the extent to which the academies were exploiting easier qualifications (Wrigley, 2011). Neither pupils in general, nor disadvantaged pupils in particular, are achieving better in these privately managed, publicly funded schools (Wrigley & Kalambouka, 2012). Evaluation in Sweden ('free schools') and the United States ('charter schools'), the other two countries that have embarked extensively on school privatization, also show no attainment gains after controlling for the changing student population (Lundahl, 2011; Lubienski & Lubienski, 2006).

School Effectiveness: What Brings Results?

There are many reasons for being critical of school effectiveness research, including its almost exclusive focus on attainment rather than a broader sense of achievement that includes personal, social, and cultural development (for example, see Slee & Weiner, 1998; Morley & Rassool, 1999). Methodologically, its claim to be scientific and reliable involves various forms of reductionism (Wrigley, 2013). It attempts to separate out, as we have shown above, school-level from classroom-level from extra-school factors rather than look at the interrelationship and interactions (Angus, 1993; Riddell, Brown & Duffield, 1998). More specifically here, we wish to question its value in identifying which school-level factors lead to higher attainment.

Repeated claims are made that School Effectiveness research has identified a small number of factors that make some schools more effective than others. With small modifications, the list has been transmitted from one report to another. Rather than these factors being derived in some automatic way from the statistics, they are the things the paradigm looks for whereas other important factors can be overlooked. The list generally mentions leadership, school ethos, expectations, teaching and learning, assessment, pupil participation, rewards, extracurricular activities, and links with parents (for example see the list in table 1 of Sammons, Hillman & Mortimore, 1995).

Lists of key characteristics are often articulated in terms of simple phrases such as *strong leadership* or *a focus on teaching and learning*. A major problem is the vagueness of many of these common sense items:

> Despite the complex detail of mathematical calculations, their truth depends on the validity of the features being observed and quantified. Many "key characteristics" of effective schools (e.g., "a clear and continuing focus on teaching and learning") are semantically incapable of being assigned unambiguously to some schools and denied to others, as would be required for valid statistical modeling. One wonders how observers are trained to identify and score such a characteristic. Furthermore, such a "focus" might involve either transmission or social constructivist pedagogies, factual or critical learning. And whereas weak leadership is undoubtedly a problem, the "strong leadership" which SE claims to be a crucial factor in successful schools could mean anything from supportive or inspirational to dictatorial. This unhelpful vagueness of terminology is concealed beneath the "certainty" conferred by mathematical precision, creating a false aura of scientific objectivity. (Wrigley, 2013, p. 6)

Descriptors such as "participation by pupils in the life of the school" are often minimally interpreted. The result is a far cry from democratic involvement in whole-school and classroom-level decision making.

Complex findings can give rise to simplistic policy dogmatically enforced. When Peter Mortimore and colleagues (1988) reported on the importance of assessment in more successful primary schools, they were referring to continuity from one year to the next involving either summative grades or portfolios containing a sample of each pupil's work. Their research certainly doesn't justify the obsession, over the past two decades, with collecting mountains of numerical data on every pupil nor the high-stakes testing imposed by government.

The presentation of "key characteristics of effective schools" operates in a seemingly neutral discourse, but it fails to reflect the engagement with social justice that marks unusually successful schools in contexts of disadvantage. Blair and Bourne's (1998) study of academically successful schools serving largely African Caribbean pupils in England highlighted, for example, the importance of headteachers taking complaints of racism seriously, even when the complaint was made against a teacher. A set of case studies of successful schools with large numbers of Asian and other bilingual pupils (Wrigley, 2000) illustrates many unusual examples of student engagement, a high profile for the creative and performing arts, ingenious ways of raising self-esteem, the celebration of identity and culture, a deep commitment to social justice, and a warm and intelligent process of relationship building with local communities. None of these is reflected in the usual lists.

The case studies in Wrigley, Thomson, and Lingard (2012) include outstanding examples of collective teacher creativity that far exceed the notion of distributed leadership emphasized in mainstream school improvement studies. The editors' conclusion highlights the importance in these schools of drawing on existing educational theory and of practical theory building, of "making philosophy practical" (pp. 205–13). It is apparent that orthodox School Effectiveness and School Improvement have been shaped through a process of paradigm formation (Wrigley, 2013) within the dominant neoliberal discourse of competitive economism.

As early as 1979, Michael Rutter's classic study highlighted the importance of looking holistically, rather than at discrete factors, in order to explain effectiveness. Alternative ecological rather than mechanistic models of school development are available (for example, see Büeler, 1998, cited in Wrigley, 2003, p. 26). The main response has, however, come in terms of widespread adoption of the concept of *school culture*, although the term is often used in a thin, apolitical view involving little sense of how power operates in institutions (see Alvesson, 2002; Wrigley, 2003, pp. 36–37; Smyth, McInerney, Lawson & Hattam, 1999, for a critique). Words such as *vision* are used in anodyne ways that don't involve a social vision or thinking about our global future, and that fail to connect organizational with pedagogical theory.

Furthermore, even when mainstream school improvement theorists are at odds with government regulations, their criticism has often been muted, leading to Thrupp and Willmott's (2003) accusation of a "subtle apologism." Typically, an introductory page is devoted to restrained commentary on the difficulties created by national policy at the macro level, but then teachers and principals are invited to simply do their best in operating within that context rather than working collectively to resist and oppose destructive regulations and interventions. There have always been exceptions, and recently a number of authoritative voices have commented on the failings of high-stakes, low-trust accountability regimes (see, for example, Ravitch, 2010; Bangs, MacBeath & Galton, 2011; Hargreaves & Fullan, 2012). A recent book by Pasi Sahlberg (2011) presents an open challenge to the international hegemony of the Anglo-American neoliberal efficiency regime from the more enlightened and collegial Finnish approach to educational development.

So, Do Schools Make a Difference?

Having devoted earlier chapters to a sustained critique of 'blame the victim' deficit theories, it might appear contradictory and perverse to deflect responsibility away from schools, at the risk of returning it to students and their families. That would be a misunderstanding of our argument.

1. While refuting arguments that seek to blame underachievement on inherited low intelligence, poor parenting, or a lack of aspirations, we are not in denial about the serious impact of exploitative class relations and, particularly, poverty. Exploitation and poverty have serious consequences for health, living conditions, leisure opportunities, and relationships. The stigma attached to poverty through underclass discourses and attacks on families dependent on welfare benefits has an enormous impact on school success. Even the inability to afford clothing bearing the right logo can tarnish self-respect.

2. Poverty has a cumulative impact through the different stages of schooling. The most advanced children from poorer families at any stage tend to be overtaken in the next stage of education by less successful children from more privileged backgrounds. The majority of those who are doing well against the odds fall back to average and fail to fulfill earlier expectations by the next major hurdle (Feinstein, 2006; Sutton Trust, 2008).

3. Next in importance to the material and symbolic damage of poverty, school resources do make a difference. Schools serving troubled neigh-

borhoods need substantial extra staffing (teachers, social workers, youth and community workers) in order to support their students' complex needs and develop a resource to support the development of the whole community.

4. It is important to recognize that statistical analyses of large numbers of real schools cannot go beyond reporting the generalities of schools *as they are*. That is, they show the extent to which schools, overall, reproduce socioeconomic divisions. It should not be assumed from this that a better kind of school is impossible and that the extent of reproduction cannot be reduced.

5. Whereas the school effect may be relatively small across large numbers of schools, a few highly successful outliers demonstrate what can sometimes be achieved. For example, Thomas and Mortimore (1994) reported differences between examination results for similar pupils of between 7 grade Es and 7 grade Cs at GCSE, though this is a comparison between schools at the *opposite* poles of effectiveness.

6. Officially authorized models of Effectiveness and Improvement, on the other hand, merely encourage schools to *follow old ways but more intensively*. Recipes have been provided for schools in challenging circumstances on how to raise their game. These are often limited, in terms of willingness to look beyond hegemonic norms of organization and school culture as well as being bleached of any political understanding of poverty, schooling, and their effects.

7. Fortunately, some 'schools in challenging circumstances' (a frequent euphemism) have recognized the futility of this and discovered ways of *doing school differently*, that is, in ways that build self-respect and satisfaction in achievement. These are schools where vision, values, and social justice really mean something (see Wrigley, 2000; Wrigley, Thomson & Lingard, 2012; Smyth & McInerney, 2007a, 2007b; Smyth, Down & McInerney, 2010; among others.)

8. Rather than seeking to place the blame, the most promising research, it seems to us, concerns the interaction between schools and society. Brookover and colleagues' (1978) focus on student perceptions of *academic futility* is particularly significant, and connects with the sense of futility and hopelessness observed in the wider social environment by Charlesworth (2000) and others.

9. If we are to understand why so many young people withdraw during the adolescent years, as they become increasingly aware of the obstacles in their path, we need to draw on theorists such as Goffman who offer insight into the symbolic interactions of marginalized participants in rigid institutions. Recognizing what makes for fruitful and supportive interactions offers a key for understanding how a combination of good fortune, determination, adult support, high quality teaching, and school climate protects a small number of young people and enables them to pursue their rightful ambitions.

CHAPTER EIGHT

Improving Schools or Transforming Them

The Politics of Social Justice

"You are all brothers," our story will tell them, "all of you in the city. But when God made you, he used a mixture of gold in the creation of those of you who were fit to be rulers, which is why they are the most valuable. He used silver for those who were to be auxiliaries, and iron and bronze for the farmers and the rest of the skilled workers." Well that's the story. Can you think of any possible way of getting people to believe it?
—Plato (2000 [c380 BCE] §415

Schools assume that middle-class students can learn, and they do. Likewise, schools assume that lower-class students cannot learn, and they don't.
—Ray Rist, 1973, p. 19

This chapter continues the argument that the dominant (shallow and apolitical) paradigm of School Improvement has little to offer the most disadvantaged schools and their students. Our opening criticisms highlight the multidimensional nature of this paradigmatic shortcoming:

- There can be no change without reinserting social class as a central element in the analysis.

- Current emphases have ignored the interests of young people and their lives.

- There has been too much wasted effort on managerialist attempts to change schools through vacuous mission statements and visions and a predilection to measure everything.

- Interventions have focused excessively on those students deemed to be easily salvageable, while allowing the most vulnerable to become collateral damage.

We are singularly uninspired by the prevailing decontextualized literature on leadership, which seems totally oblivious to its lack of direction and incapacity to deliver.

Our argument calls for a long overdue rethinking of the current pattern by *turning the school around to face the community*. School improvement cannot occur unless students are placed at the center, their families, lives, and cultures are respected, and students are provided with relationally rich experiences and opportunities. This reorientation cannot occur while school development is driven by fear, punishment, and other forms of silencing.

Central to this transformation is a notion of school culture that understands what it is trying to do in terms of changing students' lives and life chances. This can never be achieved through arithmetic calculations of test data. It requires a symbolic-interactionist attention to the mutual (mis)understandings of teachers, students, and parents. Stratifying, segmenting, and providing diminished educational opportunities for some, while reserving more rewarding experiences for others, is a recipe for social disaster. When schools become factories of failure for some students, everyone loses.

We bring our analysis to a conclusion with the modest thought that things need not be this way. There are demonstrable international examples—for instance, Finland—of countries that have very successfully gone down a very different path. In our view, real change will not be possible without having the courage and leadership necessary for *critical community engagement*.

Discourses of Educational Change

Changes in school governance outlined in the previous chapter have, in many countries, resulted in an educational market in which each school appears to operate as an autonomous entity. It is no surprise, then, that a paradigm of school improvement has become dominant that focuses on the school as a managed organization and with an inordinate emphasis on leadership and management rather than on curriculum and pedagogy (see Smyth, 2011). This paradigm shows little understanding of the interactions between what happens within the school and what happens around it. It has done little to develop understandings of educational disengagement and underachievement related to class and poverty.

There are many ways to improve schools and enhance achievement. One important way is through a curriculum development project, for example literacy or environmental education, with collaboration in an education authority or a wider voluntary network of interested teachers. In Finland, one key priority is to make sure that all pupils are well nourished—free healthy meals for every child. This is part of a nationwide healthy eating program involving the whole society. It is fair to assume that, in more divided societies such as Australia, Britain and the United States, reducing income inequalities, strengthening family services, and outlawing as a hate crime the denigration of benefit claimants would probably have a greater impact than any changes that we could devise in school management.

The concluding chapter to *Changing Schools: Alternative Ways to Make a World of Difference* (Wrigley, Thomson & Lingard, 2012, pp. 194–214), reflecting on the book's fourteen case studies, points to the crucial importance of in-depth critical thinking about pedagogy and social justice as well as school organization. This requires a sense of place as well as the ability to draw creatively upon educational theory.

A massive emphasis has been placed on school improvement in these countries in the past twenty years but with too little focus on the young people who need it most and within a completely inadequate paradigm. That is not to say that the emphasis on involving all staff in the improvement project, along with staff development and school ethos, is unimportant, but it is insufficient of itself.

Official School Improvement concentrates on the processes needed to bring about change. In principle at least, it stresses cooperative involvement and participation rather than autocratic management and the importance of involving the whole staff, if not parents and students. Without a clear sense of social purpose, however, collegiality and cooperation can mean complicity in change for the worse.

Much has been made of the need to articulate vision, mission, and values but often with little more substance, politics, or ethics than when these words are used by investment banks or arms manufacturers:

> Often "vision" means little more than minor organizational changes. This is like rearranging the deckchairs on the *Titanic*. "Values" appear in the context of "valuing good behaviour" or "placing a high value on examination results" rather than social or political values. None of this relates to the big changes taking place in the world, or to our hopes for the future, which should determine the direction of educational change.
>
> This way of talking about school improvement and leadership strengthens neo-liberal ideology. By keeping silent about human values, it reinforces the sense that monetary values are all that matters—the bottom line. By failing to discuss alternative futures, it reinforces the sense of inevitability and fatalism that neo-liberal politicians use to quell dissent. (Wrigley, 2006, p. 38)

In effect, while seeing themselves as somehow more progressive, many leading figures of school improvement have hitched their cart to the horse of School Effectiveness, which values only what it can measure and what governments and business leaders prioritize: notching up average attainment levels. This is not to suggest that test and exam results are unimportant. Indeed, if you have the wrong postal code or skin color, you need certificates more than anybody. But they are never enough. It takes a lot more to see you through.

Furthermore, your needs can be overlooked in the school's search to raise its market position. You may be entered for qualifications with limited street value, simply because they are easier to pass and will boost the school's statistics. In education systems such as England's where a school's success is measured on the basis of the percentage jumping a particular examination hurdle, there is a strong tendency to neglect both higher and lower achievers to concentrate only on those just below the bar. This has been compared to the triage system operated by nurses in accident and emergency units.

Too close a relationship with neoliberal governments has turned many improvement experts into apologists (Thrupp & Willmott, 2003) for policies that see education only in terms of macroeconomic benefits and that work against the interests of disadvantaged young people. The genre permits an introductory page that politely bemoans some damaging aspect of the system but then admonishes headteachers to carry on bravely as before.

This is also one of the principal reasons why, despite all the best intentions, the struggle to involve teachers in the improvement process turns into contrived collegiality (Hargreaves, 1994), and why distributed leadership becomes little more than principals delegating tasks they are too busy to carry out themselves:

> The neo-liberal version of the performing school requires teachers and students to be followers, but to feel good about it. . . . Teachers talk about "pseudo-participation" where views are sought as a ritual rather than a sincere attempt to listen and take note. . . . The rhetoric has been of empowerment, participation and teams, but the reality is that teachers have had to continue to do what they have always done—be empowered to do what they have been told to do. (Gunter, 2001, pp. 122 & 144)

Improving Schools for Social Justice

Improvement is one of those words—like *development, modern, community*—that only has a positive connotation. It is worth recalling that eighteenth-century English landowners who evicted farm laborers to create landscaped private parks, and Scottish aristocrats who cleared peasant farmers to make way for cattle grazing, also referred to their projects as improvement. We always need to ask—improvement for what? Improvement for whom? That holy trinity of vision, mission, and values should be taken seriously.

Without wishing to deny the importance of processes such as influencing other teachers and building teams, management in isolation becomes managerialism. A key characteristic of the officially approved school improvement paradigm is a focus on process to the neglect of context and purpose; students' lives and learning are barely considered, and so many of its academic experts appear not to have visited those other shelves of the university library dealing with sociology, curriculum, or pedagogy.

That is certainly true of the specialist literature on *leadership*, much of it vacuous and repetitive (see Smyth, 1989, for an extensive critique). Bertolt Brecht once commented, when asked about heroism, that he longed for a world where it wouldn't be necessary. We could say the same about school leadership: leadership only becomes the answer to everything in countries where teachers have been reshaped into *followers*. In England, to an extraordinary degree, the disciplining of the teaching profession through a regime of surveillance (league tables, market competition, inspection, performance-based pay) combined with teacher training pressured to deal only with pragmatics and bypass theory, has reduced many teachers' sense of judgment and agency and knowledgeable self-direction. This diminution of teacher professionalism has increased the need for leadership, but the very same forces have been at work in forming a new breed of school leaders: leadership courses that focus exclusively on pragmatics, bypassing ethical and political debate and sociological or pedagogical theory. In the discourse of the new leadership, even the term *leading learning* has been reduced into monitoring attainment; the complexities of social justice are viewed very narrowly through the lens of reducing attainment gaps.

By contrast, the headteachers and principals featured in case studies in *The Power to Learn* (Wrigley, 2000) or *Changing Schools* (Wrigley, Thomson & Lingard, 2012) work respectfully with their colleagues' professional knowledge and draw upon their social and pedagogical understanding. They articulate a situated understanding of their schools and journey within a wider social environment. Blair and Bourne's (1998) study of successful schooling for African Caribbean pupils highlights a different political orientation than the standard list of approved leadership characteristics: for example, instead of vague calls for strong leadership, we read a "strong and determined lead on equal opportunities." These headteachers, we are told:

- empathized with the political and social factors affecting the lives of their students;

- listened to and learned from students and their parents;

- tried to see things from the students' point of view; and

- created careful links with local communities.

This final point is of fundamental importance, given the distance and distrust frequently found between marginalized communities and schools. Though only one of the ten schools in Wrigley (2000) was formally designated and funded as a community school, all of them exercised this function, stretching education beyond the walls and into the community, linking up with parents, listening to their concerns, and in many cases creating opportunities for them to extend their own education.

A cliché of official school improvement is to talk about a new headteacher turning the school around. Some of the most exciting and successful school development takes this more literally: *turning the school round to face the community*.

Ethos, Discipline, and Respect

In the search for what might make schools more effective, much remains elusive. Brookover and colleagues (1978) (see chapter 7), by interviewing students rather than just teachers about their experience of the school's climate, were able to identify a cluster of factors that often make students' efforts to achieve appear futile. These involved antagonistic or indifferent attitudes from teachers and peers.

The importance of at least one supportive adult is well recognized in research on many kinds of childhood trauma (Meichenbaum, 2005), and helps to explain how some young people succeed in school 'against the odds' (Reis, Colbert & Hébert, 2005). This is one reason for the value of appointing mentors for disengaged young people, which was a key component of the Excellence in Cities initiative in England. Unfortunately mentors generally lack any power to change the school practices that are causing the disengagement which they, as mentors, have to try to repair, unless particular efforts are made to hear the message.

School ethos involves creating a climate in which students see adults as supportive, and in which plentiful opportunities exist for students to develop an attachment to the school. In the British independent school tradition, this was achieved through engagement in extracurricular activities (sport, music, etc.) and through rituals built around membership of a house as well as the school as a whole. It is much more difficult in schools in troubled areas where teachers' energies can be entirely consumed by firefighting, but there are outstanding examples of places where the collective energies of a dedicated staff have established good opportunities for belonging (see Wrigley, 2000; Smyth & McInerney, 2007b).

Partly, this is about size and scale. It is easier to feel that you belong to a school when you belong to its football team. The same logic should apply to belonging to a class of pupils, but this is not so straightforward. The typical structure of secondary schools in many countries involves pupils moving from teacher to teacher every forty to fifty minutes, encountering twelve to fifteen different subject teachers a week, several more with a pastoral or managerial role, and others exercising a disciplinary function in circulation spaces. This is not conducive to developing a sense of attachment. Conversely, for staff, teaching 200 different pupils each week makes it difficult to establish personal relationships or indeed to attend to individual needs. In schools where many young people have troubled lives, it is a recipe for disaster.

For all the attention paid to school improvement in the UK, it is surprising that these structural issues are so little considered. In the United States there is extensive experimentation with small schools and schools within schools (Conchas & Rodriguez, 2008; Toch, 2003; Meier, 2002). The Coalition for Essential Schools supports diverse organizational models but with a general norm that no teacher should be expected to teach more than about 80 students (see also Smyth & McInerney, 2007b). Similarly, Norwegian Youth Schools (lower secondary, for thirteen- to sixteen-year-olds) are generally organized so that each year group of 60–100 pupils is taught and cared for by a dedicated team of five or six teachers. Subject specialization is seen as less important than a sense of belonging and the quality of care.

Size does not, of course, resolve everything. As a recent OECD (2012) report comments:

> Changes in school size should be accompanied by reforms in the school and classroom, to allow the specific use of "small school" instruction practices. . . . It is both the frequency and quality of student/student and student/teacher interactions in small schools and classrooms that matters. (p. 122)

Instead of looking at what circumstances might aid or exacerbate a sense of belonging (Smyth & McInerney, 2007b), the emphasis in official advice for troubled schools in the UK has been to tighten up on discipline. This has a common sense appeal, since no one can learn where there is frequent disruption, and a climate of conflict damages student well-being. This is, however, dealing with the symptom but not the underlying disease. There is extensive evidence that young people whose families and communities are marginalized also feel marginalized and disrespected at school:

> A key word is respect. This is resonant in meaning, with associations with Black consciousness and resistance. Respect signifies mutuality and justice. Teachers earn respect, and show respect to their pupils. It requires that any bullying or manifestation of racism will be challenged. (Wrigley, 2000, p. 169)

Respect was almost the most frequently uttered word from the 209 young people in Smyth and colleagues' (2000) Australian study *Listen to Me, I'm Leaving*, as to why young people disconnect from schooling. The experience of respect connects with established theories of social justice, including Fraser's (1997) concept of *recognition*. It is an important corrective to suggestions that negative peer pressure is a principal cause of underachievement, which comes dangerously close to a blame-the-victim argument:

> Sewell points out that Black Caribbean boys may experience considerable pressure by their peers to adopt the norms of an "urban" or "street" subculture in order to reject the power of knowledge (Sewell, 1997). However, Warren (2005) argues that the difficult

behaviors of some Black Caribbean boys may not constitute a rejection of schooling per se, but can be a way of resisting the "inequality of respect" that they experience from some teachers. (Haynes, Tikly & Caballero, 2006, p. 579)

When young people feel disrespected, they find antischool ways of creating mutual respect among their peers (Smyth & Hattam, 2004). Sometimes these are strongly gendered or racist, including, for example, macho behavior among working-class and ethnic minority boys. They may also mobilize residual identities in complex symbolic ways. For example, Nayak (2003) explores how, in northern English towns that have suffered the loss of heavy industry, working-class boys use football as a way of perpetuating industrial masculinities. Respect operates on a number of different levels and is a key issue when evaluating the culture of a school. A lack of respect can be manifested not simply by interpersonal behavior, whether intentional or not, but also by conventions and norms easily taken for granted by teachers (see the discussion of *culture* and of *streaming* later in this chapter).

In the end, this comes down to what Smyth and McInerney (2007b) found in an Australian study of six high schools that had reinvented themselves around leadership for social justice. There were several consistent themes: (1) whole school change; (2) building authentic learning communities; (3) acting politically and strategically in the interests of students and their communities; (4) finding spaces to be innovative; and above all, (5) not being paralyzed by what the system is doing to them.

School Culture

As Raymond Williams (1983 [1976]) once commented, culture is "one of the two or three most complicated words in the English language" (p. 87), so it is not too surprising to find it used in improvement and leadership literature. In fact, we tend to find that it is undermobilized, deployed in depoliticized and anodyne ways. It has been domesticated to put it at the service of management. According to Deal and Peterson (1999), the central role of school principals is to manage culture. Headteachers are invited to recognize their own success through blandly positive indicators such as:

- shared goals—we know where we're going

- responsibility for success—we must succeed

- collegiality—we're working on this together (Stoll & Fink 1996).

The richness of the culture concept—the ways in which culture manifests the contradictions as well as the cohesion of a society and its way of life—is bleached out in this managerialist reductionism:

As the Weltanschauung of school improvement, it is bland and one-dimensional, taking little account of the many contradictions, of teachers' and pupils' lives outside, and of external pressures both political and socioeconomic. There is no concession that some innovations might be ill-conceived, that professionals have a right and duty to evaluate them critically, or that some changes should be resisted. There is a warm glow about this notion of culture, emphasizing a rather uncritical cohesion, which can conceal some of the turmoil outside. (Wrigley, 2008, p. 138)

Alvesson's (2002) studies of industrial and commercial organizations reflect the contradictions and conflict in their cultures, but in school management literature, *culture* is all about the manufacture of consent. As Ken Jones (2003) points out: "The school is separated from its complex cultural matrix in order to be presented as a potentially homogenous organization, and in order to be more easily managed" (p. 146). This does violence to the complexity of young people's lives, in a vain attempt to keep youth culture outside the boundary fence:

There is, within each school, a contest of different voices, which is what makes school development so interesting. Indeed, it is this that makes school development possible. The voice of teachers who insist upon challenging inequality, tedium, and superficial or irrelevant learning is a powerful force for change, despite attempts to silence it. The voice of the local community is crucial to the successful development of multiethnic and other urban schools. (Wrigley, 2003, p. 35)

We offer as a working definition of school culture "matter with meaning"—objects or actions that signify. We also need to include shared beliefs, but they, too, are traces of material phenomena and manifested in actions and interactions. The tacit belief system of a school can be made visible by critically observing patterns of behavior frequently taken for granted:

School improvement requires a more political and situated exploration of culture than we have managed so far. . . . For example:

- examining the cultural messages of classrooms which are dominated by the teacher's voice, closed questions and rituals of transmission of superior wisdom

- developing a better understanding of cultural difference, in order to prevent high levels of exclusion

- understanding how assumptions about ability and intelligence are worked out in classroom interactions

- discovering how assumptions about single parents, ethnic minorities and "dysfunctional" working-class families operate symbolically in classroom interactions. (Wrigley, 2003, pp. 36–37)

We cannot expect students to develop a strong affiliation to their school if we do not seriously examine the messages which its structure and culture convey.

Streaming, Setting, Tracking . . . and Expectations

One of the most visible ways in which schools reproduce social divisions is by dividing students into different 'ability groups', and many researchers since the 1960s (e.g., Douglas, 1964; Jackson, 1964) have demonstrated the impact of social class and ethnicity on the formation of these groups. Dunne and colleagues' (2007) study for England's Department for Children, Schools and Families shows a very messy relationship between learners' measured ability (i.e., prior attainment) and their allocation into sets: in their large sample around 20 percent of pupils in low sets are from the middle third by attainment and 10 percent from the top third. Conversely, 25 percent of the high set pupils are from the middle attainment band and 15 percent from the lower one. Yet allocation into sets can have a decisive influence on future curriculum and performance:

> Social class is a significant predictor of set placement. Pupils from higher socio-economic status (SES) backgrounds are more likely to be assigned to higher sets and less likely to be assigned to lower sets, over and above the effect of prior attainment. (p. 30)

Often this occurs through the influence of teachers' subjective perceptions of students' actual or possible behavior or their motivation (Araújo, 2007). Other critical studies showing the influence of SES or ethnicity on allocation into streams and sets include Troyna and Siraj-Blatchford (1993); Hallam and Toutounji (1996); Ireson and Hallam (1999); Gillborn and Youdell (2000); Luyten and Bosker (2004); and Gazeley and Dunne (2006).

There is a major contradiction in the officially approved school improvement literature and related government policy statements: the constant calls upon teachers to raise expectations is accompanied by a failure to challenge internal school divisions that actively lower them.

Research aiming to quantify whether streaming raises or lowers attainment can be useful, but it only scratches the surface. The most important issue is the symbolic effect on pupils, how they understand it, and its impact on learner identities. This is a prime example of the importance of understanding phenomena in symbolic interactionist terms.

Although sometimes it can be positively managed, dividing up children by ability through various forms of streaming, setting, and tracking generally has a depressing effect on the morale, behavior, and achievement of more disadvantaged young people. As David Hargreaves (1982) commented, "A sense of failure tends to permeate the whole personality, leaving a residue of powerlessness and hopelessness" (p. 62). He argued that ability labeling, accompanied by other aspects of traditional British secondary schooling, led to "a destruction of dignity so massive and pervasive that few subsequently recover from it" (p. 62). Those perceived as less able cease even to try, thus saving themselves from possible failure, and so are able to "retain the last vestiges of a crumbling dignity" (p. 64). Many seek other ways of achieving dignity through oppositional performances.

Lacey (1970) discovered such mechanisms at work even in a UK grammar school that admitted only the highest achieving 15 percent of the population. Despite this narrow range it streamed them after the first year into an express group plus A, B, and C streams. By the end of this second year, Lacey found distinct climates in the different classes, with 2C regarded by their peers as bullies and by their teachers as virtually unteachable.

Stephen Ball (1986) sounds a warning, however, that it is insufficient simply to abolish streaming while teachers' assumptions about ability remain unchallenged. Indeed, in *Beachside Comprehensive* (1981), he found that teachers "tended to view mixed-ability groups in terms of a threefold, normal distribution of ability—bright, average and dull" (p. 268).

West Yorkshire's director of education Alec Clegg invited 160 lower stream pupils to write about "What I like and what I do not like about being in a C or D stream." They liked being with friends, the easier work, and more personal attention, but they disliked being neglected and frequently blamed, feeling inferior, knowing they would not be able to get a good job, and being given insufficient responsibility (McCulloch, 1998, p. 119).

This notion of three levels or distinct types of ability became well engrained in policy in the early twentieth century in Britain, leading in 1945 to the establishment of three types of school, each supposedly catering for a different kind of mind. The claim that they were different but equal, and the endeavor to establish an interesting and engaging curriculum in the lowest tier secondary modern schools, predictably collapsed. When this divided system was replaced by comprehensive schools, the old divisions were initially replicated internally, despite the efforts of campaigners and teachers working to develop more inclusive pedagogies: "Evidence from the 1960s to the 1990s suggests that ability tends to be the characteristic of their pupils that is most salient" (Hart et al., 2004, p. 41). The struggle to develop more engaging and challenging pedagogies for all children was pursued by the school inspectorate in Britain throughout the 1980s, but as these extracts illustrate, this was mixed with a firm belief in distinct and relatively fixed ability bands:

> Academically less able pupils need to have plenty of opportunity to exercise their imagination and reasoning power. (DES, 1984, p. 46) . . . It is of the greatest importance to stimulate and challenge all pupils, including the most and least able. (DES, 1980, p. 15, cited in Hart, 1996, pp. 12–13)

Such a classification is never merely descriptive, it is *performative*; in other words it brings about what it claims to describe:

> If, led astray by theories of mental testing, [the teacher] believes the child's achievement is predetermined by the nature of his inborn "abilities," then all he can aim to do is to make their in-born abilities actual. (Simon, 1953, p. 105)

As Jackson (1964) argued, we create types of children by believing that there are types and consequently by treating them differently. The characteristics of a C stream child come into being through the existence of C streams, not because there is some such species to be found in the population. This continues to the present: in England the use of CAT tests to set expectations for future performance is widespread, and at least some of their apparent (albeit imperfect) reliability arises because they are a self-fulfilling prophecy, affecting the placement of pupils in courses and teaching groups and which examination courses they are assigned to.

Government policy in England makes it very difficult for schools to avoid dividing pupils into different classes by 'ability', despite the ambiguities concerning that word. Mostly this is by setting on a subject by subject basis, though there is often considerable congruence between subjects. Though setting is not compelled by law, schools were informed by the Labour government that:

> Unless a school can demonstrate that it is getting better than expected results through a different approach, we do make the presumption that setting should be the norm in secondary schools. (Department for Education and Employment, 1997, p. 38)

The government argued that setting was a more efficient strategy to raise standards than mixed ability, even though academic research refutes this (see the literature review in Ireson & Hallam, 1999).

The labeling of children by ability in the English system begins by requiring teachers to allocate each pupil to one of nine levels on each of thirteen different scales *in the year they reach the age of five*. School inspectors are briefed and trained to check that teaching is differentiated for "more able," "average," and "less able" pupils, and teachers are expected to make this explicit in their lesson plans. The National Literacy and Numeracy Strategies also endorsed ability-based grouping throughout primary schools (Hart et al., 2004, pp. 8–9).

All of this happens in the name of making schools more effective, yet lower groups are likely to be subject to more transmission teaching, with fewer demands to think for themselves, more closed questions, and more time spent copying. Large amounts of time will be consumed completing laborious decontextualized exercises; the main lesson they will learn is that learning is boring and meaningless (see, for example, Oakes, 1982, 1985; Boaler, William & Brown, 2000).

For many of these students, the reactions they show to this regime will expose them to a diagnosis of "special needs," labeling them as "attention deficit" or "moderate learning difficulties," as if these were internal characteristics that had not emerged out of pupil-teacher interactions in particular institutional contexts. McDermott (1996) fittingly calls this "the acquisition of a child by a learning disability" (pp. 269–305). The racial outcomes were exposed loudly by Bernard Coard's (1971) *How the West Indian Child Is Made Educationally Subnormal in the British School System.*

The preceding paragraphs have highlighted how pupils segregated as less able are damaged—even within schools where all the pupils have been selected as very able. The situation is much more complex in schools serving largely poor and ethnic minority students. First, their early socialization into school will involve learning a stance of passivity and how to make very brief responses, though without drawing upon the speech forms of their homes and neighborhoods. Only the most confident will continue to display verbal ability in such an environment, though at the risk of being labeled disorderly or impolite (Willes, 1983). This is part of the exchange process Bourdieu discusses as cultural capital, whereby the abilities of marginalized social groups fail to be recognized by defining institutions such as schools.

Swann et al (2012) refer to the "template of fixed ability" creating "a disposition to accept as normal, indeed inevitable, the limited achievement of a significant proportion of the school population" (p. 28):

> When they appear in our classrooms, we are not surprised. Nor are we surprised if they do not show significant progress, despite receiving extra encouragement and support. As long as this template shapes our thinking, it blocks off from our view alternative explanations for, or ways of construing, the difficulties that we perceive to be occurring. The ability template discourages us from asking important, penetrating questions about how our own practices may unwittingly contribute to the difficulties we observe; so it denies us creative opportunities continually to learn from experience, to reconstruct our practice to support and encourage learning more successfully (Simon, 1953; Dixon, 1989; Drummond, 1993; Hart, 1996, 2000). (p. 29)

In his classic ethnographic study *The Urban School: A Factory for Failure*, Ray Rist (1973) shows how this growth-stunting process arises not out of malice but from institutional norms and tacit assumptions. The well-intentioned women teachers in Rist's case study, many of them active in churches, local charities, and the Civil Rights movement, lacked the intellectual tools to challenge such assumptions, partly as a consequence of teacher training that was simply pragmatic and devoid of political understanding. As Rist argues, their training was designed merely to fit newcomers into schools that were assumed to be working well (p. 46). They see all around them that "very few black people in American society do make it" and out of this draw a "fatalistic assumption that teaching really could make no impact or reverse the skid into failure" (p. 48). Consequently

> the teachers attempted to salvage some fulfillment from their jobs by concentrating on those few students who they believed had some opportunity to escape "the streets." Overwhelmingly in the classes observed, those few students designated by the teachers as possessing the necessary traits for mobility were the children of middle-class black families trapped in the inner city by suburban racial segregation. (pp. 48–49)

> The patterns of classroom segregation were created to protect the high group from the lower groups, with their interest in the "streets," their use of "bad" language, and their lack of regard for school. One teacher, in fact, stated that the school had two types of students—those with "street blood" and those with "school blood." (pp. 244–45)

As children enroll at the school, Rist describes how well-meaning teachers and social workers would identify which children were on welfare and whether parents were "troublemakers." Already in a child's first days at school, other teachers would "pass on admonitions like 'watch out', 'don't get his old lady upset', or 'just keep him colorin'" (p. 66).

This morass of prejudice, backed up by tacit assumptions about fixed ability and operating within divisive norms of school organization, leads to deeply anti-educational pedagogical practices. Education is supposed to extend, to develop, to move a child onward to the discovery and fulfillment of new possibilities. Control takes the place of genuine education. A major review of secondary education once carried out by the Inner London Education Authority (ILEA) articulates the issue well:

> Much of the boredom cited by ILEA pupils relates to [the] view that too little effort is made to engage them in active learning, that they are required to spend too much time listening or copying, or completing worksheets. . . . Boredom leads to resentment and that resentment is expressed either by passive withdrawal of attention or by disruptive behaviour. In the case of the latter a "double-bind" situation is all too often created: rebellious pupils are seen as too irresponsible to be given opportunities for discussion, working in pairs, or in small groups, and are meted out with yet more of the very kind of silent solitary activity that has stimulated their original rebellion. . . . Our evidence suggests that pupils wish to be given much more responsibility for their own learning and to have the opportunity to negotiate much more of both its content and its process. (1984, p. 69)

Determined to extinguish such enlightened democratic thinking, Margaret Thatcher's Conservative government abolished the ILEA soon afterward.

Alternatives

A recent report from the Organisation for Economic Co-operation and Development (OECD) (2012), based on PISA 2009, points out that various forms of academic selection such as early tracking, grade repetition, and selecting pupils for different types of school have the effect of widening achievement gaps and inequities. In particular, grouping students according to their performance has "a significant negative impact on those placed in lower levels (Hattie, 2009)," while "the evidence is mixed on the impact of tracking on high achievers depending on the methodology and data used (Jakubowski, 2010)" (OECD 2012, p. 58):

> The existence of lower level tracks and streams fuels a vicious cycle in the expectations of teachers and students. Teachers can have lower expectations for some students, especially disadvantaged and/or low performing ones, and assign them slower-paced and more fragmented instruction; and students adjust their expectations and efforts, which results in even lower performance (Gamoran, 2004). Moreover, more experienced and capable teachers tend to be assigned to higher level tracks (Oakes, 2005). Students placed in lower performance groups experience a low quality learning experience, and may suffer stigmatization and a decrease in self-esteem. Also, they do not benefit from the positive effects of being around more capable peers (Hanushek & Woessmann, 2006; Ammermueller, 2005). (OECD 2012, p. 58)

Among the report's proposals, we find several compromises short of complete detracking:

- suppressing low-level tracks or groups or making these alternatives equivalent to other pathways

- delaying it until an older age range

- limiting ability grouping to specific subjects, especially those that are sequential such as mathematics or languages

- replacing it with short-term flexible grouping for specific purposes

- ensuring that all tracks give students a challenging curriculum and high quality teaching.

In Scandinavian countries, grouping by ability is rigorously avoided, at least until the upper secondary stage (ages 16–19). Even at this stage, these countries try to ensure ease of transfer between pre-university and vocational routes. It is not surprising that these are also countries where around 90 percent of young people remain in full-time education until age 18 or 19 and with low levels of SES-related underachievement.

This is not to say that grouping similar pupils together is always a bad idea. Some highly inclusive schools provide their most advanced students with opportunities to work with each other for some of the time as a supplement to mixed classes (see, for example, Wrigley, 2000, pp. 82–84.) Another strategy is to vary groupings in a subject such as math, sometimes mixed and sometimes matched, for specific learning purposes. The norm, however, should be integration through engagement in collaborative and thoughtful activities in mixed groups.

Perhaps the least useful option, in order to keep students in the same room but working at different levels, is to have them working for most of the time from individualized worksheets. This tends to remove the possibility of less advanced students learning from more advanced students or engaging collectively in problem solving.

A major European Union project, INCLUD-ED (INCLUD-ED Consortium, 2012), has concluded that two strategies are key to improving both social cohesion and achievement. These are (1) inclusive student grouping and (2) community involvement. This research identifies various forms of segregation for which it uses the generic term *streaming*, including ability groups within classrooms, segregated remedial groups, and individual assignments that limit learning and in effect deny access to the common curriculum (p. 22). They argue that human resources provided to meet the needs of low achievers can be redirected to support more inclusive arrangements, including small interactive groups. A case study (Alexiu & Sordé, 2011) describes how mixed interactive groups work intensively to acquire knowledge, each supported by a teacher or parent volunteer. This not only provides supportive interaction with adults (Vygotsky, 1978) and enables advanced students to gain by explaining to less advanced students, but it also develops intercultural community understanding.

A study of differentiation carried out for the Danish Education Ministry (Krogh-Jespersen, Methling, & Striib, 1998) proposes giving students more responsibility for defining their own tasks, based on them acquiring a strong sense of what is needed to improve through formative assessment. Initially students will depend on teachers' suggestions but develop more independence in time.

Annemarie von der Groeben (2008), reporting on practices developed at the Bielefeld Laboratory School in Germany, suggests offering a menu of alternatives that ends with "design your own." For example, inviting students' response to a character in a nineteenth-century novel, the following suggestions are offered:

- You can compile a list of this woman's qualities and ways of behaving and write some comments.

- You can imagine yourself as the woman. Maybe she sees herself differently than how the author describes her. Get her to speak: for example "If you men only knew!"

- You could conduct an interview with her.

- You could invent a conversation in which she tells her daughter what to expect in life.

- You can write a letter to her, in which you explain how women live nowadays.

- You can . . .

If learning is structured in more open ways, for example, through project method or storyline, in an extended simulation, or by producing a video or website, students will set their own targets, supported and challenged by the teacher's proposals and feedback. There will be no need for educational apartheid.

Many of the same principles emerge from the case studies in *Learning without Limits* (Swann et al., 2012). These show that providing a choice of tasks or routes toward a goal encourages more thoughtful participation in which students accept greater responsibility. One strategy is

> to set a broad question or task and allow students to construct their own ways through it. For example, working collaboratively in pairs or groups, students often design their own ways into a text, working from a set of assessment criteria that allow them into the secret of exactly what I am looking for in judging their knowledge and understanding. These are often oral tasks, including discussion, role play and dramatic interpretation. For example, one of the oral tasks used in our study of *Talking in Whispers*, a novel by James Watson (1983), asked students, in self-selecting groups, to present their final interpretation of the moral and message of the novel. . . . The resulting presentations ranged from interviews in role with the author, hot-seating a range of characters, to a dramatised presentation of key moments from the novel. (p. 153)

The observations and interviews with teachers in the book bring out the relationships between task-setting, openness about evaluation criteria, challenging students to think and see connections, creating mutual support in the classroom, providing helpful feedback, and understanding how different students learn.

Clearly the old scripts of school effectiveness and school improvement are not working, and Smyth, Angus, Down, and McInerney (2008) sketch out the contours of an alternative through detailed ethnographic accounts of two Australian communities—Wirra Wagga and Bountiful Bay. What they find are some refreshing notions about culture and community (pp. 153–56), pedagogy and curriculum that connect to young lives (pp. 156–60), and school structure and organization (pp. 160–63) that is built around "social cohesion, empathy, caring, respect, reciprocity and trust" (p. 160).

Critical Community Engagement

An appropriate way of bringing this chapter toward a conclusion is to look at community engagement. What we have been arguing is that *school improvement*, while a progressive sounding term, has actually been hijacked by those whose real agenda is managerialist and economistic—that is to say, making schools more easily controlled and compliant and harnessing them to national imperatives of economic competitiveness. At heart is a problematic that has to be robustly confronted:

> It is becoming increasingly clear that communities suffering debilitating and inter-generational disadvantage are not going to experience the kind of changes necessary to improve their conditions unless there is reform at the level of both schools and communities. (Smyth, 2009, p. 10)

Furthermore, it seems that the core of the problem, apart from the tokenistic involvement of teachers in the decision-making process, is that community members as the other major players have been misled by spurious neoliberal arguments to jettison their role as *citizens* and become *consumers*.

What we have shown in this chapter is how educative relationships have been distorted, corroded, and corrupted. We believe they have been replaced by a set of exchange relationships of a provider-consumer kind, through notions such as school choice, value added, league performance tables, and the like. The effect has been the subjugation of schools to the ideology and practices of commercial interests—schools as zones of marketization, consumption, and exploitation, to put it bluntly.

The remaining areas of possible resistance—beyond students, who are mostly captives by virtue of the compulsory nature of schooling—are parents and communities. But even parents and communities have been co-opted into this corrosive ideology of the market as largely fearful consumers, forced to act in their own individual self-interests in securing the best deal for their children.

This uniformly depressing situation is not inexorable—it can be difficult, but pursuing this goal involves having the courage to create the conditions in which to enact two crucial imperatives: (1) community voice and (2) a critical approach to leadership. They are not mutually exclusive but are both part of an approach we call "critical community engagement"—where the term *critical* signifies an unwillingness to accept the status quo and to adopt an activist approach.

Case studies from the CREA (Centre of Research in Theories and Practices That Overcome Inequalities) project, based at the University of Barcelona, demonstrate the importance for school improvement of collaborative research involving community members, particularly those from marginalized groups (families in poverty, migrants, Roma, etc.). These projects were based on principles of "critical communicative methodology" (Puigvert, Christou & Holford, 2012) such as

> the *absence of interpretative hierarchy* which means that all interpretations that emerge in the research process are equally valued regardless of the social position of the person expressing them [and] *equal epistemological level* [which] implies that while researchers bring knowledge from the scientific community, research participants provide knowledge based on their experience, and both types of information are considered equally valid. (pp. 514–55)

This is not to suggest, in a relativistic way, that all conclusions are equally valid, since the purpose of this dialogism is social transformation:

Freire's theory of dialogic action (1970) stresses the role of dialogue as a powerful tool in raising social actors' critical consciousness and in leading to transformation and emancipation. Through dialogue and communication human beings problematize their reality and reflect critically on how they can be empowered to alter oppressive social structures. Freire's work is embedded in CCM, as research participants are perceived as subjects of their own transformation through dialogue and reciprocity with researchers. (p. 515)

The authors see this as crucial to overcoming the problem of educational research generally having very little impact on practice (p. 513).

According to Oliver and colleagues (2011), successful community involvement in school change requires a belief in cultural intelligence, namely, that those whose situation is being researched have the ability to interpret their own situation. This premise also demonstrates that they can provide alternatives that may reverse the inequalities they face; their CI [cultural intelligence] makes them uniquely able to transform their own situation (p. 268). Many rich examples can be found in Ramon Flecha's book *Sharing Words* (2000). Christou and Puigvert (2011) argue that 'other women' (those from non-dominant groups) who are normally asked to participate in schools in a recreational way, for example, cooking or making costumes for events, must be brought into involvement in classroom learning and in school decision making. Among other benefits, this develops teachers' cultural understanding and appreciation of children's hidden abilities. A critical approach to leadership in these situations involves a strong belief that people can learn and participate, regardless of their educational level.

These families can do it. It is important to change the attitude of "the family cannot do it," because sometimes we hold this [idea]: "they don't know how to speak, [so] they don't know how to write." Certainly they don't know how to speak our language, possibly they don't know how to write it, but that does not mean that they cannot work on reading with their children. (interview cited in Diez, Gatt & Racionero, 2011, p. 190)

One way of envisaging what these twin imperatives might look like practically— and the ideas that underpin them have been drawn from the practices of actual schools, ordinary publicly funded ones—is through the ideological lenses of three overlapping archetypes.

First, the *socially just school*—wherein the leadership of the school has "a central unswerving passion and commitment to making the school work in the interests of the least advantaged" (Smyth, 2010a, p. 80). This is something that schools ought to do but that gets quickly expunged when the overriding concern is with presenting the school as a high achieving one in the ruthless competitive rush to survive through securing market share.

Second, with only a slightly different inflection, the *student-voiced school*— where students are far from being domesticated but have a real say in what, where and how they learn (Smyth, 2010a, p. 80). This involves an authentic voice; negotiating curriculum and learning around students' lives and interests; connecting what goes in the classroom to popular culture; providing flexibility around students' out-of-school lives especially around work and family caring commitments; taking students' emotional lives seriously; creating an atmosphere of trust in which [the development of] school policies . . . involve[s] young people in their formulation and understanding of their rationale. (pp. 81–82)

Third, there is the notion of *relational school*—where the "leadership [of the school] positions itself in ways in which students have *relational power*" (Smyth, 2010a, p. 82). Put simply this means they are shown what it means to have people around them who act respectfully toward one another and toward their students, their families, and communities. According to the assistant principal of a school that foregrounds respect, in his school the overriding concern is with

"knowing the kids and their homes" and where they are coming from with all of its colorfulness and tragic fragments . . . [which translated meant] "here the kids learn you first, then they learn your subject." (p. 82)

To put it another way, learning depends on students believing that teachers really care about them, their lives, and families. Only then are students prepared to make the social, emotional, and psychic investment necessary for learning. At the center, then, is the question of who has power—in this case over how relationships are to be enacted. What occurs in the school and classrooms obviously spills over in the way the school deals with parents and the community.

Within each of these three visions of schools, there is a strong sense that the community, in the broadest sense of the term, has a major and authentic role in giving expression to their aspirations and the place they want their school to have in their lives and those of their children (see Smyth & McInerney, 2007a, 2007b).

To give an illustration of how these notions can play out in an actual school setting, the Emily Carr Elementary School in Canada had a view of itself as "a school *as* a community" as well as "a school *in* community" (Vibert et al., 2002, p. 109). This was a school that was committed to making itself feel more like a family than an institution. For example:

What happened at this school was a sort of de-institutionalizing of relations. Normal routines of in-school relations did not entirely hold. Relations . . . appeared characterized by ordinary (and therefore extraordinary) humanity, not dictated by position and role. (Vibert et al., 2002, p. 111)

Rather than being a place that dutifully followed government edicts or diktats, there was quite a different philosophy:

A flattening of the normal hierarchies; the de-institutionalized relationships to the extent that people were frank and open with each other in a substantive way; the degree of participation of all members of the school community; the shared projects in the world beyond the school . . . ; the discussions and activities on issues of real concern . . . ; [and] the focus on questions of how to live well together. (p. 111)

This was a school that found it difficult to see itself as "separate from community" (p. 111):

> The community was in the school, involved in decisions of substance (e.g., drafting discipline policies, writing funding applications, establishing and running a preschool and after school literacy program), and the relationship between the school and community was participatory. (p. 111)

As Smyth (2008) put it:

> Without over-romanticizing things, it was not that decisions were always consensual, harmonious, or unanimous, but rather the case that when conflicts and disagreements occurred, as we would expect, "they were the subject of dialogue and negotiation" (Vibert et al., 2002, p. 111). In other words, what community meant at *Emily Carr* "was produced by the openness with which conflict among members was approached" (Vibert et al., 2002, p. 111). (p. 248)

One incident may serve to demonstrate that Emily Carr Elementary School leaders had a sense of what it meant to exercise critical leadership, as well as providing the space for community voice. This concerned the adverse stereotyping of the school by the media:

> When a newspaper article on Emily Carr Elementary identified it as a high-poverty school, middle-class community members wrote letters objecting. Instead of treating the incident as a public relations issue, some administrators and teachers brought articles and letters into the classroom and undertook with students a study of the social construction of poverty. (Vibert et al., 2002, p. 104)

Emily Carr Elementary is by no means an isolated example. Smyth and McInerney (2007a) present a revealing study of an Australian primary school they call Plainsville, located within a neighborhood of protracted disadvantage beset with all kinds of problems. The community and the school embarked on a process of transforming the school in ways that were designed to ensure that it worked for the most excluded students but with benefits for the community as well. As Smyth (2008) puts it:

> The stark reality was a preparedness by the school to acknowledge the stark reality that the overall undemocratic context in which schooling operated, was clearly impacting badly on this disadvantaged community, already suffering from the tilted playing field. A radically different approach was required. What was needed was a raising of expectations and the creation of a sense of worth in a community that had been repeatedly "done to" so often that failure and exclusion were normal expectations. The axis for change was around

the idea that schooling could be a rewarding experience for these children, that they could succeed, and that this would benefit the whole community.

The center-piece for the transformation from "old world" (their nomenclature for the system that was aggravating, alienating, dispiriting and disempowering) to the "new world," in which they had dignity, pride, success and power over their lives, was around the idea of "*student-initiated curriculum.*" Student-initiated curriculum was *Plainsville* code for a set of educative experiences in which students had power over what they learned, where, how and with whom. Students developed *learning plans* or individual blueprints, with the assistance of adults in the school setting who helped them pursue worthwhile learnings that were not only of interest to them but that would put them on worthwhile career pathways. (p. 248)

The complexity of bringing about socially just school transformation, in a school like Plainsville, in a deep and concerted way, was summarized thus:

If there were two simple words that underscored what was unique, it would be the dynamic duo of courage and leadership. By this we mean, the courage to admit that schools are not working for the increasing numbers of disadvantaged children. [T]his meant a preparedness to think outside the square and to literally put every aspect of the school under scrutiny regarding how it was serving students and their lives and futures. . . . [I]t also meant having an abundance of the leadership skills to be able to envisage an alternative, and the passion to convince others of the indispensability of student inclusiveness in their reworked vision of schooling—and to carry all constituents along with that idea in practice over a sustained period of time. (Smyth & McInerney, 2007a, pp. 1163–64).

Confronting some Murky Territory

One of the most seductive buzz words in relation to disadvantaged communities is the term *community engagement*. Like its close cousin *neighborhood renewal*, it has become the new Trojan horse for shifting the responsibility for complex social problems from the state onto communities least able to respond to the structural inequality that disfigures their lives. While this is not the place for an extensive historical rendition, some genesis of the ideas is important if we are to better understand how to respond.

The short story is that the British New Labour government of Tony Blair in 1997 wanted to respond quickly to the social destruction wreaked under Thatcher. For the first time in many years the incoming government responded to the "recalcitrant socio-economic problems of urban Britain" (Johnstone & Whitehead, 2004, p. 3) with a White Paper titled *Our Towns and Cities: The Future—Delivering an Urban Renaissance* (Department of Environment, Transport and Regions, 2000). The following paragraph encapsulates its central aim:

The purpose of this White Paper was to provide on integrating framework and ideological vision for urban policy development. . . . At the heart of this document was the desire to instigate a social, cultural, economic and political renaissance within English cities . . . [Its essence was] a broader *Third Way*—one which sought to synthesize the economic rationales of neo-liberalism with the social concerns of the old Left. (Johnstone and Whitehead 2004, p. p. xii)

The overriding discourses as Atkinson (1999) notes were those of partnership and empowerment. As Blair revealingly put it in the foreword to a consultation paper by the Social Exclusion Unit (2001) for *A New Commitment to Neighborhood Renewal: A National Strategy Action Plan*: "Unless the community is fully engaged in shaping and delivering regeneration, even the best plans will fail to deliver in practice" (p. 5).

However, as Imrie (2004) argues, what is going on here when all the political rhetoric is stripped away is that measures are being crafted and targeted at "people perceived to be defective citizens" (p. 129), who are treated "not for what they do or what they have been made into but for what they lack" (Cruikshank, 1999, p. 123).

This is a fake partnership in which people are sold the cruel hoax that if they become involved in seeking out local solutions, then somehow their lives will be repaired and they will escape from the debilitating cycles of poverty they have become caught up in. As Smyth, McInerney, and Harrison (2011) put it, the issue is a lot more complicated:

> Community engagement is one of those apparently commonsense plausible ideas that no one in their right mind could possibly be opposed to. It is such a compelling idea—that those who are excluded from the mainstream of society, should be restored, and made a prosperous part of it by being given a kind of relational makeover. What we need to do, so the thinking goes, is find ways of getting people who have fallen off the track back on it, into productive and rewarding (i.e., working) lives. Lives that have become fractured and fragmented have to be repaired and they have to be provided with better alternative models to choose from. Along the way, they have to be better isolated and targeted in terms of the identification of "risk factors" so that the unfortunate "cycles of disadvantage" they have become caught up in can be interrupted. (p. 3)

> We don't endorse most of the definitions that abound on this topic. . . . We believe that one of the features of community engagement, as we envisage it, is the space it provides for deeper mutual understanding—between communities that are deemed "disadvantaged," but who proudly disavow and deny this derogatory-sounding label. . . . We, therefore, prefer to think of community engagement as a *learning space* as well as an *arena for possibilities* within which to level a playing field. (p. 4)

We need to work against the danger of "opening up free space for the choices of individual actors while enwrapping these atomized actors within new forms of control" (Imrie, 2004, p. xxiii, citing Rose, 1999). To achieve this, Smyth, McInerney, and Harrison (2011) developed a process, in their critical community engagement work, of continual interrogation in context around the following key questions and assertions:

- Who is community engagement for?
- Who gets to speak?
- The community has to be in the driver's seat.
- Unless the community has important leadership roles, it is going to fall over.
- People can't be coerced into community engagement.

This is a very different notion to one that positions parents as passive clients. As Smyth (2009, summarized it:

> The notion of *parental engagement*, or to put it another way "parents in community," goes considerably beyond taking an interest in and supporting the school for what it will return in terms of individual educational capital. Parental engagement is predicated on a socially activist, collectivist, socially critical, equity-oriented, and community-minded view of participation that is committed to improving the learning of all students in the community, not just the few. This is an approach that is located in a "citizen politics" (Boyte, 1989).(p. 17)

CHAPTER NINE

Poor Kids Need Rich Teaching

We do not profess to give these children an education that will raise them above their station and business in life.
        —Robert Lowe, 1862, Parliamentary Debates CLXV cols 237–8

The rich get richer, the poor get direct instruction.
        —Curt Dudley-Marling and Pat Paugh, 2005, p. 156

The opening quotations neatly announce the central issue for this chapter— How can we overcome the tendency for poorer kids to fall further behind during their school years? How can we contest the assumption that these students are incapable of anything more challenging than 'the basics'? How do we prevent this assumption becoming the self-fulfilling prophecy that shackles their development and stifles their thinking and creativity?

This is not to suggest that key skills are unimportant or that they will be acquired automatically, but we vigorously reject the idea that a curriculum can be based predominantly on 'basic skills' taught outside an engaging context. Lisa Delpit (1995) makes this essential point:

> Black teachers . . . see the teaching of skills to be essential to their students' survival. . . . Their insistence on skills is not a negation of their students intellect . . . I run a great risk in writing this . . . that those who subject black and other minority children to day after day of isolated, meaningless, drilled "subskills" will think themselves vindicated . . . [But skills are] useful and usable knowledge which contributes to a student's ability to com-

municate effectively in standard, generally acceptable literary forms [and] are best taught through meaningful communication, best learned in meaningful contexts. (pp. 18–19)

The expansion of education from the preserve of a privileged minority to compulsory schooling for the masses has been a contradictory process. One strand in this history has been progressive and democratic, but the other has been premised on the need to domesticate and control working-class children. The vestiges of this are still present, including forms of testing and payment by results within current accountability systems. Nor are these matters innocent, since they attempt to impose order and maintain social control. How can we collaborate to challenge the mind-numbing MacDonaldization of schooling that has been imposed in the name of school improvement?

Our central concern in this chapter, therefore, is to articulate and exemplify some key principles that will liberate the learning of young people and particularly enable those growing up in poverty to achieve success. It includes a critical account of what has been called *pedagogies of poverty*, but it brings with it many rich examples of meaningful and engaging teaching and learning.

Education: Liberation or Control?

The expansion of schooling in modern times, from its minority beginnings in the medieval monasteries and cathedral schools, is marked by two contradictory trends, one democratizing, the other disciplinarian. These two directions reflect the dichotomy presented by Freire in terms of education for liberation or domestication.

We can trace a reform movement stretching from Comenius to the dissenting academies in eighteenth-century England and then Robert Owen, through the great European reformers such as Froebel and Pestalozzi, to Dewey, Vygotsky, and Freire, among many others. This strand was grounded in the Protestant Reformation's aspiration for universal literacy, and later in republicanism and socialism; we should also not forget that many of these pioneers developed their ideas in situations of severe disadvantage. Common threads include an emphasis on active learning, the learner's engagement and understanding, making learning accessible to all, adjustment to the natural processes of child development, and a less authoritarian school ethos.

The contrary strand, a kind of counter-reform, is concerned with the shaping of docile minds and bodies. Foucault (1977) traces this back to Jean-Baptiste de La Salle and his Christian Brothers schools in Catholic France in the late seventeenth century, though there are doubtless other starting points. Detailed regulations were produced not only for how to hold the pen when writing but also for the exact position of the legs, arms, and head. Learning was about acting on command rather than achieving independent understanding. This strand continued through the Anglican and nonconformist monitorial schools of Bell and Lancaster in nineteenth-century industrial Britain, providing a model for compulsory mass schooling on the cheap. It survives, in some important respects, in reductionist notions of 'effective teaching' within high-stakes testing regimes such as England and the United States today.

This second strand is especially evident in schooling designed to impose order on impoverished working-class children who, since the start of industrial capitalism, have been viewed as unruly, dangerous, and badly brought up. In late nineteenth century Britain, school inspections were used to police a system of 'payment by results' that ensured that these children received only the most basic instruction restricted largely to the '3 Rs' (reading, writing, and arithmetic), and always at a mechanical level (accurate calculation, neat handwriting, correct spelling, and memorizing poems rather than creative writing or problem solving).

In our own period, various researchers have identified a "pedagogy of poverty" (Haberman, 1991) prevalent in schools located in poorer areas and in the lower streams of more mixed schools (see also Anyon, 1981; Wexler, 1992, among others). Teachers transmit information, assign practice exercises, ask closed questions, and check the acquisition of a set of basic facts:

> Essentially, it is a pedagogy in which learners can 'succeed' without becoming either involved or thoughtful (Kohn, 2011).

Nearly twenty years after coining the expression *pedagogy of poverty*, Haberman (2010) saw fit to add:

> the overly directive, mind-numbing, mundane, useless, anti-intellectual acts that constitute teaching not only remain the coin of the realm but have become the gold standard. (p. 45)

Test-driven school systems actively encourage the acquisition of low-level skills and knowledge, placing so much pressure on teachers that many feel unable to venture beyond it. As Andy Hargreaves (2003) has pointed out, this particularly affects schools in poorer areas since test-failure is more of a risk there.

As Kozol (2008) explains, this has social and cultural consequences as well as academic: "The children of the suburbs learn to think and to interrogate reality; the inner-city kids meanwhile are trained for nonreflective acquiescence"(p. 121). Of course technical skills are important, but crucially the pedagogy of poverty restricts learning to these basics and bars the road to mature citizenship, better employment, and cultural engagement. It certainly closes down any possibility of students gaining an understanding of their own economic situation and how this might be changed (see Johnson, 1979).

Pedagogies of Poverty

"The rich get richer, the poor get direct instruction." With this provocative heading, Dudley-Marling and Paugh (2005) put a finger on forms of teaching that result in low-achieving students falling even further behind. They were identified by Jean Anyon (1981) and Philip Wexler (1992) in case studies of schools in poor areas in the United States, and labeled by Martin Haberman (1991) as a 'pedagogy of poverty' (see also the Haberman Foundation website). Unfortunately high-stakes testing regimes in systems such as England and the United States have reinforced such practices across the majority of publicly funded schools.

In Anyon's (1981) case study of working-class schools, we see the self-fulfilling prophecy of low ability at work when some teachers decide to limit what they teach because the children do not know much:

> Most spoke of school knowledge in terms of facts and simple skills. . . ."They're lazy. I hate to categorize them, but they're lazy." . . . "History is a fact-oriented subject. But I really don't do much. I do map skills, though. It's practical—it's good for measuring and it's math." A fifth-grade teacher in the other school said she did social studies by putting notes on the board which the children then copied. I asked why she did that, and she said, "Because the children in this school don't know anything about the US, so you can't teach them much." The male fifth-grade teacher in this school said, "You can't teach these kids anything." A second-grade teacher when asked what was important knowledge for her students said, "Well, we keep them *busy*." (p. 7)

The accusation of 'low expectations' frequently aimed at teachers in low socio-economic status (SES) schools has some resonance here, but clearly it is not just a technical matter of demanding higher marks: something deeply political is at work.

Mathematics, in Anyon's (1981) study, is "often restricted to the procedures or steps to be followed in order to add, subtract, multiply, or divide" (p. 7). Although the text book contained numerous pages calling for "mathematical reasoning, inference, pattern identification or ratio setup, for example" (p. 7), these were avoided as they were believed to be too hard; one teacher called them "the thinking pages" (p. 7), choosing to concentrate instead on "the basics," that is "how you multiply and divide" (p. 8). Another said, "These pages are for creativity—they're the extras" (p. 8). The teachers often set tasks requiring students to follow precise instructions but without any explanation or understanding of the purpose of the activity.

Teachers chose social studies textbooks that avoided inquiry and independent research in favor of memorizing a limited set of facts:

> There are one to four paragraphs of history in each lesson, a vocabulary drill, and a review and skills exercise in each to check "recall and retention" (p. 8).

The guidance given by one textbook speaks of conditioning students to make organized responses and calls for the students to be "trained in the techniques of assembling information" (pp. 8–9). Anyon (1981) describes these textbooks as the least honest in their representation of American society and history:

> There was less mention of potentially controversial topics than in the series of books used in other schools. Both texts refer to the economic system as a "free enterprise" system. There are five paragraphs on minority and women's rights and history in one text and ten in the other. . . . There is little information on the working class in either book. In one class, the teacher had bought a supplementary booklet called *The Fabulous Fifty States*, and every day wrote such facts on the blackboard to copy out, for example, "Idaho grew 27 billion potatoes in one year. That's enough potatoes for each man, woman and..." (p. 9)

Anyon sums up the approach to knowledge and learning:

> It seems to be the case that what counts as school knowledge in these two working-class schools is not knowledge as concepts, cognitions, information or ideas about society, language, math, or history, connected by conceptual principles or understandings of some sort. Rather, it seems that what constitutes school knowledge here is (1) fragmented facts, isolated from context and connection to each other or to wider bodies of meaning, or to activity or biography of the students; and (2) knowledge of 'practical' rule-governed behaviors—procedures by which the students carry out tasks that are largely mechanical. Sustained conceptual or 'academic' knowledge has only occasional, symbolic presence here. (p. 12)

Similar issues have been identified by researchers in various countries. An extreme example from South Africa can be found in Hoadley (2008) with students expected to repeat and copy without even attempting to understand. In Australia, Johnston and Hayes (2008) point to little variation in routine, minimal opportunities to read and make sense of texts, intellectually undemanding tasks (at the factual-procedural end of the Bloom taxonomy), and student-teacher talk that is generally instructions or questions expecting one- or two-word answers.

Cognitive Challenge and Key Skills

It is often argued that direct instruction in the basics is the best way to remedy weak skills of literacy or numeracy among poor or ethnic minority students. This invariably results in decontextualized exercises and further disaffection, and it is part of the reason why these students fall further and further behind during their school years. Compensatory programs in the United States funded under the Chapter 1 or Title 1 rubric encouraged an intense concentration on basic literacy and numeracy techniques, and with some apparent success, but students with low-level reading skills were spending most of their time in low-level remedial work. A major evaluation (U.S. Department of Education, 1998) concluded that the program did not help students develop the ability to analyze and communicate complex ideas.

Although it is easy to produce evidence to show the efficacy of a direct instruction approach, the deep flaw is that effectiveness is judged in limited curriculum areas and against limited outcomes such as word-level decoding, the literal meaning of individual words, and accuracy in arithmetic procedures. Such research is circular and tautological: it proves that certain methods are effective provided you use tests focused on those same procedures.

Working within the school effectiveness paradigm, Muijs and Reynolds (2001) claim to have identified the most effective ways of teaching, strongly favoring direct teaching approaches: it is only on page 175 of the book that one discovers that much of the evidence is restricted to elementary maths:

> Underpinning Direct Instruction is a . . . model of reading that equates reading with a set of discrete skills (e.g., phonemic segmentation, sound blending) that are assumed to be fundamental to the reading process. Assumptions about what it means to read are also embedded in the assessments that are used to determine the efficacy of programs like DI. . . . Essentially, Direct Instruction accomplishes its own goals. It teaches what its proponents define as basic skills—the knowledge evaluated on standardized measures of achievement. (Dudley-Marling & Paugh, 2005, pp. 163–64)

Darling-Hammond and colleagues (2008) have also undertaken a critique of such research.

The alternative to teaching technical skills initially and separately is to combine them with the exploration of challenging and meaningful ideas. This has been implemented systematically in networks such as Accelerated Schools (see Finnan et al., 1995). Kohn (2011) also cites the New York Performance Standards Consortium and Big Picture schools, which "start with students' interests and questions" and where success is judged "by authentic indicators of thinking and motivation, not by multiple-choice tests."

Lisa Delpit (1995) is adamant that you cannot leave acquisition of technical skills to chance but rejects the notion of a choice between authentic activities and decontextualized exercises. In writing, for example, she points to the particularly strong impact of mini lessons consisting of direct instruction about some technical convention when located within meaningful writing for real audiences and real purposes. She is also a firm believer in making the politics of literacy explicit to students: that the rules are arbitrary cultural conventions but they are important for getting listened to in the wider society.

The Faulty Politics of Raising Standards

Paradoxically, a back-to-basics curriculum has frequently been promoted under the flag of raising standards. High-stakes testing focused on 'rigorous' application of basic skills usually has the combined effect of narrowing the curriculum and driving many students out of school (Kohn, 2011).

In the name of raising standards, the current Conservative-led government in England is busy raising pass marks rather than dealing with the heart of the problem—alienated learning with little opportunity for holistic or critical thinking. There is a crucial error here of mistaking accuracy for quality, a failure to look at the nature of the task. Bureaucratic bullying is used to 'drive up standards', including relabeling the 40 percent of schools previously judged 'satisfactory' as 'needing to improve'.

Ironically, the problematic teaching methods this produces are recognized at the top of the Inspectorate but without acknowledging that the accountability system, including the draconian inspection system itself, is exacerbating the problem. The Chief Inspector's annual report (Ofsted, 2011), points out that less successful schools relied too heavily on worksheets and a narrow range of textbooks and that teachers often spent too much time talking and set low-level tasks that failed to develop pupils' knowledge. Planning was "too focused on covering content rather than being clear what the pupils should learn," and activities were "insufficiently challenging . . . and often based on procedural and descriptive work." Lessons were "not well paced" with "time lost on unproductive activities such as copying out the objectives for the lesson, completing exercises without sufficient reason, or simply spending too long on one activity." There was an "emphasis on low-level tasks which do not develop their knowledge and understanding systematically." When least successful, tasks "occupy rather than engage and challenge and develop understanding" (pp. 51–53).

The report (Ofsted, 2011) also pointed to a critical link between weak teaching and poor behavior: bored children lose attention, demonstrate poor attitudes to learning, and eventually interrupt the learning of others, then teachers end up continually managing low-level disruption at the expense of providing interesting and relevant opportunities for pupils to learn—a vicious circle.

Among features of good teaching highlighted by the Chief Inspector were:

- lessons that "deal with contemporary issues and developments of relevance to the pupils, and include a range of activities, including practical sessions and out-of-classroom activities which help to motivate pupils and maximize learning";

- a "creative and appropriate balance between teacher-directed and independent learning . . . which allows pupils to explore questions and solve problems in more depth";

- "opportunities for enquiry through research, discussion, collaboration and initiative"; and

- teachers probing pupils to "explore the ideas more deeply" (Ofsted, 2011, p. 52).

Ironically, in this school system based on intimidation, teachers tend to 'play safe' and avoid more creative methods from fear of inspectors' adverse judgments.

Authentic or Alienated Learning?

Although schools are designed as a separate space for concentrated learning, removed from many of the daily pressures of life, meaningful learning also requires a connectedness to the wider world in real or simulated modes. This throws up a particular challenge for teachers in areas of deprivation: how to maintain an orderly space for learning while ensuring that students feel they are doing something meaningful and relevant to their lives rather than worn-out routines of which students feel little ownership.

There is a strong parallel between traditional tasks in schools and alienated labor in industrial settings. At the heart of Marx's humanist vision was a concern about alienation (Swain, 2012; Mészáros, 2005). Since work—our creative and productive interaction with nature—is a central characteristic of humanity, alienated labor prevents our satisfaction and self-fulfillment. It denotes a deep separation from our true human nature. Alienated labor is endemic under capitalism, where most people produce commodities in exchange for wages, with little concern for how their products are used and little say in what they make or how they make it. They are alienated from their own work, from what they produce, from nature, and from themselves and other people.

Similarly, in many traditional classrooms, students are told what to do and how to do it, when to start and stop; they hand over a product not to a genuine user or audience but to the teacher as assessor, eventually getting back a mark or grade as a kind of surrogate wage. In Marx's terms, they have a sense of exchange value but not use value, extrinsic but not intrinsic reward (Wrigley, 2006). This must particularly affect pupils who lack a clear sense of the eventual rewards that might arise from hard work, including lower attainers, those with few role models of academic and economic success, and young people whose outside lives are so full of problems that school is a lower priority. In adolescence, many of them look elsewhere for more immediate and tangible rewards.

Peter McInerney (2009) points out that alienation occurs when students lack meaningful connection to their studies, see little relevance in the content, and when individualized modes of work disconnect them from others. Assessment reinforces this when it is seen as satisfying the teacher or institution, not the individual. He argues that it is too easy to pathologize this as an individual deficit, a *failure* to engage, as *disaffection*.

Fortunately there are alternative modes of school learning that avoid reinforcing and reproducing it. One of the recurrent features in the case-study schools of *The Power to Learn* (Wrigley, 2000) was learning that led to a shared product, presentation, or performance. Pupils frequently worked in groups, writing their ideas and findings on large posters to show to others, often with illustrations to emphasize the point. Improvised drama was common, to explore an issue or experience, and then presented to the whole class or a wider audience. Students regularly worked in small groups to solve a problem before presenting their proposals to the class. They were also frequently involved in designing an activity or working out how to tackle a problem.

The creative arts, systematically marginalized by high-stakes testing regimes, had a high profile in these schools, providing many opportunities for deliberation, collaboration, and presentation. Students also engaged in investigations and campaigns around social and environmental issues of deep concern to them.

The Ramiro Solans School in Zaragoza, featured in *Another School Is Possible* (Wrigley, 2006), was clearly a school that had been in difficulties. Absenteeism had been as high as 50 percent, but a complete transformation reduced this to 10 or 12 percent. The school had come to be seen by pupils and parents as a low-status school in the local pecking order. As the headteacher expressed it:

> This is the Gypsies' School. That's what people call it, and that's what it is. We have 130 pupils, of whom 75 percent are from Gypsy families, 20 percent immigrants and the other 5 percent Spanish. But you have to realize that we receive the very poorest Gypsies—only one market trader—the rest survive on social security and what they can find. (p. 124)

The teachers were well aware of some very basic problems (unhealthy diet, poor concentration, low self-esteem, etc.), but when they investigated the children's interests, they found many areas of potential motivation:

> a taste for manual activities, visual language, computers, story telling, drama, songs and games, pets and the world of animals—and they wanted to appear in any way possible in the regional newspaper. (p. 125)

The teachers redesigned the curriculum so that every month a major theme led to a performance or festival involving parents and sometimes a public event in the city, with a song specially composed for each occasion. A high profile was given to the creative and performing arts: the other subjects were sometimes taught separately and sometimes linked into the monthly theme. At the end of each month, the work was exhibited and performed in an open afternoon for parents, with dances, poetry, dramatic performance, and an exhibition, and some months it became part of a traditional citywide or district festival:

This is a very important way for parents to get involved in the school, and particularly because of our pupils' characteristics. Some teachers objected—they didn't like the fuss and confusion, they said it was too much like a street parade—but the pupils insisted: "We like our families coming to see what we do at school. We like them hearing us sing and seeing that we're real artists." (p. 126)

The music teacher wrote or adapted a song for each monthly theme, with an eye to opportunities to connect the curriculum and the wider culture:

We try to use a wide range of multicultural genres, as a way to connect with the world. They are passionate about rumba, but we also use jazz, reggae, rap, waltzes, traditional music and so on. The song and its dance are fundamental to the project. In the music class we work on the words, the rhythm, the score, the instrumentation. Some pupils already know how to play an instrument, and others learn here. We learn and practise dance steps, adapted to the age of pupils. Music becomes a real motor of learning.

The kids get involved so they're motivated to learn other things. For example, in the Pilar festival [a city procession], we make large heads, and that involves all kinds of learning, not just modelling—we use mathematics and explore different units of measurement. Using karaoke with a copy of the lyrics is a great way to get them reading and writing, and we have used a song from Liberia as the starting point to study the war in that country. (p. 126)

Open Architectures and Authentic Assessment

This example of a curriculum built round a monthly theme and event is clearly an ambitious transformation, but there are more modest structures of learning that encourage learner initiative and collaboration. Wrigley (2007) refers to some of these as *open architectures* because they have a clear structure while allowing space for students to make their own decisions. They provide a valuable solution to many of the problems of alienated learning.

Some years ago, Wrigley (2003, p. 134) discovered in official Danish guidelines for social studies (Ministry of Education, Denmark, 1995) a methodology that actively encourages student independence while sustaining a shared learning community in the class. It combines structure with openness, creating the opportunity to combine students' ideas and perceptions with concepts and processes from various academic disciplines.

Teachers are discouraged from writing too fixed a plan for the year, so they can keep open opportunities for students to propose topical themes for class study. Stage 1 involves either the teacher or a group of students stimulating the class's interest. After this initial impetus, it is important not to truncate stage 2: this involves plenary discussion in the class during which students can share their experiences and attitudes, and in which the teacher presents relevant concepts and methods from social science disciplines. Only at the end of this stage are students encouraged, individually or in small groups, to decide on specific issues for their independent or group research (stage 3). After that, stage 4 (plenary) involves groups not only disseminating what they have discovered but also actively generating further class discussion. Although the Danish document does not discuss this, there is, logically, also the possibility of a fifth stage in which students take their ideas out of the classroom and into the wider community as a discussion, event, or social action. Smyth and McInerney (2007a) describe essentially the same kind of process in an Australian school they refer to as "Plainsville."

This is a particular form of what is often called *project method*, with origins in Dewey and Kilpatrick's work around 1910. The method is infinitely adaptable and is particularly useful to engage students in issues of citizenship. For example, a project on refugees can begin with a simulation as its initial stage to stir up interest. The plenary discussion (stage 2) reveals the different levels of knowledge and conflicting attitudes of students and allows them to choose issues for independent investigation at stage 3.

Project method is only one of many 'open architectures'. Another very popular form, particularly in Northern Europe, is *storyline*, a narrative-based form (Bell, Harkness & White, 2007; see below). The open architectures umbrella could also include large-scale simulations, producing a video film, critical mathematics (Gutstein, 2012), and many variants of place-based learning (e.g., Smith, 2012; McInerney, Smyth & Down, 2011; Tooth & Renshaw, 2012; Thomson, 2006).

Storyline, a situated and embodied form of learning, was originally invented for young children but is used extensively in Scandinavia for all ages. It typically begins with a location, presented to children as a mural. Pupils invent roles for themselves, and they mark up their presence on the mural. The teacher creates a sequence of events in a loose plot, to which the pupils respond. For example, a storyline about Vikings begins with a scene of an apparently uninhabited bay somewhere in Scotland. The pupils are told it is more than 1,000 years ago. They form family groups, and after researching in history books, they paint cottages and huts to place around the bay. When the pupils arrive in class the next day, the pupils find a ship at sea and heading toward their village. Later stages explore the experiences, mutual perspectives, dilemmas and crises which result, using drama, writing and research. It would be easy to adapt this storyline to the first arrival of European conquerors and settlers in Australia or America.

Since inappropriate assessment procedures can easily undermine curriculum and pedagogy, it is also important to explore forms of authentic assessment that support rather than negate authentic learning (see Lingard et al., 2003; Hayes et al., 2006; Newmann, Secada & Wehlage, 1995). The Queensland New Basics project (Queensland Department of Education, 2001) developed a concept of assessment through rich tasks—assessment activities that are meaningful and worthwhile in themselves, collaborative rather than competitive, and involve presentations to an invited audience. Examples include:

- *Endangered plant or animal*—eleven-year-olds investigate, use their knowledge to take constructive action, and create a persuasive and informative multimedia presentation

- *The shape we're in*—sixteen-year-olds explore various shapes for a container, a domestic object, a mechanical device, and an object from nature, then present an alternative design for one of these, explaining the maths

- *National identity*—a project that involves planning, producing, and presenting a filmed documentary, including information from research and interviews with people from different cultural backgrounds.

Similar approaches to assessment meaningful to students, but also intellectually challenging, were pioneered by Debbie Meier and colleagues in New York (2002); see also discussion and examples on the websites of the Performance Assessment Consortium and the Big Picture schools.

Connecting Cognition with Experience

The preceding examples illustrate a major question of assessibility: how to build a bridge between abstract academic knowledge and personal experience. This is not an either-or, since a Vygotskian understanding of learning entails both. Vygotsky (1978) emphasizes how we draw on cultural tools, and particularly language, to mediate our encounters with the world. We can also reverse this model: teachers use learners' experience to mediate and give access to scientific concepts. The successful learning of academic concepts requires experience but cannot be achieved by immersion in experience alone.

This recognition is at the heart of Cummins' (1997) approach to the teaching of bilingual pupils and, we maintain, has a wider relevance to pupils who are not fluent in the formal discourses of academic learning. Rather than the blind alley of decontextualized exercises (low in cognitive challenge, weak in experience), Cummins proposes challenging problem solving that is well supported by experience, including mediation through key visuals such as diagrams (high in cognitive challenge, strong in experience). This is equally important for monolingual pupils whose lack of curriculum-related experiences (museums, visits to historic sites, television documentaries) or specialist vocabulary might make it difficult to follow abstractly presented academic explanations. It is vital if we are not to allow a weak command of formal academic registers to stand in the way of challenging and interesting ideas.

A similar principle emerged from the reform of English teaching originating in London in the 1960s and 1970s. One of its central figures, Harold Rosen—in many respects a parallel to Paulo Freire—began to articulate this in the 1950s as head of English at Walworth Road School in South London, one of the earliest comprehensive schools. The norm for school-based writing in English lessons had been essays, on quite random subjects, as the conventional way of practising technical skills and organizing ideas, and ultimately to display these skills in formal examinations:

> Philip Hartog in 1947 had complained of "the absurdity of asking children to write 'essays' as if they were addressing the civilized world" and "the purposeless meandering served up to us by pupils asked to write, without notice, in the space of an hour, on such subjects as Sugar, Spies, Etiquette, The North Sea, or Beasts of Burden—with no purpose and with no audience in view except the examiners who . . . are bored stiff." (cited by Medway & Kingwell, 2010, p. 764)

The Walworth Road approach was rooted in the urban environment, in family life, in the local streets, thus "asserting the validity as curricular topics of local and specific urban realities . . . affirming the worth of the ordinary experience of working-class children and dignifying it through improvised drama, classroom discussion and literary and argumentative writing" (Medway & Kingwell, 2010, p. 764). Medway and Kingwell point out that descriptive writing in English lessons had traditionally been situated in rural locations. Students developed from there to consider emergent political issues such as the quality of housing and slum clearance. This sprouted out of descriptive or narrative genres and eventually the balance would shift toward genres of argument and explanation, though remaining rich in illustration.

English teaching was also characterized by a seamless flow between language and literature, the spoken and written word, high and popular culture, scripted and improvised drama, all around a theme or situation of interest to the learners. A major step toward overcoming alienated learning was to find plentiful occasions for presentation and performance, such as classroom discussions and pupils reading their work aloud at school assemblies.

This early work was developed and shared through the teachers network LATE (London Association for Teachers of English, later part of the national association NATE), and the writings of Harold Rosen, Douglas Barnes, and James Britton among others became internationally known. Key principles were the centrality of autobiography and the urban environment, ordinary speech as the foundation for more formal genres of expression, and exploratory discussion often in small groups. This group of educators, having moved into university posts, researched the ways in which teachers commonly dominated classroom exchanges through closed questions that invited only the briefest response and a widespread failure to build on learners' existing knowledge. The movement was resolutely opposed to what Britton called "meaningless busy-work." Connections were soon drawn with Vygotsky's and Freire's ideas as they became available in English. However, whereas Freire spoke of a culture of silence among the poor of Brazil, Rosen and colleagues never saw the urban working class as silent—rather that they were being actively silenced by the norms of traditional schooling.

Real Literacy: Liberating Voice, Agency and Identity

There has been a considerable emphasis on 'student voice' in English-speaking countries, based on observations of how rarely students have a say in the running of their schools and in the ways they learn (e.g., Fielding, 2001b; Rudduck & Flutter, 2004). It is, however, important to discuss *voice* in tandem with the concept of *agency*. Both are clearly as vital in the critical communicative methodology used in CREA's research to transform education in marginalized communities (see Flecha, 2000; Puigvert, Christou & Holford, 2012; and other examples in chapter 8).

Schools typically close down on learning at three levels of operation, the organization and disciplining of relations, the curriculum as a selection of content, and the normative modes of teaching and learning. The voice and agency of the learner (especially those from working-class and minority communities) are systematically denied on all three levels in traditional schools. Finding space for the voice and agency of marginalized learners is crucial if we are to help them work against the sense of shame and futility discussed in early chapters.

The question reaches into all areas of the curriculum. It is one of the reasons why the performing and creative arts are so important, though neglected in more instrumental versions of the neoliberal curriculum, or at best addressed in terms of preparation for technical or administrative work in the culture industry. It is of the utmost importance in conceptualizing literacy.

The denial of voice and agency impinges on the formation of identity. When disadvantaged young people, suffering from a sense of stigma and futility, have to endure schooling that demands passivity and labels them as academic failures, the circle is complete: the school is reinforcing the lessons of social-structural inequality to which they are subject outside school. The effects of this closing down of learning have been documented by Smyth and McInerney (2012) in their book *From Silent Witnesses to Active Agents*, in which young people vividly describe the conditions that propelled them out of school and the very different set of conditions that made it possible for them to resume learning.

Stephanie Jones' book *Girls, Social Class and Literacy* (2006; see review by Vicars, 2010) points to the double damage when students are forced to read about a cozy privileged world but without the opportunity to speak back to it from their own experience and lifeworlds:

> Because [kids in St Francis] see things all the time—and they read these little stories in school about all these perfect lives, and mommy and daddy work and blah—*that* is not how it *is*. You have a mom who gets a check once a month, whose daddy's on the street corner selling *drugs*, whose kid is—you know, sittin' there with people comin' in and out of the house who buy drugs, and they see this, yet they're going to school learnin' about perfect little Jill's life and this and that—and that's *bullcrap* because that's not how it is. (p. 112, italics in original)

Vicars (2010) quotes Nakata (1999, p. 15):

> If I can't speak about the world, then how am I to understand my position, or hold my position, or negotiate my position, or change my position in the face of others? (p. 271).

This problem demands a richer view of literacy, extending into improvised drama, media, and visual arts, with opportunities for learners to re-enact situations from their own lives and how they could be different. Language is not just representation, in the sense of mirroring reality; the very structure of human language invites us to make new connections, to construct alternatives, to conceive of living differently. Returning to the issue of alienation, we should recall Marx's powerful metaphor of the difference between human beings and other animals:

> What distinguishes the worst architect from the best of bees is this, that the architect raises his structure in imagination before he erects it in reality (Marx, 1987[1867], chapter 7, section 1).

Versions of literacy that squeeze out interpretation and self-expression in favor of the technical features of reading and writing simply dumb down human development, despite the recurrent argument that such practices are necessary to raise standards. Critical literacy involves raising questions about the intended readership of texts, the absences and omissions, the positionality of the text, what it privileges, the knowledge the reader would bring to it, the social and cultural realities it assumes, possible interpretations that could be made, and (in Freirean terms) reading of the self in the world as offered by the word of the text.

In both England and the United States, literacy teaching has recently suffered from a dogmatic insistence on systematic synthetic phonics, not as a component of learning to read but displacing all else. It is interesting to note that the two Scottish experiments in synthetic phonics (Johnston & Watson, 2005; MacKay, 2007; see also Rosen, 2006; Wyse & Styles, 2007) that triggered its forced adoption across England led to dramatic improvements in decoding words and reading them aloud but hardly any improvement in terms of comprehension when measured a few years later.

Cummins (2003) pinpoints in the following paragraphs the awful damage perpetrated by such policies. This has obvious relevance to our arguments about all young people who are marginalized by class position and poverty, whatever their ethnic background. It is worth quoting at length:

> Nowhere in this anemic instructional vision is there room for really connecting at a human level with culturally diverse students. When we frame the universe of discourse only in terms of children's deficits in English and in phonological awareness (or deficits in any other area), we expel culture, language, identity, intellect, and imagination from our image of the child. In contrast . . . an instructional focus on empowerment, understood

as the collaborative creation of power, starts by acknowledging the cultural, linguistic, imaginative, and intellectual resources that children bring to school.

Effective citizenship requires active intelligence, critical literacy, and a willingness to challenge power structures that constrict human possibility. . . . Identity, intellect, imagination and power are absent from the new regime of truth because they potentially challenge the smooth operation of coercive power structures. (pp. 56–57)

Today's young people are thrown into a world where the "saturation of youth consciousness by the media" (McInerney, 2009, p. 28) constantly undermines the potential for active political engagement. Critical literacy is an essential means to challenge students to "build a critical understanding of their presence in the world" as "active critical investigators into their own lives and society" (p. 27). As Lisa Delpit (1995) reminds us, literacy teaching limited to technical skills is incapacitating:

Students need technical skills to open doors, but they need to be able to think critically and creatively to participate in meaningful and potentially liberating work inside those doors. Let there be no doubt; a 'skilled' minority person who is not also capable of critical analysis becomes the trainable, low-level functionary of the dominant society, simply the grease that keeps the institutions which orchestrate his or her oppression running smoothly. (p. 19)

Curriculum Reform: The Dilemma of Relevance

Throughout this book, we have argued that a dialectical or symbolic interactionist approach is needed to understand (under)achievement or (dis)engagement from school. This necessarily involves the question of how learners relate to the curriculum.

Unfortunately, some of the most interesting debates concerning the curriculum have suffered from an entrenchment into one or other pole of a crudely defined binary: teacher-centered or child-centered, formal or informal, subject-based or interdisciplinary. The principle of accessibility calls for a curriculum well rooted in the students' local experience, but will this trap them within limited horizons?

This problem confronted the Liverpool Education Priority Area of the 1970s in its attempt to transform inner-city schools. This exemplary reform program worked on schools' connections with neighborhood life, including community schools, playgroups, and adult education: its director Eric Midwinter soon raised the question of a community curriculum, but others condemned this as ghettoization.

The first thing we should say is that a curriculum rooted in local experiences is not necessarily worse than exposure to random scraps of formal knowledge. Midwinter (1975) rightly ridiculed the inert and random forms in which fragments of a common culture are often passed on:

"If you would ask me to repeat the symptoms of the Black Death, recite *Cargoes* or write an essay on the Masai tribe, I should be happy to oblige." . . . Given the massive factor of perpetuation in education, teachers sometimes discover themselves transmitting an artificial heritage—the one, in fact, transmitted to them. There is bric-a-brac of this and that, bits and pieces of history, shreds and patches of geography, dribs and drabs of scripture, bubbles and squeaks of science, odds and sods of maths, poems and stories, a ragbag of shoddy oddments with little meaning outside the school. It's not only remote and sterile, it tends to be backward looking and romanticist. It is romanticist about the dainty, twee Victoriana of poesy and the country. (pp. 226–27)

But second, using the local environment as a starting point should not restrict the establishment of universal concepts or prevent teachers making connections with other places and times and societies. A good example was found in the Bradford primary school (Wrigley, 2000, pp. 111–120), where firsthand explorations of the local area were counterposed to a reading of *Katie Morag and the Two Grandmothers*, set on a remote Scottish island. One wall of the classroom was covered in symbolic representations of Bradford (posters and messages in English, Urdu, and other languages; photographs and maps of the neighborhood), and another with a giant map of Katie Morag's island.

We should be arguing for a curriculum that is both accessible and far reaching, rooted in the present but opening diverse possibilities for the future, global as well as local. This is, necessarily, a complex pedagogical process concerning the reflective reworking and revaluation of culture rather than the conservation of a heritage. As Midwinter (1972) argued:

> Those who think the community-based curriculum is a recipe for resignation have totally missed the point. By stretching the children intellectually and creatively on the social issues that confront them, one hopes to produce adults provoked and challenged into a positive and constructive response.
>
> In short, it is an outward looking attitude not an introverted one. It is intended that, from the stable base of an understanding of their own locale, children can look outwards to wider frames of reference. (p. 30)

More recently, within a neoliberal policy environment, the binary divide around relevance to working-class students has repeatedly been articulated in terms of a contrast between academic and vocational. This opposition is misleading, since the word *vocational* is never used to denote preparation for high-status professions such as law or medicine; moreover, *academic* studies are increasingly being viewed in instrumentalist fashion in terms of their career potential, losing sight of other educational purposes.

Clearly we cannot build a curriculum that does not relate to young people's expectation to earn a living. Without allowing a divide, the upper secondary curriculum should include a vocational element, arguably for all young people whatever their academic and social standing. However, we need to think through the possibilities of a critical vocationalism, one that would explore workplace conflicts, environmental damage, economic inequalities, and tensions with family life as well as the best ways to enter working life.

Australian academics Kemmis, Cole, and Suggett (1983) have pointed out that both academic ('neoclassical') and vocational curricula share a conservative orientation of fitting students into society as it stands. By contrast, a socially critical curriculum involves both closeness and critical distance—bringing learning closer to the realities of the local community and enabling students to view the world from different perspectives, including the perspectives of those marginalized by poverty or racism.

A socially critical curriculum would, for example, involve taking up an enquiring stance with regard to the consumer culture which relentlessly constructs children as consumers, fusing identity, pleasure, and purchase:

> You buy delights . . . kids rule . . . adults are dim . . . and schools are dull. These are the canons of globalizing consumer cultures. In the places where kids, commodities and images meet, education, entertainment and advertising merge. Kids consume this corporate abundance with an appetite. Young people are being turned into "desiring machines." (Kenway, 2001; see also Kenway and Bullen, 2001). (Wrigley, 2003, p. 99)

A socially critical curriculum requires opening up space for critical thought without signaling disrespect for young people's lifestyles or choices (see McInerney, Smyth & Down, 2011).

This principle has been further developed through the concept of place-based education. We can situate this concept in a world marked by the complex global flows of ideas, commodities, and people but where global capitalism often appears to delete and homogenize the local. Pat Thomson (2006; 2010) explains and illustrates forms of learning that have both immediacy and reach:

> A place-based curriculum forges new social bonds: it offers opportunities for schools to explicitly and critically foster identity work through events and tasks that allow students to encounter embedded social practices and agents that they would normally avoid. In doing so, it also avoids a narrow, insular, and potentially inequitable localism (Gruenewald, 2003); by connecting students with different peoples in their local neighborhoods, teachers and students are imbricated in the trajectories of everyday lives which are not simply local, but are also "stretched-out" relations, practices and narratives (Massey, 1994; Childress, 2000; Davies, 2000). . . . Students are taught to critically question the relationship of people and nature and the histories of oppression of indigenous peoples (Bowers, 2005). (Thomson, 2010, p. 131)

This involves drawing on the community's funds of knowledge as both an object of study and a cognitive tool (Gonzalez, Moll & Amanti, 2005)—knowledge of which teachers are often unaware. Families and neighborhoods are seen as sources of potential assets for learning. Using Australian examples, Thomson (2006) shows us how local investigations and interventions can open up a critical global understanding, serving both to "affirm and unsettle identities and place." Lew Zipin (2009) has further insisted that we should not shy away from "darker" aspects of students' lives but create opportunities for students to grapple with them in transformative ways.

All of this involves not just getting closer to reality, as encapsulated in calls for greater relevance, but also a critical distance, a space to reflect and debate matters of concern, to see structures of power below the surface and possibilities for change.

When Policy Makes Matters Worse

This chapter has focused on some of the ways in which schools can enhance the learning of underachieving students. It has proposed some important principles for curriculum formation and teaching and included rich illustrations of successful innovative practice.

We have come across so many inspiring and committed teachers over the years who have creatively developed new approaches to teaching that engage disadvantaged young people and help them to achieve: we have also highlighted these inspirational examples in various other books. We have good reason to believe in the difference that outstanding teaching makes.

The chapter has also described some of the features of a pedagogy of poverty which limit engagement and restrict progress. We have not undertaken this in a spirit of blame—there is far too much of that about—but in recognition of the extreme pressures teachers are under. Unfortunately, political interventions ostensibly intended to bring about improvement have frequently made matters worse.

There is a long history of teachers being driven toward limited patterns of teaching by oppressive bureaucratic control. Let us recall some British examples. In the late nineteenth century, the payment by results system policed by inspectors rewarded low-level skills acquisition (arithmetic calculations, reading aloud, neat handwriting, and accurate spelling and punctuation) to the exclusion of all else. For much of the twentieth century, the vast majority of manual workers' children were segregated into lower-level, poorly resourced schools, and provided with only a rudimentary secondary education. The curriculum consisted of basic literacy and numeracy, fragments of scientific, geographic, and historical knowledge, and forms of technical work such as needlework and woodwork, which were strongly gendered and indeed archaic in terms of industrial relevance. All of this helped shape the teaching profession's collective habits and its view of what was feasible and appropriate in urban schools.

Though it is possible for teachers to resist the narrowness such systems reward, this takes particular courage and a degree of protection by school management; it is less likely to happen in lower-achieving schools and poorer environments where there is more risk of being deemed a failure. The narrow forms of learning rewarded by the system build a collective professional habitus, defining the norms of teaching for areas of deprivation. In some periods this has been reinforced by the requirement to teach large classes or to accommodate some troubled young people in the mainstream classroom without adequate assistance.

The neoliberal era has increasingly sought to control schools through tests of basic literacy and numeracy, resulting in a neglect of critical and creative activity and of many other curriculum areas. In England particularly, this has been reinforced by the publication of league tables of test results, by an intimidatory inspection regime, and by performance-related pay for teachers.

On the surface, tightly constrained activities keep children busy and with the appearance of being 'on-task'. This approach has been reinforced by a selective espousal of Effectiveness research and an uncritical appeal for 'evidence-based practice'. Despite the availability of research supporting alternative teaching methods (see, for example, Darling-Hammond et al., 2008), Effectiveness research that reinforces pedagogies of poverty gets the widest circulation.

For all this, while teachers should not carry the blame, it is crucial to stress a professional ethical responsibility for thinking through the implications of limited classroom methods. Questioning the dominant methods also entails questioning the deficit discourse that is often used to justify them.

Of course, while schools can make a difference, they cannot overcome the damage of exploitation and poverty by themselves. The great pioneers of socially just pedagogy, as well as many ordinary teachers struggling to educate well in difficult situations, have often combined thinking outside the box of standard methods with a political commitment that opposes unjust social structures. It is no accident that curricular and social activism so often go together.

Schools for Social Justice

Theories of Good Practice

I am, somehow, less interested in the weight and convolutions of Einstein's brain than in the near certainty that people of equal talent have lived and died in cotton fields and sweatshops.
—Stephen Jay Gould, 1983, p. 126.

Schools can be humane and still educate well. They can be genuinely concerned with gaiety and joy and individual growth and fulfillment without sacrificing concern for intellectual discipline and development. They can stress aesthetic and moral education without weakening the three Rs.
—Charles Silberman, 1971, p. 208

The central purpose of this book has been to examine conflicting explanations of how social class and poverty affect schooling and to respond to problems of disengagement and underachievement in schools. We have developed a rigorous critique of inadequate and damaging theories and an introduction to more fruitful ideas and practices. Though theory cannot provide a blueprint for practice, it can help teachers and policymakers avoid repeating the same mistakes and provide an inspiration for planning socially just change in schools.

The situations we have described in this book cannot remain unchanged—we need to *do school differently*! It is an illusion that the education system is anything like a level playing field. Continuing to prop up the myth that schools provide a fair reward for diligence and an equal opportunity to develop talent, while increasing numbers of young people are sidelined and marginalized, can only result in continuing damage to the young people who are being sold this cruel hoax (see Smyth, 2010b).

In this closing chapter we want to bring together the basic principles of an alternative framework—one that we do not believe is in any way utopian, but that is very much alive in the culture and practice of some existing schools. This is an organic project that is never complete and is always in the process of becoming, so we are fully aware that it will open up further debate as well as stimulating learning through action. Before we do that we need to revisit some key issues.

The Emotions of Class

Our starting point is that social class is grounded in relationships of power linked to the ownership and control of the economy—a system whereby a tiny minority own the means of production (factories, land, technology, and so on) and determine the employment of most of the world's population. Poverty sits within this as a consequence of exploitation and marginalization, not the result of personal or cultural inadequacies or individual misfortune.

Nevertheless, both class and poverty have wide-ranging cultural and psychological effects. For example, low pay, limited skills, and a subordinate position at work can produce feelings of low self-esteem, particularly when one is in unfamiliar or exalted surroundings. The memories of school failure, perhaps, resonate with other thwarted ambitions and frustrated hopes and reinforce a sense that there is little you can do to change your social status or well-being. All of this impacts on the education of young people.

Most acutely, we know from people living in neighborhoods of concentrated and acute poverty, especially where there is chronic unemployment and fragile employment, that they often experience a complex of emotions and experiences we have summarized as *shame* and *futility*. A sense of shame—humiliation, low self-esteem, and so on—results from the internalization of low social status, a marginal role in production, or the humiliation of having to claim (and sometimes plead for) welfare benefits. The sense of futility, in these circumstances, is sharpened by having to abandon personal plans for lack of finance or by one's own and others' experiences of training courses that still don't result in employment. Political and media attacks on 'benefit scroungers' make the situation even more intolerable.

It is a central part of our argument that traditional patterns of schooling can actually *reinforce these experiences of shame and futility*. Poverty and a low class status are reproduced by a sense of poor self-esteem and sometimes active humiliation through the disciplinary processes and relations of schools. Students marked out as having low ability and little chance of success and tracked into a repetitive and decontextualized curriculum within schools dominated by patterns of alienated learning become disengaged and fatalistic about the possibilities of personal success. Disruption and antagonism often appear the only ways to regain some degree of respect and recognition from peers. However, these forms of agency and opposition usually bring little direct benefit.

This is not, of course, the whole picture. Many people struggle through periods of poverty, take great care of their children, and help them to stay safe and focused at school. Dignity is maintained in a spirit of "don't let the buggers grind you down!" Even the politics of Austerity have not extinguished solidarity and class struggle, as we see from Cairo to Chicago, from Athens to Madrid. Teachers, too, continue to fight for children's right to learn, individually, in their schools, and collectively through their trade unions.

At the other end of the social spectrum, though, power and wealth can buy children an education leading not only to academic success but also to a belief in their right to rule.

False Beliefs and Harmful Policies

Earlier chapters of this book provide a critique of inadequate and misleading explanations. Broadly speaking, these theories are characterized by deficit images of young people, families, and neighborhoods, compounded of late by abusive characterizations of teachers and schools as ineffective or failing. There is a paradox in this mixture, as children's poet Mike Rosen (2012) pointed out in his satirical attack on reactionary government rhetoric and policy:

> When somebody posts a comment in a newspaper, all the guys come out of the woodwork to explain why it happens. So here are some of the explanations:
>
> (1) "People are born stupid, not so stupid, not stupid, quite bright, bright, very bright and genius, and this is fixed from the moment they're born for the rest of their lives."
>
> (2) "A great number of teachers are bad at teaching and create stupidity schools, which produce unskilled stupid people."
>
> Some people can hold those two ideas in their minds at exactly the same time. *People are born stupid* but *teachers produce stupidity?* You'd have thought there was a contradiction!

First, we have been at pains to unmask the assumption that most children undergo a tedious and meaningless curriculum because it suits their limited capabilities (see chapters 4 and 9). We have shown that there is no substance to the claim that young people brought up in poverty are incapable of serious learning and so need to be fed an emaciated and dumbed-down educational diet. In the worst cases, it appears that these young people are regarded as hopeless cases for whom schools can only be sites of incarceration. There is, unfortunately, a widespread assumption that these so-called 'disconnected youth' (MacDonald & Marsh, 2005) who grow up in poor neighborhoods underachieve in education because of irretrievable parental histories of failure and moral decay that feed into intergenerational lack of ambition and aspiration (chapters 3, 5, and 6). We robustly contest the view that these young people are bundles of pathologies.

Second, we also contest 'joined up' welfarist responses as ineffectual and demeaning. They fail to recognize that poor people are not marginal because of unwise lifestyle choices (chapter 3), but rather they are *actively marginalized* by economic and political forces over which they have no control (chapters 1 and 2). The failure to understand the ways in which people are *made* poor leads to a recycling of disciplinary processes of shaming and punishing or at best a curriculum oriented toward moral regeneration and coping with adversity. Lessons on 'enterprise' simply compound the deceit.

Third, we have contested existing theories that purport to explain the reproduction of class and poverty by pinning the blame on some alleged defect—lack of intelligence, poor parenting, or low aspirations (chapters 4–6). Such pathologies are constructed by reifying and essentializing the consequences of low socioeconomic status and poverty as if they were its causes. Focusing on alleged inadequacies and failings serves only to reinforce low self-esteem and a sense of worthlessness.

The problem is viewed in terms of the absence of certain personal qualities rather than the dynamics of social and school relationships, and issues are separated rather than making connections between them. Our thinking is that these complex issues can only be properly understood dialectically, which involves looking at the symbolic interaction between the students' lifeworld and the school. This is one of the meanings behind this book's title *Living on the Edge*—students are engaged in constant negotiation of the demands of school and community. For understanding this, we believe it is particularly helpful to draw upon Bourdieu and Goffman as social theorists whose work focuses on the complexities of interaction in situations of severe inequality (see Introduction). These two sociologists provide important intellectual tools for pursuing enquiry into the relationship of schools to society.

Some Directions for Research

Bourdieu enables us to recognize the unequal exchange whereby schools honor the interests and knowledge, discourse and behavioral style of children from higher-status families so that it becomes 'cultural capital', whereas they overlook, misunderstand, or denigrate the lifestyle and knowledge and interests of lower-status families. Within weeks of entering primary schools, this unfair trade can very quickly become the basis on which teachers attribute different levels of ability to the children in their class, often placing the 'more able' and the 'less able' on different tables for literacy and numeracy. In effect, children are consigned to a different curriculum, different expectations, and a different way of being seen, seeing each other and seeing themselves.

We need to find ways to explore what kind of evidence is drawn upon in these early judgments, including any preconceptions or prejudice. We also need to discuss with teachers what they believe ability or intelligence means, where it comes from, and whether and how it can be enhanced. The impact of early labeling needs to be followed through with the aim of breaking the spiral of self-fulfilling prophecy.

Goffman's (1959) study of social interaction focused closely on everyday situations in which people try to manage the impressions others have of them. They interpret each other's intentions, attempt to influence one another, and create and sustain a good impression of themselves by presenting a front or keeping face. In *The Presentation of Self in Everyday Life*, Goffman uses the extended metaphor of theater and concepts such as performance, role, learning a script, playing a part, props (clothes, etc.), and 'stage managing' events to ensure they give the right message. All these are powerful conceptual tools for understanding interactions in schools.

The situations Goffman describes frequently involve inequalities of power, such that more powerful individuals are able to define and interpret the actions of subordinates; the subordinates in their turn struggle either to maintain a good impression, to challenge the validity of the definition, or, more commonly, pursue a complex strategy of outward conformity to the rules imposed by superiors while creating shared messages of resistance among peers. The struggle to maintain self-respect is studied with greater intensity by Goffman (1963) in *Stigma: Notes on the Management of Spoiled Identity*, which again has relevance for many school situations. Humiliation by a teacher in front of other students has to be challenged in order to maintain peer respect, even at the cost of putting at risk one's place in the school.

In the introduction to *Asylums*, Goffman (1968[1961]) defines 'total institutions' as places where individuals expect to reside for long periods of time—mental hospitals, barracks, monasteries, prisons, or boarding schools. Entry into such institutions often requires a shedding of the identity one has developed in the outside world and an adjustment to apparently arbitrary and meaningless norms. The adjustments to life in total institutions are challenging enough, but, as we argued earlier, the daily transitions in and out of a normal school can be even more wearing and conflictual, especially where there is a wide gap between the culture of the school and the customs of the neighborhood.

It has been a long time since the publication of such classic ethnographic studies of schooling as those of Stephen Ball (1981), David Hargreaves (1967), and best known of all, Paul Willis in *Learning to Labour* (1977). We believe Goffman's concepts provide rich insights when applied to observations of schools serving neighborhoods of poverty within the present circumstance of marketized schools. We can learn a great deal, too, from the approaches pioneered in Spain by the CREA network, which directly involve members of marginalized communities in research for educational change (see references in chapter 8).

Given the way schools are traditionally structured and the miscuing that occurs when schools fail to understand and connect to young lives, what frequently gets played out is cultural misunderstanding, miscommunication, and victim blaming—what Freebody, Ludwig, and Gunn (1995) refer to as "interactive trouble" (p. 297). What occurs as a consequence are variants of educational displacement, disconnection, disengagement, disaffection, and alienation among young people, and feelings of shame and failure on the part of families. All of this reinforces the sense of humiliation and futility in marginalized and poor communities. Through close observation of everyday encounters as well as critical incidents, viewed through the lens of symbolic interactionism, we may achieve a better understanding of the struggle for mutual understanding and the sources of confusion surrounding the exchange and processing of knowledge.

Rethinking Schools for Social Justice

All of this impels us to argue for quite a different way of doing education—one in which the structure and culture of schools and what goes on in them are radically reconstructed. We have seen many fine examples of schools in these contexts that work in ways that are respectful, that recognize differences and celebrate successes, that acknowledge multiple ways of learning, employing improvisational rather than homogenized or standardized ways of teaching. There are common principles and values, but no blueprint: 'what worked' yesterday may not work today.

Making a difference, therefore, involves *actively recognizing difference* by:

- listening openly to the lives of young people

- valuing and respecting communities with their histories, cultures, and aspirations

- employing pedagogies that are connected to the local but open up an understanding of the complex effects of global issues.

In our previous writings we have used various labels to characterize these schools: schools of hope (Wrigley, 2003) or the socially just school (Smyth, 2004; Smyth, 2012; Smyth, 2013; Smyth, Down & McInerney, 2010; Smyth, Angus, et al., 2009), and similar labels invoked by others (May, 1994; Goodman, 1992; Vibert et al., 2001, to mention just a few). We are not referring here to the whole gamut of alternative schools, though these can be inspirational in exploring and modeling very different forms of organization and modes of learning. Rather we have in mind the diverse manifestations of a socially just philosophy we have found in ordinary schools that teachers, students, and families have had the imagination to transform. The specifics may be diverse, but they are expressions of a remarkably similar nexus of underlying values and pedagogical beliefs.

The authors of this book began to develop our thinking separately but at roughly the same time. For Smyth, the journey of articulating what this orientation might look like began seriously in *Schooling for a Fair Go* (Smyth, Hattam & Lawson, 1998). It drew its title from the Australian idiom of "a fair go," referring to egalitarian support for the underdog (the expected loser) in any competitive context. The notion of 'a fair go' is steeped in Australian mythology, but in essence it captures the popular view that people should not be excluded from participation in culture, work, sport, or other pursuits because of class, race, gender, or sexual orientation. It is a value statement that is often more imaginary than real in the way social structures are created and sustained, and Australia has one of the most inequitable education systems anywhere in the Western world despite all its egalitarian exhortations. In espousing 'a fair go', it is important not to fall into a meritocratic ideology of individual upward mobility for a few, though schools must make this possible. However we also need to look at how schools can improve the collective lives of all their students (see, for example, the schools described in Smyth, 2013).

For Wrigley, the ideas began to emerge when visiting successful multiethnic inner-city schools. Despite a control and surveillance approach to school improvement pervading the wider school system, the culture in these schools was a very genuine kind of empowerment, hence the title *The Power to Learn* (Wrigley, 2000). The ten case studies became an exploration of the many different ways in which respectful and motivating attitudes were being realized in the different areas of school life: ethos and organization, curriculum, pedagogy, connections with the wider community, and the change process itself.

Systems of Inequality

The scope of teachers and school leaders to respond to inequalities of class and to the needs of young people in poverty can be heavily constrained by the education system they have to operate within. Somewhat hypocritically, systems that actively reinforce inequalities often operate under cover of a rhetoric demanding improved attainment from the most disadvantaged.

Australia displays one of the most deformed and grotesque social distortions of any country in the world, with almost 40 percent of secondary-aged children attending nonpublic (independent and Catholic) schools, reflecting the unrestrained operation of school choice and marketization. Public schools are at a very grave risk of becoming residualized ghettoes.

All parts of Britain are also marked by high levels of inequality and family poverty, producing major differences in attainment. England, where pupils with free meal entitlement have only half as much chance of a successful outcome at age 16, has experienced the systematic undermining of comprehensive secondary schools and a rapid handover of schools to private corporations. The system actively encourages competition between schools rather than collaboration, including naming and shaming less successful schools, which are predominantly located in poorer neighborhoods.

Both education systems, exceeded only by the United States, exemplify versions of the Global Educational Reform Movement or *GERM*, as Pasi Sahlberg (2011, pp. 99–106) has called it. Sahlberg contrasts this approach to school governance and development with the highly successful collaborative approaches of his native Finland. The dogged commitment to market competition and corporatist forms of accountability that characterize GERM, and that have influenced policy in many countries to varying degrees, is neither edifying nor a sustainable pathway to be following. In particular, there is great confusion between data collection to identify the need for support (whether for individuals or for schools), and data collection designed to segregate individuals and punish schools.

Things need not be this way, and the fact that these powerful English-speaking countries manifest shamefully high levels of inequality yet appear deaf to any alternatives says much about the ideologically driven nature of this particular reform paradigm. The lessons from Finland could not be more stark, and while impossible to transplant or copy, they stand as demonstrable evidence that a commitment to equitable school provision and more democratic systems of quality control pays off handsomely in high levels of achievement and without any of the social disfigurement experienced in countries where schooling is blighted by the neoliberal project.

Some Principles of Renewal

The dominant neoliberal model of school evaluation and improvement (Sahlberg's GERM model) is characterized by managerial*ism*. By this we do not wish to condemn skillful management or enlightened leadership, but rather a blind reliance on top-down direction that has emerged from marketized school systems. Education systems that use assessment data not to prompt respectful and supportive intervention but to shame schools into improving scores, produce headteachers who respond through ad hoc and often ill-informed 'improvements'.

By contrast, our starting point has been to learn from schools that genuinely create the 'power to learn' through all aspects of the way they work: school ethos, relationships, and organization; relationships with the wider community; curriculum and pedagogy; and the change process.

The process of school self-evaluation (MacBeath, 1999; MacBeath et al., 2000) is fundamental to a reorientation of school change and needs to be intelligently focused on questions of social justice. While we wince somewhat at the language of *audit,* we think a smart game can be played in speaking back to the neoliberal project on our own terms through a "social justice audit" (Gewirtz, 2002, p. 138).

The notion of *what to look for* in a socially just school (Smyth, Lawson & Hattam, 1998, pp. 115–24) is meant as a practical heuristic to help us interrogate why education is not working for the increasing numbers of young people who are being shunted to the margins. In line with the central arguments in this book, we suggest that such an enquiry should have in mind:

1. the tangled and confused nexus between the new realities of adolescent lives and the out-of-touch realities of educational policy regimes;

2. the complex set of processes and pressures impacting young lives, with particular reference to poverty, social class, and schooling;

3. the conflicting explanations, variously locating the problem outside and inside schools, that are shaping and affecting young people living on the edge; and

4. the driving need to counter the sense of shame and futility that blights the lives of many young people, through educational relationships and practices that are *respectful, affirmative, identity building, engaging, meaningful,* and *hopeful.*

We turn now to explore these in more detail with reference to what a socially just school ought to look like. We should reiterate that these are not ideas plucked from the air but derive from the many fine schools we have been privileged to visit and be involved with.

Ethos: Enacting Democratic Forms of Practice

In all the activities and encounters within the school, there is an overwhelming emphasis on relationships of respect, trust, and care. This is based on positive interactions with students which acknowledge the diversity and richness of their talents, articulated through active (and activist) forms of learning. Schools should be places in which unforced agreements can be negotiated, including the curriculum. In particular, the school should be struggling to open up spaces for the voices of the most disenfranchised members of the school community.

Socially just schools should be safe and welcoming spaces for the interaction of all their members. This involves developing a culture where pejorative representations of gender and sexualities, physical characteristics, ethnic and cultural differences, and families affected by poverty, are openly challenged. Students should be able to engage actively in discussion of school policies and practices and carry the outcomes of these discussions through their representatives to the school decision-making body.

The philosophical principle is that debate, contestation, and discussion should be a normal part of the life of the school. Cooperation is a key organizational, curricular, and pedagogical concept; there is a strong belief that more will be gained through working together than competing.

The approach to school organization emphasizes flexibility, with students being treated as adults, and processes and structures that 'fit around' students. Behavior management policies are developed inclusively, and school culture is presented as a genuine alternative to the more damaging aspects of street culture experienced by some young people. Relational and resource inequalities are not tolerated but are confronted, exposed, and challenged.

Questions of school size and structure can be particularly important to marginalized or vulnerable young people, including those experiencing poverty. Their success and engagement, and ability to overcome crises, depend on close relationships with supportive adults. This is difficult to achieve in very large schools, or where students lack a smaller learning community where they feel at home. The traditional organization of the secondary school curriculum, whereby students have twelve to fifteen different teachers, makes it difficult to cater in any coherent way for the complex academic and social needs of more vulnerable young people.

Schools need to find new ways of recognizing value in diversity and building aspirational and reflective identities within a pedagogic community. Instead of segregating students of different levels of prior attainment into separate groups and classes, a variety of formations should be explored for interactive and cooperative learning within the wider learning community of the school.

The atmosphere in the classroom and the school should emphasize possibilities arising from learning, the reward that comes from understanding what the world is like, how it came to be that way, how things work, what could be done differently, and how everyone might share more fully and equitably. So, we expect students to be excited about the discoveries they are making, to show pride in the outcomes of their investigations, and to be eager to engage this learning in discussion with parents, along with actions that might help to change the wider world.

Being Community-Minded

Socially just schools strive to achieve a shared consciousness of the situated and located nature of the learning process. This involves working to be relevant to the community around the school, and being partisan in response to local people's struggles to live worthwhile lives within a wider culture of solidarity, teamwork, partnership, and collaboration. It also means breaking the hermetic seal that frequently contains school life and instead regarding communities as *having* and *being* significant "funds of knowledge" (Moll et al., 1992). Establishing school projects based in the community, or adults learning in the school, helps engender community trust in the school.

Schools of hope regard themselves as located in the immediate society and responsive to its needs. They also have a global perspective so that students engage in practical and ethical discovery and action across both these levels. The curriculum should include opportunities to examine problems posed by community representatives and offer responses and solutions. It should develop young people as active citizens and enable them to work intellectually and critically on their social and environmental concerns.

The principles underpinning school ethos extend to, and are influenced by, the school's relationship with the wider community. Conceived in this way, schools need to provide spaces and structures within which teachers and the wider community can discuss and develop policy and practice. Such gatherings allow for the critical examination of policy and practice, for the expression of different views, and for working through issues. Where schools are planned to serve a range of functions in addition to young people's learning, and particularly where there is democratic control of adult learning and social provision, it becomes easier to engage parents as equal partners in their children's learning and to involve them in school activities and curriculum.

The Curriculum and Pedagogy

In reconstructing the school curriculum, we need to find a positive reconciliation of conflicting needs. It must:

- be meaningful to young people but provide them with knowledge for adult life;

- provide for their development as free citizens as well as opening up possibilities for satisfying employment;

- build on and relate to local knowledge, including ethnic and youth cultures, while opening up wider horizons;

- enable learners to acquire key skills of literacy, numeracy, and ICT within meaningful contexts, and to overcome any limitations of technique while engaging with challenging and interesting ideas and activities; and

- initiate them into the knowledge and methods associated with major academic disciplines while developing a capacity for critical reading of established beliefs and dominant ideologies.

The curriculum should maintain a balanced response to the various aims of education. This means avoiding an early division into academic and vocational tracks. It should avoid the danger of vocational studies displacing social studies and creative arts, and should also develop a critical approach to familiarization with the world of work. As a result of our experiences of successful schools in challenging environments, we place a high value on a critical understanding of the natural and social world, and of students learning to express themselves through various media, including print, ICT, and the creative and performing arts.

Assessment needs to be formative and authentic, providing helpful feedback for future learning rather than labeling and segregating and instead be linked to meaningful activities for all students. Models of authentic assessment such as 'rich tasks' based on investigations, challenges, and presentations provide alternatives to individual competitive exams. Such assessment processes also enable the connection of knowledge and skills from different disciplines along with community-based knowledge.

Teaching that empowers learners avoids the set routines of pedagogies of poverty (an excess of direct instruction, closed questions which invite two or three word answers, and individual practice through decontextualized exercises). To avoid demotivation through alienated learning, students of all ages should be involved in discussing the what, how, and why of learning; they should learn high-level academic concepts in familiar and interesting contexts; be engaged in problem solving; and work toward meaningful and motivating products, presentations, and performances.

To increase opportunities for students to exercise voice and agency, a range of open architectures should be investigated, for example, project method, storyline, design challenges, media production, simulations, expeditionary, and place-based learning. Learning should not be a mysterious activity. Students should be engaged in finding out about their own and other people's lives. In other words, learning needs to be driven by an overwhelming culture of curiosity where taking risks and failing is a normal course of events. This requires the gradual acquisition of more rigorous methods of enquiry: acquiring frameworks for perception; knowing how to analyze information, transform it, and store it in an accessible way; being able to search for and use it to solve and resolve problems; learning how to present findings in satisfying and interesting ways so as to engage others.

Students will gradually understand that they can regulate their own learning and that there are multiple pathways to completing tasks. Reflecting on how learning occurs is crucial. Teachers in these schools are only one of many sources of learning—who teaches and who has expertise depends upon the circumstances. Pedagogical expertise is not fixed—it all depends on the issues and the situation.

The education of democratic citizens requires critical and political literacies, not just functional skills training that leads to technical literacy. Schools must be centrally concerned with literacies for active local and global citizenship, including a critical view of the world of work. Learning to read and write should be based on an understanding that literacy is a social practice and that making meaning requires "reading the world and the word" (Freire & Macedo, 1987). Put another way, reading is about interpretation, how things are constructed, and how they came to be that way: even the simplest narratives require us to bring a reading of the world to the words.

The Change Process: Meaningful Collaboration and Purposeful Leadership

School development oriented to social justice requires meaningful collaboration among the teachers but also involving other staff, students, and parents (see Smyth, 1990). As McLaughlin (1990) put it: "You can't mandate what matters" (p. 12), an idea subsequently popularized by Fullan (1993). In other words, the effectiveness of governing by command and instruction is limited to trivial change; real transformation requires deeper understanding arrived at through open debate. The necessary critical challenge to unjust norms and harmful cultures is stifled by authoritarian management and education systems.

The commitments we have listed so far need to be held together in the organization of the school and developed across time. This task of development and coherence is a function of leadership but should not be understood only in terms of senior administrative positions: many teachers in the successful schools we have studied contribute significantly to the leadership of the school, though invariably the principals and deputies play key roles. An important source of leadership is found in colleagues who enjoy a close community involvement, as well as students and influential community members.

Schools that experience success against the odds show a close engagement with the complex and often troubled realities of students and their families but also a willingness to innovate thoughtfully and an openness to new ideas and practices. Though the words *vision, mission,* and *values* have often been trivialized in school improvement literature, the level of reflection they suggest is indispensable in any worthwhile process of educational change. This is a philosophical and cultural process, involving a grappling with meanings, the meanings of words and actions, the significance of everyday phenomena often taken for granted, the aims of education, the direction of social change, and our hopes for the society and world we inhabit (Wrigley et al., 2012).

Leaders do not need to be charismatic. They do need a clear sense of purpose, strongly held values, and a sense of vision—that things can become different than they are (Smyth, 1989). Crucially, they encourage others to contribute *their* ideas and influence. Working in challenging situations requires a close relationship with local people and a "helicopter view of leadership that can see both in the distance and up close" (Wrigley, 2000, p. 160). Enormous value is derived from drawing on the experience and initiative of those closest to the local community, whether support staff, parents, or students themselves.

Hierarchy, regardless of how it is expressed—status, position, gender, race, ethnicity, class, age—will be continually challenged in schools committed to social justice. Unless this occurs, we will find "corrosive leadership" (Thornton,

2004) that contradicts and undermines the spirit of justice supposedly driving the school's educational work. Sometimes the struggle for social justice requires the courage and preparedness to challenge undemocratic relations and dogmatic viewpoints (Smyth, Down & McInerney, 2010, p. 206).

The democratic, critically engaged school has effective policies and procedures for including all students and protecting their rights. All students are expected to succeed, and the school provides the resources and structures that allow this expectation to be fulfilled for all students across the full range of abilities and activities. Education and schooling should be a way toward economic capability for independence in adult life for all students.

Teachers need to share and develop ways of teaching and learning that will help to overcome barriers to learning. Their professional development should be collaborative and critical, involving self-evaluation and peer support through observation and coaching (Smyth, 1990). It needs to be well grounded in practice within the school but open to new ideas from outside. Like their students, they should be excited about the discoveries they make. We are not arguing here for mere concern with the avant-garde or the popular. We are pointing to the importance of building on students' desires to understand their world and to act on it in ways that change it—in other words, innovation, thoughtful experimentation, and a willingness to take some risks.

Final Words

This returns us to our central concern with overcoming the sense of humiliation and futility from living on the edge. We must acknowledge the difficulties faced by schools in areas of poverty, despite politicians who compound the problem of marginalization by attacking those who teach there.

We recognize the central need to transform economic relations based on exploitation and a monopoly of power. At the same time, we need to find respectful ways of challenging faulty expectations, norms, and pedagogies that help to reproduce poverty and marginalization.

We need to find new ways of reasserting a sense of possibility and hope and rising to the challenge posed by poverty in affluent countries.

Since social justice cannot be achieved by schools alone, this will involve new combinations of action within schools and in the wider society. We have to exert collective power to bring about serious change in schools and struggle alongside marginalized young people for their right to life beyond the edge.

References

Adey, P., & Shayer, M. (1994). *Really raising standards*. London: Routledge.

Ainscow, M. (2010). Achieving excellence and equity: Reflections on the development of practices in one local district over 10 years. *School Effectiveness and School Improvement, 21*(1), 75–92.

Alexiu, T., & Sordé, T. (2011). How to turn difficulties into opportunities: Drawing from diversity to promote social cohesion. *International Studies in Sociology of Education, 21*(1), 49–62.

Allen, J., Massey, D., & Cochrane, A. (1998). *Rethinking the region*. London: Routledge.

Alvesson, M. (2002). *Understanding organizational culture*. London: Sage.

Angus, L. (1993). The sociology of school effectiveness. *British Journal of Sociology of Education, 14*(3), 333–345.

Anyon, J. (1981). Social class and school knowledge. *Curriculum Inquiry, 11*(1), 3–43.

———. (2005) *Radical possibilities: Public policy, urban education and a new social movement*. New York: Routledge.

Appadurai, A. (1996). *Modernity at large: Cultural dimensions of globalization*. Minneapolis: University of Minnesota Press.

———. (2004). The capacity to inspire: Culture and the terms of recognition. In V. Rao & M. Walton (Eds.), *Culture and public action* (pp. 59–84). Stanford, CA: Stanford University Press.

Araújo, M. (2007). "Modernising the comprehensive principle": Selection, setting and the institutionalisation of educational failure. *British Journal of Sociology of Education, 28*(2), 241–257.

Aronson, R. (2001). When at-risk students defy the odds. *Improving Schools, 4/3*, 9–22.

ATD Fourth World. (2000). *Participation works: Involving people in poverty in policy making*. London: ATD Fourth World, http://www.atd-uk.org/resources/uk

Atkinson, R. (1999). Discourse of partnership and empowerment in contemporary British urban regeneration. *Urban Studies, 36*(1), 59–72.

Au, W. (2009). *Unequal by design: High-stakes testing and the standardization of inequality*. London: Routledge.

Ball, S. (1981). *Beachside comprehensive*. Cambridge: Cambridge University Press.

———. (1986). The sociology of the school: Streaming and mixed-ability and social class. In R. Rogers (Ed.), *Education and social class* (pp. 83–100). London: Falmer.

———. (2003). *Class strategies and the education market: The middle classes and social advantage*. London: RoutledgeFalmer.

———. (2006). The risks of social reproduction: The middle class and education markets. In S. Ball (Ed.), *Education policy and social class: The selected works of Stephen J. Ball* (pp. 264–276). London: Routledge.

———. (2008). *The education debate*. Bristol, UK: Policy.

———. (2013) The education debate 2nd edition. Bristol: Policy Press

Ball, S., & Vincent, C. (1998). "I heard it on the grapevine": "Hot" knowledge and school choice. *British Journal of Sociology of Education, 19*(3), 377–400.

Bangs, J., MacBeath, J., & Galton, M. (2011). *Reinventing schools, reforming teaching: From political visions to classroom reality*. London: Routledge.

Barnes, D., Britton, J., Rosen, H., & LATE. (1969). *Language, the learner and the school* (Rev. ed.). Harmondsworth: Penguin.

Bauder, H. (2001). Culture in the labour market: Segmentation theory and perspective of place. *Progress in Human Geography, 25*(1), 37–52.

Bauman, Z. (1998). *Work, consumerism and the new poor*. Buckingham, UK: Open University Press.

———. (2001). *Community: Seeking safety in an insecure world*. Cambridge: Polity.

———. (2011). *Collateral damage: Social inequalities in a global age*. Cambridge: Polity.

Baumert, J., & Schümer, G. (2002). Family background, selection and achievement: The German experience. *Improving Schools 5*(3), pp. 13–120.

BBC News website. (2008, September 30). Millions of UK young in poverty.

BBC News website. (2012, February 21). Pooper Store. [quoting Nick Clegg].

BBC News website. (2012, August 3). Olympics "dominated by privately educated." www.bbc.co.uk/mews/education-19109724

Beck-Gernsheim, E. (1996). Life as a planning project. In C. Lash, B. Szersynski & B. Wynne (Eds.), *Risk, environment and modernity* (pp. 139–153). London: Sage.

Bell, S., Harkness, S., & White, G. (2007). *Storyline past, present and future*. Glasgow: University of Strathclyde.

Benn, M. (2011). *School wars: The battle for Britain's education*. London: Verso.

Bereiter, C., & Engelmann, S. (1966). *Teaching disadvantaged children in the preschool*. Eaglewood Cliffs, NJ: Prentice-Hall.

Bereiter, C., Engelmann, S., Osborn, J., & Reidford, P. (1966). An academically oriented pre-school for culturally deprived children. In F. Hechinger (Ed.), *Pre-school education today: New approaches to teaching three-, four- and five-year-olds* (pp. 105–135). New York: Doubleday.

Bernstein, B. (1971) *Class, codes and control. Vol. 1: Theoretical studies towards a sociology of language*. London: Routledge and Kegan Paul.

———. (1972). A critique of the concept of compensatory education. In B. Cazden, V. John & D. Hymes (Eds.), *Functions of language in the classroom* (pp. 135–151). New York: Teachers College Press.

———. (1975). *Class, codes and control: Towards a theory of educational transmissions*. London: Routledge & Kegan Paul.

———. (1986). A sociolinguistic approach to socialization; with some reference to educability. In J. Gumperz & D. Hymes (Eds.), *Directions in sociolinguistics: The ethnography of communication* (pp. 465–497). New York: Blackwell.

Binet, A. (1905). Various papers published in *L'Annee Psychologique 12*.

——. (1973[1909]) Les idées modernes sur les enfants (with preface by Jean Piaget). Paris: Flammarion.

Bisseret, N. (1979). *Education, class language and ideology*. London: Routledge & Kegan Paul.

Blair, M., & Bourne, J. (1998). *Making the difference: Teaching and learning strategies in successful multi-ethnic schools*. Sudbury, UK: DfEE/Open University.

Blair, T. (1998). *The third way: New politics for the new century. Fabian Pamphlet 588*. London: Fabian Society.

Blumer, H. (1969). *Symbolic interactionism: Perspective and method*. Berkeley: University of California Press.

Boaler, J., William, D., & Brown, M. (2000). Students' experiences of ability grouping—disaffection, polarisation and the construction of failure. *British Educational Research Journal 26*(5), 631–648.

Bok, J. (2010). The capacity to aspire to higher education: "It's like making them do a play without a script." *Critical Studies in Education, 51*(2), 163–178.

Bomer, R., Dworin, J., May, L., & Semingson, P. (2008). Miseducating teachers about the poor: A critical analysis of Ruby Payne's claims about poverty. *Teachers College Record, 110*(12), 2497–2531.

Boring, E. (1923). Intelligence as the tests test it. *New Republic, 34*, 35–36.

Boulton, J. (1979). *The letters of D. H. Lawrence, Vol. 1*. Cambridge: Cambridge University Press.

Bourdieu, P. (1977). *Outline of a theory of practice*. Cambridge: Cambridge University Press.

——. (1984a). *Distinction: A social critique of the judgment of taste*. London: Routledge.

——. (1984b). Social space and the genisis of "classes." Reprinted in Bourdieu, P. *Language and symbolic power*. Cambridge: Polity.

——. (1991). Social space and the genesis of "classes." In J. B. Thompson (Ed.), *Language and symbolic power* (pp. 229–51). Cambridge, MA: Polity.

Bourdieu, P., Accardo, A., et al. (Eds.). (1999). *The weight of the world: Social suffering in contemporary society*. Cambridge, MA: Polity.

Bourdieu, P., & Wacquant, L. (1992). *An invitation to reflexive sociology*. Chicago: University of Chicago Press.

——. (2001). Neoliberal newspeak: Notes on the new planetary vulgate. *Radical Philosophy, 105*. http://loicwacquant.net/assets/Papers/NEOLIBERALNEWSPEAK.pdf

Bowles, S., & Nelson, V. (1974). The inheritance of IQ and the intergenerational reproduction of economic inequality. *Review of Economics and Statistics, 56*, 39–51.

Boyte, H. (1989). *Commonwealth: A return to citizen politics*. New York: Free Press.

Bradbury, B., & Jäntti, M. (1999). *Child poverty across industrialised nations. Innocenti Occasional Papers, Economic and Social Policy Series No. 71*. Florence: UNICEF.

Bradley, R., Corwyn, R., McAdoo, H., & Coll, C. (2001). The home environments of children in the United States. Part 1: Variations by age, ethnicity and poverty status. *Child Development, 27*(6), 1844–1867.

Bradshaw, J. (2000). Child poverty in comparative perspective. In D. Gordon & P. Townsend (Eds.), *Breadline Europe* (pp. 223–250). Bristol, UK: Policy Press.

——. (2011). *Growing up in Scotland: Changes in child cognitive ability in the pre-school years*. Edinburgh: Scottish Executive Education Department.

Bromley, C. (2009). *Growing up in Scotland: The impact of children's early activities on cognitive development*. Edinburgh: Scottish Executive Education Department.

Brookover, W., Schweitzer, J., Schneider, J., Beady, C., Flood, P., & Wisenbaker, J. (1978). Elementary school social climate and school achievement. *American Educational Research Journal, 15*(2), 301–318.

Brown, P. (2006). The opportunity trap. In H. Lauder, P. Brown, J.-A. Dillabough & A. Halsey (Eds.), *Education, globalization and social change* (pp. 381–97). Oxford: Oxford University Press.

Burchardt, T. (2000). *Enduring economic exclusion: Disabled people, income and work.* York, UK: Joseph Rowntree Foundation.

———. (2003). *Being and becoming: Social exclusion and the onset of disability.* London: CASE.

Carter-Wall, C., & Whitfield, G. (2012). *The role of aspirations, attitudes and behaviour in closing the educational attainment gap.* York, UK: Joseph Rowntree Foundation.

Cassen, R., & Kingdon, G. (2007). *Tackling low educational achievement.* York, UK: Joseph Rowntree Foundation.

Castro, J. (1971). Untapped verbal fluency of black schoolchildren. In E. Leacock (Ed.), *The culture of poverty: A critique* (pp. 81–108). New York: Simon & Schuster.

Cavalcanti, R., Goldsmith, C., Lea, J., Measor, L., Squires, P., & Wolff, D. (2011). *Youth and community: Connections and disconnections.* Arts & Humanities Research Council, UK: Connected Communities Programme.

Chadderton, C., & Colley, H. (2012). School-to-work transition services: Marginalising "disposable" youth in a state of exception? *Discourse Studies in the Cultural Politics of Education, 33*(3), 329–343.

Chamberlayne, P., & Rustin, M. (1999). *From biography to social policy.* London: Centre for Biography in Social Policy.

Charlesworth, S. (2000). *A phenomenology of working class experience.* Cambridge: Cambridge University Press.

Child Poverty Action Group. (2011). *Poverty in the UK: A summary of facts and figures.* Retrieved November 2011, from http://www.cpag.org.uk/povertyfacts

Chitty, C. (2009). *Eugenics, race and intelligence in education.* London: Continuum.

Christou, M., & Puigvert, L. (2011). The role of "other women" in current educational transformations. *International Studies in Sociology of Education, 21*(1), 77–90.

Ciupak, Y., & Stich, A. (2012). The changing educational opportunity structure in China: Positioning for access to higher education. In L. Weis & N. Dolby (Eds.), *Social class and education: Global perspectives.* New York: Routledge.

Coard, B. (1971). *How the West Indian child is made educationally subnormal in the British school system: The scandal of the black child in schools in Britain.* London: New Beacon for the Caribbean Education and Community Workers' Association.

Coleman, J. (1966). *Equality of educational opportunity.* Washington, DC: Government Printing Office.

———. (1973). Equality of opportunity and equality of results. *Harvard Educational Review, 43*(1), 129–137.

Conchas, G., & Rodriguez, L. (2008). *Small schools and urban youth: Using the power of school culture to engage students.* Thousand Oaks, CA: Corwin.

Condron, D. (2011) Egalitarianism and educational excellence: Compatible goals for affluent societies? *Educational Researcher.* 40, 47–55.

Connell, R. W. (1989). Cool guys, swots and wimps: The interplay of masculinity and education. *Oxford Review of Education, 15*(3), 291–303.

Cowburn, W. (1986). *Class, ideology and community education.* London: Croom Helm.

Craig, G. (2002). Ethnicity, racism and the labour market: A European perspective. In J. Anderson & P. Jensen (Eds.), *Labour markets, welfare, policies and citizenship* (pp. 149–181). Bristol, UK: Policy.

Creegan, C. (2008). *Opportunity and aspiration: Two sides of the same coin?* York, UK: Joseph Rowntree Foundation.

Cruikshank, B. (1999). *The will to empower: Democratic citizens and other subjects.* Ithaca, NY: Cornell University Press.

Cummins, J. (1997). *Negotiating identities: Education for empowerment in a diverse society.* Stoke-on-Trent, UK: Trentham.

———. (2003). Challenging the construction of difference as deficit: Where are identity, intellect, imagination, and power in the new regime of truth? In P. Trifonas (Ed.), *Pedagogies of difference: Rethinking education for social change* (pp. 41–60). London: Routledge.

Daly, M., & Leonard, M. (2002). *Against all odds: Family life on a low income in Ireland.* Dublin: Institute of Public Administration/Combat Poverty Agency.

Daniel, P., & Ivatts, J. (1998). *Children and social policy.* Basingstoke, UK: Macmillan.

Darling-Hammond, L. (2010) *The flat world and education: How America's commitment to equity will determine our future.* New York: Teachers College Press.

Darling-Hammond, L., Barron, B., Pearson, D., Schoenfeld, A., Stage, E., Zimmerman, T., et al. (2008). *Powerful learning: What we know about teaching for understanding.* San Francisco: Jossey-Bass.

Davis, A., & Hill, P. (2001). *Poverty, social exclusion and mental health.* London: Mental Health Foundation.

Davis, M. (2006). *Planet of slums.* London: Verso.

Deal, T., & Peterson, K. (1999). *Shaping school culture: The heart of leadership.* San Francisco: Jossey-Bass.

Delpit, L. (1995). *Other people's children: Cultural conflict in the classroom.* New York: New Press.

Department for Children Schools and Families (DCSF). (2007). *The children's plan.* London: Stationery Office.

Department for Education (DfE). (2010). *The importance of teaching: Schools white paper.* CM 7980. London: DfE.

Department for Education and Employment (DfEE). (1997). *Excellence in schools.* London: HMSO.

Department for Work and Pensions. (2012). *Households below average income 2010/2011.* London: Department of Work and Pensions.

Department of Education. (2011). *Michael Gove: Face reality, reform urgently.* Speech to national College for School Leadership June 2011. Retrieved December 3, 2012, from http://www.education.gov.uk/inthenews/inthenews/a0077837/michael-gove-face-reality-reform-urgently

Department of Environment, Transport and Regions. (2000). *Our towns and cities: The future—delivering an urban renaissance.* London: HMSO.

Devine, F., & Savage, M. (2005). The cultural turn, sociology and class analysis. In F. Devine, M. Savage, M. Scott, & R. Crompton (Eds.), *Rethinking class: Culture, identities and lifestyle* (pp. 1–23). London: Palgrave Macmillan.

Dickens, C. (1989 [1849]). *Hard times.* Oxford: Oxford University Press.

Diez, J., Gatt, S., & Racionero, S. (2011). Placing immigrant and minority family and community members at the school's centre: The role of community participation. *European Journal of Education, 46*(2), 184–196.

Dillabough, J.-A., Kennelly, J., & Wang, E. (2007). Warehousing young people in urban Canadian schools: Gender, peer rivalry and spatial containment. In K. Gulson & C. Symes (Eds.), *Spatial theories of education: Policy and geography matters* (pp. 131–154). London & New York: Routledge.

Dixon, A. (1989). Deliver us from eagles. In G. Barrett (Ed.), *Disaffection from school* (pp. 13–24). London: Routledge.

Douglas, J. (1964). *The home and the school: A study of ability and attainment in the primary school.* London: MacGibbon & Kee.

Dowler, E., & Leather, S. (2000). Spare some change for a bite to eat? In J. Bradshaw & R. Sainsbury (Eds.), *Experiencing poverty* (pp. 200–218). Aldershot, UK: Ashgate.

Drucker, E. (1971). Cognitive styles and class stereotypes. In E. Leacock (Ed.), *The culture of poverty: A critique* (pp. 41–62). New York: Simon & Schuster.

Drucker, P. (1994). *Post-capitalist society*. New York: HarperBusiness.

Drummond, M. (1993). *Assessing children's learning*. London: David Fulton.

Dudley-Marling, C. (2007). Return of the deficit. *Journal of Educational Controversy* (www.wce.wwu.edu/eJournal)

Dudley-Marling, C., & Paugh, P. (2005). The rich get richer; the poor get direct instruction. In B. Altwerger (Ed.), *Reading for profit* (pp. 156–171). Portsmouth, NH: Heinemann.

Dunne, M., Humphreys, S., Sebba, J., Dyson, A., Gallannaugh, F., & Muijs, D. (2007). *Effective teaching and learning for pupils in low attaining groups*. London: Department for Children, Schools and Families, Research Report DCSF-RR011.

Eagleton, T. (2000). *The idea of culture*. Oxford: Blackwell.

———. (2011). *Why Marx was right*. New Haven, CT: Yale University Press.

Editors (1973). Perspectives on inequality. *Harvard Educational Review, 43*(1), 37–50.

Edmonds, R., Billingsley, A., Comer, J., Dyer, J., Hall, W., Hill, R., et al. (1973). A black response to Christopher Jencks's inequality and certain other issues. *Harvard Educational Review, 43*(1), 76–91.

Edwards, A. (1976). *Language in culture and class*. London: Heinemann.

Edwards, J. (1970). *Language and disadvantage*. London: Arnold.

Eggleston, J. (1996). *Teaching design and technology*. Buckingham: Open University Press.

Ehrenreich, B. (1989). *Fear of falling: The inner life of the middle class*. New York: Pantheon.

Entwistle, H. (1978). *Class, culture and education*. London: Methuen.

Farrell, C., & O'Connor, W. (2003). *Low income families and household spending*. Leeds, UK: DWP/Corporate Document Services.

Feinstein, L. (2006). Social class and cognitive development in childhood in the UK. In H. Lauder, P. Brown, J.-A. Dillabough, & A. Halsey (Eds.), *Education, globalization and social change* (pp. 409–419). Oxford: Oxford University Press.

Feuerstein, R., Rand, Y., Hoffman, M., & Miller, M. (1980). *Instrumental enrichment: An intervention programme for cognitive modificability*. Baltimore: University Park Press.

Fielding, M. (1999). Target setting, policy pathology and student perspectives: Learning to labour in new times. *Cambridge Journal of Education, 29*(2), 277–87.

———. (2001a). Target setting, social pathology and student perspectives. In M. Fielding (Ed.), *Taking education really seriously: Four years hard labour* (pp. 143–154). London: RoutledgeFalmer.

———. (2001b). Student voice. Special issue of *Forum 43*(2).

Fine, B. (2010). Because you're worth it? *New Humanist, 125*(5). Retrieved November 8, 2012, from http://newhumanist.org.uk/2400/because-youre-worthit

Finn, J., & Achilles, C. (1999). Tennessee's class size study: Findings, implications and misconceptions. *Educational Evaluation and Policy Analysis, 21*, 97–110.

Finnan, C., St. John, E., McCarthy, J., & Slovacek, S. (1995). *Accelerated schools in action: Lessons from the field*. London: Corwin.

Fischer, C., Hout, M., Jankowski, M., Lucas, S., Swidler, A., & Voss, K. (1996). *Inequality by design: Cracking the bell curve myth*. Princeton, NJ: Princeton University Press.

Flecha, R. (2000). *Sharing words: Theory and practice of dialogic learning*. Lanham, MD: Rowman & Littlefield.

Flynn, J. (1999). Searching for justice: The discovery of IQ gains over time. *American Psychologist, 54*, 5–20.

Fordham, S., & Ogbu, J. (1986). Black students' school success: Coping with the burden of "acting white." *Urban Review, 18,* 176–206.

Foucault, M. (1977). *Discipline and punish: The birth of the prison* (A. Sheridan, Trans.). Harmondsworth: Penguin.

Fraser, N. (1997). *Justice interruptus: Critical reflections on the "postsocialist" condition.* London: Routledge.

———. (2000, May–June). Rethinking recognition. *New Left Review.* 107–20.

Fraser, N., & Hooneth, A. (2003). *Redistribution or recognition? A political-philosophical exchange.* London: Verso.

Freebody, P., Ludwig, C., & Gunn, S. (1995). *Everyday literacy practices in and out of schools in low socio-economic urban communities.* Vol. 1. Melbourne: Curriculum.

Freire, P. (1972). *Pedagogy of the oppressed.* Harmondsworth: Penguin.

Freire, P., & Macedo, D. (1987). *Literacy: Reading the word and the world.* South Hadley, MA: Bergin & Garvey.

Fullan, M. (1993). *Change forces: Probing the depth of educational reform.* London: Falmer.

Galloway, K. (2002). *A Scotland where everyone matters.* Manchester: Church Action on Poverty.

Galton, F. (1869). *Hereditary genius: An inquiry into its laws and consequences.* London: Macmillan.

Gamoran, A. (2004). Classroom organization and instructional quality. In M. Wang & J. Walberg (Eds.), *Can unlike students learn together? Grade retention, tracking and grouping* (pp. 141–155). Greenwich, CT: Information Age.

Gamoran, A., & Long, D. (2006). *Equality of educational opportunity: A 40-year retrospective.* Wisconsin Center for Education Research Working Paper no. 2006–9.

Gardner, H. (1983). *Frames of mind: The theory of multiple intelligences.* London: Fontana.

Gazeley, L., & Dunne, M. (2006). *Addressing working class underachievement.* http://www.multiverse.ac.uk/viewArticle.aspx?contentId=11862.

Gee, J. (2004). *Situated language and learning: A critique of traditional schooling.* London: Routledge.

Gewirtz, S. (2002). *The managerial school: Post-welfarism and social justice in education.* London & New York: Routledge.

Gibb, N. (2012, January 26). *New data reveals the truth about school performance.* London: Department for Education press notice.

Gieryn, T. (2000). A space for place in sociology. *Annual Review of Sociology, 26,* 463–496.

Gillborn, D., & Youdell, D. (2000). *Rationing education: Policy, practice, reform and equity.* Buckingham & Philadelphia: Open University Press.

Gilliat, S. (2001). *How the poor adapt to poverty in capitalism.* New York: Edwin Mellen.

Goddard, H. (1919). *Psychology of the normal and subnormal.* New York: Dodd, Mead.

Goffman, E. (1959). *Presentation of self in everyday life.* New York: Anchor.

———. (1963). *Stigma: Notes on the management of spoiled identity.* Englewood Cliffs, NJ: Prentice-Hall.

———. (1968 [1961]). *Asylums: Essays on the social situation of mental patients and other inmates.* New York: Doubleday.

Goldsmith, C. (2012, February). *"It just feels like it's always us": Young people, safety and community.* Paper presented at the Youth in Crisis Conference, University of the West of Scotland.

Gonzalez, N., Moll, L., & Amanti, C. (2005). *Funds of knowledge: Theorizing practices in household, communities and classrooms.* Mahwah, NJ: Lawrence Erlbaum.

Goodman, A., & Gregg, P. (2010). *The importance of attitudes and behaviour for poorer children's educational attainment.* York, UK: Joseph Rowntree Foundation.

Goodman, J. (1992). *Elementary schooling for critical democracy.* Albany: State University of New York Press.

Gordon, J. (1981). *Verbal deficit: A critique.* London: Croom Helm.

Gough, J., & Eisenschitz, A., with McCulloch, A. (2006). *Spaces of social exclusion*. London: Routledge.

Gould, S. (1983). *The panda's thumb*. Harmondsworth: Penguin.

———. (1996). *The mismeasure of man*. New York: W. W. Norton.

Grace, G. (Ed.). (1984). *Education and the city—Theory, history and contemporary practice*. London: Routledge & Kegan Paul.

Gregg, P., Harkness, S., & Machin, S. (1999). *Child development and family income*. York, UK: Joseph Rowntree Foundation.

Gunter, H. (2001). *Leaders and leadership in education*. London: Paul Chapman.

Gutman, L., & Feinstein, L. (2008). Parenting behaviours and children's development from infancy to early childhood: Changes, continuities and contributions. *Early Child Development and Care, 180*(4), 535–556.

Gutstein, E. (2012). Using critical mathematics to understand the conditions of our lives. In T. Wrigley, P. Thomson & B. Lingard (Eds.), *Changing schools: Alternative ways to make a world of difference* (pp. 181–193). London: Routledge.

Haberman, M. (1991). The pedagogy of poverty versus good teaching. *Phi Delta Kappan, 73*(4), 290–294.

———. (2010). Eleven consequences of failing to address the "pedagogy of poverty." *Phi Delta Kappan, 92*(2), 45.

Hall, S. (1974) Education and the crisis of the urban school. In J. Raynor (Ed.), *Issues in Urban Education* (pp. 7–17). Milton Keynes, Open University Press.

Hallam, S., & Toutounji, I. (1996). *What do we know about the groupings of pupils by ability?* London: Institute of Education.

Hargreaves, A. (1994). *Changing teachers, changing times: Teachers' work and culture in the postmodern age—Professional development and practice*. New York: Teachers College Press.

———. (2003). Professional learning communities and performance training cults: The emerging apartheid of school improvement. In A. Harris, et al. (Ed.), *Effective leadership for school improvement* (pp. 180–195). London: RoutledgeFalmer.

Hargreaves, A., & Fullan, M. (2012). *Professional capital: Transforming teaching in every school*. London: Routledge.

Hargreaves, D. (1967). *Social relations in a secondary school*. London: Routledge & Kegan Paul.

———. (1982). *The challenge for the comprehensive school*. London: Routledge & Kegan Paul.

Harrison, T. (2011). *An Australian "Rules for Radicals"—Community Activism and Genuine Empowerment*. Draft Doctor of Philosophy Degree, School of Education and Arts, University of Ballarat.

Hart, B., & Risley, T. (1995). *Meaningful differences in the everyday experience of young American children*. Baltimore: Paul Brookes.

Hart, B., and Risley, T. (2003). The early catastrophe: The 30 million word gap. *American Educator, 27*(1), pp 4-9

Hart, S. (1996). Differentiation and equal opportunities. In S. Hart (Ed.), *Differentiation and the secondary curriculum: Debates and dilemmas* (pp. 9–25). London: Routledge.

———. (2000). *Thinking through teaching*. London: David Fulton.

Hart, S., Dixon, A., Drummond, M., & McIntyre, D. (2004). *Learning without limits*. Maidenhead, UK: Open University Press.

Harvey, D. (1993). Class relations, social justice and the politics of difference. In M. Keith & S. Pile (Eds.), *Place and the politics of identity* (pp. 41–66). London: Routledge.

———. (1996). *Justice, nature and the geography of difference*. Oxford: Blackwell.

———. (2001). *Spaces of capital: Towards a critical geography*. Edinburgh: Edinburgh University Press.

————. (2005). *A brief history of neoliberalism.* Oxford: Oxford University Press.

Hattie, J. (2009). *Visible learning: A synthesis of over 800 meta-analyses relating to achievement.* London: Routledge.

Hayes, D., Mills, M., Christie, P., & Lingard, B. (2006). *Teachers and schooling making a difference: Productive pedagogies, assessment and performance.* Sydney: Allen & Unwin.

Haynes, J., Tikly, L., & Caballero, C. (2006). The barriers to achievement for white/black Caribbean pupils in English schools. *British Journal of Sociology of Education, 27*(5), 569–583.

Herrnstein, R., & Murray, C. (1994). *The bell curve: The reshaping of American life by difference in intelligence.* New York: Free Press.

Hill, M., Turner, K., Walker, M., Stafford, A., & Seaman, P. (2006). Children's perspectives on social exclusion and resilience in disadvantaged urban communities. In E. Kay, M. Tisdall, J. Davis, M. Hill & A. Prout (Eds.), *Children, young people and social inclusion: Participation for what?* (pp. 39–56). Bristol, UK: Policy.

HM Treasury and DCSF (Department for Children Schools and Families). (2007). *Aiming high for young people: A ten-year strategy for positive activities.* London: HM Treasury and DCSF.

Hoadley, U. (2008). Social class and pedagogy: A model for the investigation of pedagogic variation. *British Journal of Sociology of Education, 29*(1), 63–78.

Hoggart, R. (1957). *The uses of literacy.* London: Chatto & Windus.

Howarth, C., Kenway, P., Palmer, G., & Morelli, R. (1999). *Monitoring poverty and social exclusion 1999.* York, UK: Joseph Rowntree Foundation.

Imrie, R. (2004). Governing the cities and the urban renaissance In C. Johnstone & M. Whitehead (Eds.), *New horizons in British urban policy: Perspectives on New Labour's urban renaissance* (pp. 129–142). Aldershot, UK: Ashgate.

INCLUD-ED Consortium. (2012). *Final INCLUD-ED Report. Strategies for inclusion and social cohesion in Europe from education.* INCLUD-ED Project, Universitat de Barcelona. http://creaub.info/included/wp-content/uploads/2010/12/D25.2_Final-Report_final.pdf

Inglis, F. (2000). A malediction upon management. *Journal of Education Policy, 15*(4), 417–429.

Ingram, N. (2009). Working-class boys, educational success and the misrecognition of working-class culture. *British Journal of Sociology of Education, 30*(4), 421–434.

Inner London Education Authority (ILEA). (1984). *Improving secondary schools.* London: ILEA.

Ireson, J., & Hallam, S. (1999). Raising standards: Is ability grouping the answer? *Oxford Review of Education, 25*(3), 343–358.

Jackson, B. (1964). *Streaming: An education system in miniature.* London: Routledge & Kegan Paul.

Jackson, C. (2006). *Lads and ladettes in school, gender and fear of failure.* Maidenhead, UK: Open University Press/McGraw-Hill Education.

Jakubowski, M. (2010). Institutional tracking and achievement growth: Exploring difference-in-differences approach to PIRLS, TIMSS, and PISA Data. In J. Dronkers (Ed.), *Quality and inequality of education: Cross-national perspectives* (pp. 41–81). Rotterdam: Springer.

James, S. (1992). The good-enough citizen. In G. Bock & S. James (Eds.), *Beyond equality and difference.* London: Routledge.

Jencks, C., Smith, M., Ackland, H., Bane, M., Cohen, D., Gintis, H., et al. (1973). *Inequality: A reassessment of the effect of family and schooling in America.* New York: Basic.

Jensen, P. (1968). Social class and verbal learning. In M. Deutsch, I. Katz & A. Jensen (Eds.), *Social class, race and psychological development.* New York: Holt, Rinehart & Winston.

Johnson, R. (1979). Really useful knowledge. In J. Clarke et al. (Ed.), *Working-class culture: Studies in history and theory* (pp. 75–102). London: Hutchinson.

Johnston, K., & Hayes, D. (2008). "This is as good as it gets": Classroom lessons and learning in challenging circumstances. *Australian Journal of Language and Literacy, 31*(2), 109–127.

Johnston, R., & Watson, J. (2005). *The effects of synethetic phonics teaching on reading and spelling: A seven year longitudinal study.* Edinburgh: Scottish Executive Education Department. Retrieved December 4, 2012, from http://www.scotland.gov.uk/Resource/Doc/36496/0023582.pdf

Johnstone, C., & Whitehead, M. (2004). Horizons and barriers in British urban policy. In C. Johnstone & M. Whitehead (Eds.), *New horizons in British urban policy: Perspectives on New Labour's urban renaissance* (pp. 3–21). Aldershot, UK: Ashgate.

Jones, K. (2003). Culture reinvented as management: English in the new urban school. *Changing English, 20*(2), 143–153.

Jones, O. (2011). *Chavs: The demonization of the working class.* London & New York: Verso.

Jones, S. (2006). *Girls, social class and literacy: What teachers can do to make a difference.* Portsmouth, NH: Heinemann.

Kamin, L. (1972). *Heredity, intelligence, politics and psychology.* Unpublished presidential address to meeting of the Eastern Psychological Association.

———. (1974). *The science and politics of IQ.* New York: Erlbaum.

Katz, M. (1971). *Class, bureaucracy and schools: The illusion of educational change in America.* New York: Praeger.

Keddie, A. (2007). Games of subversion and sabotage: Issues of power, masculinity, class, rurality and schooling. *British Journal of Sociology of Education, 28*(2), 181–194.

Kelsh, D. (2010). Cultureclass. In D. Kelsh, D. Hill & S. Macrine (Eds.), *Class in education: Knowledge, pedagogy, subjectivity* (pp. 6–38). Abingdon, UK: Routledge.

Kemmis, S., Cole, P., & Suggett, D. (1983). *Orientations to curriculum and transition: Towards the socially-critical school.* Melbourne: Victorian Institute of Secondary Education.

Kenway, J. (2001). Keynote: ICSEI. *Improving Schools, 4*(1), 3–7.

Kenway, J., & Bullen, E. (2001). *Consuming children: Education, entertainment, advertising.* Buckingham & Philadelphia: Open University Press.

Kenway, J., Kraack, A., & Hickey-Moody, A. (2006). *Masculinity beyond the metropolis.* New York: Palgrave Macmillan.

Kintrea, K., St Clair, R., & Houston, M. (2011). *The influence of parents, places and poverty on educational attitudes and aspirations (Full Report).* York, UK: Joseph Rowntree Foundation.

Kohn, A. (2011). *Poor teaching for poor children . . . the name of reform.* Haberman Educational Foundation, Retrieved October 4, 2012, fromhttp://www.habermanfoundation.org/Articles/Default.aspx?id=97

Kozol, J. (2008). *Letters to a young teacher.* New York: Three Rivers.

Krogh-Jespersen, K., Methling, A., & Striib, A. (1998). *Inspiration til undervisningsdifferentiering (Inspiration for differentiating education).* Copenhagen: Undervisningsministeriet (Folkeskole-afdelingen).

Labov, W. (1969). The logic of nonstandard English. In P. Giglioli (Ed.), *Language and social context* (pp. 179–215). Hammondsworth, UK: Penguin.

Lacey, C. (1970). *Hightown Grammar: The school as a social system.* Manchester: Manchester University Press.

Lareau, A. (2003). *Unequal childhoods: Class, race and family life.* Berkeley: University of California Press.

Lawler, S. (2005). Disgusted subjects: The making of middle class identities. *Sociological Review, 53*(3), 429–446.

Leacock, E. (Ed.). (1971). *The culture of poverty: A critique.* New York: Simon & Schuster.

Leeds, A. (1971). The concept of the "culture of poverty": Conceptual, logical and empirical problems, with perspectives from Brazil and Peru. In E. Leacock (Ed.), *The culture of poverty: A critique* (pp. 226–284). New York: Simon & Schuster.

Lefebvre, H. (1991). *The production of space.* Oxford: Blackwell.

Levin, H. (1992). At-risk students in a yuppie age. *Educational Policy, 4,* 283–295.

Levitas, R. (2005). *The inclusive society? Social exclusion and New Labour* (2nd ed.). London: Palgrave Macmillan.

Lewis, H. (1971). Culture of poverty? What does it matter? In E. Leacock (Ed.), *The culture of poverty: A critique* (pp. 345–363). New York: Simon & Schuster.

Lewis, O. (1966). *La Vida: A Puerto Rican family in the culture of poverty—San Juan and New York.* New York: Random House.

———. (1968). *A study of slum culture: Backgrounds for* La Vida. New York: Random.

Ley, D. (1988). Interpretive social research in the city. In J. Eyles (Ed.), *Research in human geography* (pp. 121–138). Oxford: Blackwell.

Lingard, B., Hayes, D., Mills, M., & Christie, P. (2003). *Leading learning: Making hope practical.* Buckingham, UK: Open University Press.

Lipsky, M. (1980). *Street-level bureaucracy: Dilemmas of the individual in public service.* New York: Russell Sage Foundation.

Lister, R. (2004). *Poverty.* Cambridge: Polity.

Lowe, R. (1862). Parliamentary Debates CLXV cols. 237–8.

Lubienski, C., & Lubienski, S. (2006). *Charter, private, public schools and academic achievement: New evidence from NAEP mathematics data.* New York: Teachers College, Columbia University.

Lundahl, L. (2011). The emergence of a Swedish school market. In R. Hatcher & K. Jones (Eds.), *No country for the young* (pp. 37–50). London: Tufnell.

Lupton, R. (2003). *Neighbourhood effects: Can we measure them and does it matter.* CASE paper no. 73. London: CASE.

———. (2010). Area-based initiatives in English education: What place for place and space? In C. Raffo, A. Dyson, H. Gunter, D. Hall, L. Jones & A. Kalambouka (Eds.), *Education and poverty in affluent countries* (pp. 111–123). New York & London: Routledge.

Luyten, J., & Bosker, R. (2004). Hoe meritocratish zijn schooladviezen? *Pedagogische Studien, 81*(2), 89–103.

MacBeath, J. (1999). *Schools must speak for themselves: The case for the school self-evaluation.* London: RoutledgeFalmer.

MacBeath, J., with Schratz, M., Meuret, D., & Jakobsen, I. (2000). *Self-evaluation in European schools: A story of change.* London: RoutledgeFalmer.

MacDonald, R. (Ed.). (1997). *Youth, the "underclass" and social exclusion.* London & New York: Routledge.

MacDonald, R., & Marsh, J. (2005). *Disconnected youth?: Growing up in Britain's poor neighbourhoods.* Basingstoke, UK: Palgrave.

MacKay, T. (2007). *Achieving the vision: The final research report of the West Dumbartonshire Literacy Initiative.* Dumbarton, UK: West Dumbarton Council.

Madanipour, A. (1998). Social exclusion and space. In G. Cars, A. Madanipour & J. Allen (Eds.), *Social exclusion in European cities* (pp. 75-94). London: Jessica Kingsley.

Maguire, M. (2010). Leaving school and moving on: Poverty, urban youth, and learning identities. In C. Raffo, A. Dyson, H. Gunter, D. Hall, L. Jones & A. Kalambouka (Eds.), *Education and poverty in affluent countries* (pp. 135–147). New York & London: Routledge.

Mahoney, P., & Hextall, I. (2000). *Reconstructing teaching: Standards, performance and accountability.* London: RoutledgeFalmer.

Mann, M. (1973). *Consciousness and action among the Western working class.* London: Macmillan.

Marx, K. (1987[1867]). *Capital.* Retrieved October 4, 2012, from www.marxists.org/archive/marx/works/1867-c1/ch07.htm

Marx, K., & Engels, F. (1845). *The German ideology.* www.marxists.org/archive/marx/works/1845/german-ideology/ch01d.htm

Marx, K., & Engels, F. (1996 [1848]). *The Communist manifesto*. London: Phoenix.

Massey, D. (1993). Power-geometry and a progressive sense of place. In J. Bird, B. Curtis, T. Putnam, G. Robertson & L. Tickner (Eds.), *Mapping the futures: Local cultures, global change* (pp. 59–69). London: Routledge.

———. (1994). *Space, place and gender*. Cambridge: Polity.

———. (1995, Autumn). Making spaces: or, geography is political too. *Soundings, 1*, 193–208.

———. (2005). *For space*. London: Sage.

———. (2007). *World city*. Cambridge: Polity.

May, S. (1994). *Making multicultural education work*. Clevedon, UK: Multilingual Matters.

McCulloch, G. (1998). *Failing the ordinary child? The theory and practice of working-class secondary education*. Buckingham & Philadelphia: Open University Press.

McDermott, R. (1996). The acquisition of a child by a learning disability. In S. Chaiklin & J. Lave (Eds.), *Understanding practice: Perspectives on activity and context* (pp. 269–305). New York: Cambridge University Press.

McGregor, G., Mills, M., & Thomson, P. (2012). Educating in the margins, lessons for the mainstream. In T. Wrigley, P. Thomson & B. Lingard (Eds.), *Changing schools: Alternative ways to make a world of difference* (pp. 47–60). London: Routledge.

McInerney, P. (2009). Toward a critical pedagogy of engagement for alienated youth: Insights from Freire and school-based research. *Critical Studies in Education, 50*(1), 23–35.

McInerney, P., Smyth, J., & Down, B. (2011). "Coming to a place near you." The politics and possibilities of a critical pedagogy of place-based education. *Asia-Pacific Journal of Teacher Education, 39*(1), 3–16.

McLaughlin, M. (1990). The Rand change agent study revisited: Macro perspectives, micro realities. *Educational Researchers, 19*(9), 11–16.

McNamee, S., & Miller, R. (2004). *The meritocracy myth*. Lanham, MD: Rowman & Littlefield.

Medway, P., & Kingwell, P. (2010). A curriculum in its place: English teaching in one school 1946–1963. *History of Education, 39*(6), 749–765.

Meichenbaum, D. (2005). *Understanding resilience in children and adults: Implications for prevention and interventions*. Miami: Melissa Institute for Violence Prevention and Treatment. http://www.melissainstitute.org/documents/resilienceinchildren.pdf

Meier, D. (2002). *The power of their ideas: Lessons for America from a small school in Harlem*. Boston: Beacon.

Mészáros, I. (2005). *Marx's theory of alienation*. London: Merlin.

Midwinter, E. (1972). Curriculum and the EPA community school. In E. Midwinter (Ed.), *Projections: An educational priority area at work*. London: Ward Lock.

———. (1975). Curriculum and the EPA community school. In M. Golby, J. Greenwald & R. West (Eds.), *Curriculum design* (pp. 225–237). London: Taylor & Francis.

Milbourne, L., Macrae, S., & Maguire, M. (2003). Collaborative solutions or new policy problems: Exploring multi-agency partnerships in education and health work. *Journal of Education Policy, 18*(1), 19–35.

Mills, C., & Gale, T. (2011). Re-asserting the place of context in explaining student (under) achievement. *British Journal of Sociology of Education, 32*(2), 239–256.

Ministry of Education, Denmark. (1995). *Samfundsfag*. (Curriculum guidelines for citizenship education).

Mocombe, P. (2011). Role conflict and black underachievement. *Journal for Critical Education Policy Studies, 9*(2), 2011.

Moll, L., Amanti, C., Neff, D., & Gonzalez, N. (1992). Funds of knowledge for teaching: Using a qualitative approach to connect homes and classrooms. *Theory into Practice, 31*(2), 132–141.

Moogan, Y. (2011). An analysis of school pupils' (with low socioeconomic status) perceptions of university, regarding programs of study. *Educational Studies, 37*(1), 1–14.

Morley, L., & Rassool, N. (1999). *School effectiveness: Fracturing the discourse.* London & New York: Falmer.

Morrow, V. (2001). Young people's explanations and experiences of social exclusion: Retrieving Bourdieu's concept of social capital. *International Journal of Sociology and Social Policy, 21*(4–6), 37–63.

———. (2008). Conceptualising social capital in relation to the well-being of children and young people: A critical review. *Sociological Review, 47*(4), 744–765.

Mortimore, P., Simmons, P., Stoll, L., Lewis, D., & Ecob, R. (Eds.). (1988). *School matters: The junior years.* Somerset: Open Books (reprinted in 1995 by Paul Chapman, London).

Mortimore, P., & Whitty, G. (1997). *Can school improvement overcome the effects of disadvantage?* London: Institute of Education, University of London.

Muijs, D., & Reynolds, D. (2001). *Effective teaching: A handbook of evidence-based methods.* London: Paul Chapman.

Mumford, A., & Power, A. (2003). *East Enders: Family and community in East London.* Bristol, UK: Policy.

Murray, C. (1996). *The emerging British underclass.* London: Institute of Economic Affairs.

Nakata, M. (1999). History, cultural diversity and English language teaching. In P. Wignell (Ed.), *Double power: English literacy and indigenous education language* (pp. 5–22). Melbourne: Language Australia.

National Coalition of Advocates for Students. (1985). *Barriers to excellence: Our children at risk.* Boston: National Coalition of Advocates for Students.

National Commission on Excellence in Education. (1983). *A nation at risk: The imperative for educational reform.* Washington, DC: Government Printing Office.

Nayak, A. (2003). Last of the "real geordies"? White masculinities and the subcultural responses to deindustrialisation. *Environment and Planning D: Society and Space, 21*, 6–25.

Newmann, F., Secada, W., & Wehlage, G. (1995). *A guide to authentic achievement and assessment: Vision, standards and scoring.* Madison: Wisconsin Center for Education Research.

Oakes, J. (1982). The reproduction of inequity: The content of secondary school tracking. *Urban Review, 14*(2), 107–120.

———. (1985). *Keeping track: How schools structure inequality.* New Haven, CT: Yale University Press.

Ofsted. (2011). *Annual report 2010–11. Maintained schools.* London: Office for Standards in Education.

Ogbu, J. (1991). Low school performance as an adaptation: The case of blacks in Stockton, California. In M. Gibson & J. Ogbu (Eds.), *Minority status and schooling: A comparative study of immigrant and involuntary minorities* (pp. 129–186). New York: Garland.

Oliver, E., deBotton, L., Soler, M., & Merrill, B. (2011). Cultural intelligence to overcome educational exclusion. *Qualitative Inquiry, 17*(3), 267–276.

Organisation for Economic Co-operation and Development (OECD. (2012). *Equity and quality in education: Supporting disadvantaged students and schools.* http://dx.doi.org/10.1787/9789264130852-en

Pahl, R. (1989). Is the emperor naked? Some questions on the adequacy of sociology theory in urban and regional research. *International Journal of Urban and Regional Research 13*(4), 709–720.

Patterson, C. (2009, January). Heaven help the white working class now. *Independent, 242,*

Payne, R. (2005). *A framework for understanding poverty* (4th ed.) Highlands, TX: RFT.

Perkins, D. (1995). *Smart schools: Better thinking and learning for every child.* New York: Free Press.

Perlman, J. (1974) *The myth of marginality: urban poverty and politics in Rio de Janeiro*. Berkeley: University of California Press

Pickering, M. (2001). *Stereotyping*. Basingstoke, UK: Palgrave.

Plato (2000 [c380 BCE] *The Republic*. trans. T. Griffith. Cambridge: Cambridge University Press.

Plowden Report. (1967). *Children and their primary schools. A report of the Central Advisory Council for Education (England)*. London: Her Majesty's Stationery Office.

Polakow, V. (1993). *Lives on the edge: Single mothers and their children in the other America*. Chicago: University of Chicago Press.

Pollard, A., & Filer, A. (2007). Learning, differentiation and strategic action in secondary education: Analyses from the "Identity and Learning Programme." *British Journal of Sociology of Education, 28*(4), 441–458.

Portes, A. (1998). Social capital: Its origins and applications in modern sociology. *Annual Review of Sociology, 24*, 1–24.

Portes, A., & Landolt, P. (2000). Social capital: Promise and pitfalls of its role in development. *Journal of Latin American Studies, 32*(2), 529–547.

Power, S., Edwards, T., Whitty, G., & Wigfall, V. (2003). *Education and the middle class*. Maidenhead, UK: Open University Press.

Power, S., & Gewirtz, S. (2001). Reading education action zones. *Journal of Education Policy, 16*(1), 39–51.

Power, S., Rees, G., & Taylor, C. (2005). New Labour and educational disadvantage: The limits of area-based initiatives. *London Review of Education, 3*(2), 101–116.

Prout, A. (2000). Children's participation: Control and self-realisation in British late modernity. *Children and Society, 14*(4), 304–305.

Puigvert, L., Christou, M., & Holford, J. (2012). Critical communicative methodology: Including vulnerable voices in research through dialogue. *Cambridge Journal of Education, 42*(4), 513–526.

Putnam, R. (1993, Spring). The prosperous community: Social capital and public life. *American Prospect, 13*, 35–42.

———. (2000). *Bowling alone: The collapse and revival of American community*. New York: Simon & Schuster.

Queensland Department of Education. (2001). *New basics: Rich tasks*. Brisbane: Education Queensland.

Raffo, C. (2011). Educational equity in poor urban contexts—Exploring issues of place/space and young people's identity and agency. *British Journal of Educational Studies, 59*(1), 1–19.

Raffo, C., & Dyson, A. (2007). Full service extended schools and educational inequality in urban contexts—New opportunities for progress? *Journal of Education Policy, 22*(3), 263–282.

Raffo, C., Dyson, A., Gunter, H., Hall, D., Jones, L., & Kalambouka, A. (2010). The mapping framework, research literature, and policy implications within a functionalist framework. In C. Raffo, A. Dyson, H. Gunter, D. Hall, L. Jones & A. Kalambouka (Eds.), *Education and poverty in affluent countries* (pp. 41-55). London: Routledge.

Ravitch, D. (2010). *The death and life of the American school system: How testing and choice are undermining education*. Philadelphia: Basic.

Reay, D., & Lucey, H. (2000). "I don't really like it here but I don't want to be anywhere else": Children and inner city housing estates. *Antipode, 32*(4), 410–428.

———. (2003). The limits of "Choice": Children and inner city schooling. *Sociology, 37*(1), 121–142.

Reis, S., Colbert, R., & Hébert, T. (2005). Understanding resilience in diverse, talented students in an urban high school. *Roeper Review 27*(2), http://www.gifted.uconn.edu/sem/pdf/understanding_resilience.pdf

Richardson, L. and Mumford, K. (2002) 'Community, neighbourhood, and social infrastructure', in J. Hills, J. LeGrand and D. Piachaud (eds) *Understanding Social Exclusion* (pp. 202–225). Oxford: Oxford University Press.

Riddell, R. (2010). *Aspiration, identity and self-belief: Snapshots of social structure at work*. Stoke-on-Trent, UK: Trentham.

Riddell, S., Brown, S., & Duffield, J. (1998). The utility of qualitative research for influencing policy and practice on school effectiveness. In R. Slee & G. Weiner with S. Tomlinson (Eds.), *School effectiveness for whom? Challenges to the school effectiveness and school improvement movements* (pp. 170–186). London & Bristol, PA.: Falmer.

Ridge, T. (2002). *Childhood poverty and social exclusion: From a child's perspective*. Bristol, UK: Policy.
———. (2006). Childhood poverty: A barrier to social participation and inclusion. In E. Kay, M. Tisdall, J. Davis, M. Hill & A. Prout (Eds.), *Children, young people and social inclusion: Participation for what?* (pp. 23–38). Bristol, UK: Policy.

Riessman, F. (1962). *The culturally deprived child*. New York: HarperRow.

Riggins, S. (1997). The rhetoric of othering. In S. Riggins (Ed.), *The language and politics of exclusion* (pp. 1-30). Thousand Oaks, CA: Sage.

Rist, R. (1973). *The urban school: A factory for failure*. Cambridge, MA: MIT Press.

Rizvi, F. and Lingard, B. (2010) *Globalizing education policy*. London: Routledge.

Robbins, P., & Aydede, M. (2009). *The Cambridge handbook of situated cognition*. Cambridge: Cambridge University Press.

Rose, D. (1995). Official social classifications in the UK. *Social Research Update, 9*. Retrieved August 28, 2011, from http://sru.soc.surrey.ac.uk/SRU9.html

Rose, N. (1999). *Powers of freedom: Reframing political thought*. Cambridge: Cambridge University Press.

Rose, S. (1998). *Lifelines: Biology, freedom, determinism*. Harmondsworth, UK: Penguin.

Rose, S., Lewontin, R., & Kamin, L. (1984). *Not in our genes: Biology, ideology and human nature*. London: Penguin.

Rosen, H. (1972). *Language and class: A critical look at the theories of Basil Bernstein*. Bristol, UK: Falling Wall.

Rosen, M. (2006, June 6). *What's politics got to do with it?* The Annual Education Lecture, King's College, London.
———. (2012). Dear Mr. Gove. Talk recorded at Marxism conference. www.youtube.com/watch?v =trFOqilQiB0&list=PL5AE70FB0F5E7C1D9&index=29&festure=plpp_video

Rudduck, J., & Flutter, J. (2004). *How to improve your school: Giving pupils a voice*. London: Continuum.

Rutter, M. (1983). School effects on pupil progress—Findings and policy implications. *Child Development, 54*(1), 1–29.

Rutter, M., Maughan, B., Mortimore, P., & Outston J., with Smith, A. (1979). *Fifteen thousand hours: Secondary schools and their effects on children*. London: Open.

Sahlberg, P. (2011). *Finnish lessons: What can the world learn from educational change in Finland?* New York: Teachers College Press.

Salomon, G. (Ed.). (1993). *Distributed cognitions: Psychological and educational considerations*. Cambridge: Cambridge University Press.

Sammons, P., Hillman, J., & Mortimore, P. (1995). *Key characteristics of effective schools: A review of school effectiveness research*. London: Ofsted.

Sarra, C. (2012). Reflections of an Aboriginal school principal on leading change in an Aboriginal school. In T. Wrigley, P. Thomson & B. Lingard (Eds.), *Changing schools: Alternative ways to make a world of difference* (pp. 61–70). London: Routledge.

Savage, M. (2005). Working-class identities in the 1960s: Revisiting the affluent work study. *Sociology, 39*(5), 929–949.

Savage, M., Barlow, J., Dickens, P., & Fielding, T. (1992). *Property, bureaucracy and culture: Middle class formation in contemporary Britain.* London: Routledge.

Sayer, A. (2005). *The moral significance of social class.* Cambridge: Cambridge University Press.

Schatzman, L., & Strauss, A. (1955). Social class and modes of communication. *American Journal of Sociology, 60*(4), 329–338.

Sennett, R., & Cobb, J. (1977). *The hidden injuries of class.* Cambridge: Cambridge University Press.

Seyan, K., Greenhalgh, T., & Dorling, D. (2004). The standardised admission ratio for measuring widening participation in medical schools: Analysis of UK medical school admissions by ethnicity, socioeconomic status, and sex. *BMJ,* 2004;328: 1545. www.bmj.com/cgi/content/full/328/7455/1545.

Shaw, G. (2009 [1912]). *Pygmalion.* Rockville, MD: Wildside.

Shaw, M., Dorling, D., Gordon, D. and Davey-Smith, G. (1999) *The Widening Gap: health inequalities and policy in Britain.* Bristol: Policy Press.

Shayer, M., & Adey, P. (2002). *Learning intelligence: Cognitive acceleration across the curriculum from 5 to 15 years.* Buckingham, UK: Open University Press.

Shropshire, J., & Middleton, S. (1999). *Small expectations: Learning to be poor?* York, UK: Joseph Rowntree Foundation.

Sibley, D. (1995). *Geographies of exclusion: Society and difference in the West.* London & New York: Routledge.

Siisiäinen, M. (2000, July). *Two concepts of social capital: Bourdieu vs. Putnam.* Paper presented at the ISTR Fourth International Conference, Dublin.

Silberman, C. (1971). *Crisis in the classroom.* New York: Random House

Simon, B. (1953). *Intelligence testing and the comprehensive school.* London: Lawrence & Wishart.

———. (1960). *Studies in the history of education 1780–1870.* London: Lawrence & Wishart.

———. (1965). *Studies in the history of education. Education and the Labour Movement 1970–1920.* London: Lawrence & Wishart.

Skeggs, B. (1997). *Formations of class and gender.* London: Sage.

———. (2004). *Class, self, culture.* London: Routledge.

———. (2005). The re-branding of class: Propertizing culture. In F. Devine, F. Savage, R. Crompton & J. Scott (Eds.), *Rethinking class: Identities, cultures and lifestyles* (pp. 46–68). London: Palgrave.

Slee, R., Weiner, G., with Tomlinson, S. (Eds.). (1998). *School effectiveness for whom? Challenges to the school effectiveness and school improvement movements.* London & Bristol, PA: Falmer.

Smith, A. (2005 [1776]). *An inquiry into the nature and causes of the wealth of nations.* London: Routledge.

Smith, G. (2012). The promise of place and community-based education. In T. Wrigley, P. Thomson & B. Lingard (Eds.), *Changing schools: Alternative ways to make a world of difference* (pp. 85–97). London: Routledge.

Smyth, J. (Ed.). (1989). *Critical perspectives on educational leadership.* London & New York: Falmer.

———. (1990). *Teachers as collaborative learners: Challenging dominant forms of supervision.* Milton Keynes, UK: Open University Press.

———. (Ed.). (1993). *Socially critical view of the self-managing school.* London: Falmer.

———. (2004). Social capital and the "socially just school." *British Journal of Sociology of Education, 25*(1), 19–33.

———. (2008). Listening to student voice in the democratisation of schooling. In E. Samier, with Stanley, G. (Ed.), *Political approaches to educational administration and leadership* (pp. 240–251). London & New York: Routledge.

———. (2009). Critically engaged community capacity building and the "community organizing" approach in disadvantaged contexts. *Critical Studies in Education, 50*(1), 9–22.

———. (2010a). Inclusive school leadership strategies in disadvantaged schools based on student and community voice: Implications for Australian education policy. In C. Raffo, A. Dyson, H. Gunter, D. Hall, L. Jones & A. Kalambouka (Eds.), *Education and poverty in affluent countries: Mapping the terrain and making the links to educational policy* (pp. 72–84). London & New York: Routledge.

———. (2010b). Speaking back to educational policy: Why social inclusion will not work for disadvantaged Australian schools. *Critical Studies in Education, 51*(2), 113–128.

———. (2011). The disaster of the "self-managing school"—Genesis, trajectory, undisclosed agenda, and effects. *Journal of Educational Administration and History, 43*(2), 95–117.

———. (2012). The socially just school and critical pedagogies in communities put at a disadvantage. *Critical Studies in Education, 53*(1), 9–18.

———. (2013). Losing our way? Challenging the direction of teacher education in Australia and re-framing it around the socially just school. *Asia-Pacific Journal of Teacher Education, 41*(1), 115–126.

Smyth, J., Angus, L., Down, B., & McInerney, P. (2008). *Critically engaged learning: Connecting to young lives.* New York: Peter Lang.

———. (2009). *Activist and socially critical school and community renewal: Social justice in exploitative times.* Rotterdam: Sense.

Smyth, J., Down, B., & McInerney, P. (2010). *"Hanging in with kids" in tough times: Engagement in contexts of educational disadvantage in the relational school.* New York: Peter Lang.

Smyth, J., & Hattam, R. (2004). *"Dropping out," drifting off, being excluded: Becoming somebody without school.* New York: Peter Lang.

Smyth, J., Hattam, R., Cannon, J., Edwards, J., Wilson, N., & Wurst, S. (2000). *Listen to me, I'm leaving.* Adelaide: Flinders Institute for the Study of Teaching.

Smyth, J., Hattam, R., & Lawson, M. (Eds.). (1998). *Schooling for a fair go.* Sydney: Federation.

Smyth, J., Lawson, M., & Hattam, R. (1998). What to look for in your neighbourhood school. In J. Smyth, R. Hattam & M. Lawson (Eds.), *Schooling for a fair go* (pp. 115–124). Sydney: Federation.

Smyth, J., & McInerney, P. (2007a). "Living on the edge": A case of school reform working for disadvantaged adolescents. *Teachers College Record, 109*(5), 1123–1170.

———. (2007b). *Teachers in the middle: Reclaiming the wasteland of the adolescent years of schooling.* New York: Peter Lang.

———. (2012). *From silent witnesses to active agents: Student voice in re-engaging with learning.* New York: Peter Lang.

———. (2013). Making "space" for disengaged young people who are *put at* a disadvantage to re-engage with learning. *British Journal of Sociology of Education, 34*(1), 39–55.

Smyth, J., McInerney, P., & Harrison, T. (2011). *What to look for in genuine community engagement: A toolkit.* Ballarat, Victoria: University of Ballarat.

Smyth, J., McInerney, P., Lawson, M., & Hattam, R. (1999). *School culture as the key to school reform* (Teachers' Learning Project Investigation Series). Adelaide: Flinders Institute for the Study of Teaching.

Social Exclusion Unit. (2001). *A new commitment to neighbourhood renewal: A national strategy action plan.* London: Social Exclusion Unit.

Soja, C. (1989). *Postmodern geographies: The reassertion of space in critical social theory.* London: Verso.

———. (1996). *Thirdspace: Journeys to Los Angeles and other real-and-imagined places.* Oxford: Blackwell.

Squires, P. (1990). *Anti-social policy*. New York: Harvester Wheatsheaf.

St. Clair, R., Kintrea, K., & Houston, M. (2011). *The influence of parents, places and poverty on educational attitudes and aspirations* (Summary Report). York, UK: Joseph Rowntree Foundation.

Stack, C. (1974). *All our kin: Strategies for survival in a black community*. New York: Basic.

Standing, G. (2011). *The precariat: The new dangerous class*. London: Bloomsbury Academic.

Sternberg, R. (1977). *Intelligence, information processing and analogical reasoning: The componential analysis of human abilities*. Hillsdale, NJ: Erlbaum.

Stewart, W. (2011, October 28). Aiming high but with no idea how to get there. *Times Educational Supplement*. Retrieved from http://www.tes.co.uk/teaching-resource/Aiming-high-but-with-no-idea-how-to-get-there-6124335/

Stoll, L., & Fink, D. (1996). *Changing our schools*. Buckingham & Philadelphia: Open University Press.

Stubbs, M. (1980). *Language and literacy: The sociolinguistics of reading and writing*. London: Routledge & Kegan Paul.

Sutton Trust. (2008). *Wasted talent? Attrition rates of high-achieving pupils between school and university*. www.suttontrust.com

Swain, D. (2012). *Alienation—An introduction to Marx's theory*. London: Bookmarks.

Swann, M., Peacock, A., Hart, S., & Drummond, M. J. (2012). *Creating learning without limits*. Maidenhead, UK: Open University Press.

Sylva, K., Melhuish, E., Sammons, P., Siraj-Blatchford, I., & Taggart, B. (2007). *Promoting equality in the early years: Report to the Equalities Review*. London: Institute of Education (EPPE Project). www.theequalitiesreview.org.uk

Taubman, P. (2009). *Teaching by numbers: Deconstructing the discourse of standards and accountability in education*. London: Routledge.

Terman, L. (1916). *The measurement of intelligence*. Boston: Houghton Mifflin.

———. (1921). The intelligence of school children. *Journal of Educational Psychology, 12*, 127–133.

Therborn, G. (1983, March–April). Why some classes are more successful than others. *New Left Review 138*. Retrieved from http://newleftreview.org/I/138/goran-therborn-why-some-classes-are-more-successful-than-others

Thomas, S., & Mortimore, P. (1994). *Report on value added analysis of 1993 GCSE examination results in Lancashire*. London: Research Papers in Education. Curriculum Studies Department, University of London Institute of Education.

Thompson, E. P. (1980[1963]). *The making of the English working class*. London: Penguin.

Thompson, G. (2010). Acting, accidents and performativity: Challenging the hegemonic good student in secondary schools. *British Journal of Sociology of Education, 31*(4), 413–430.

Thomson, P. (2006). Miners, diggers, ferals and show-men: School-community projects that affirm and unsettle identities and place? *British Journal of Sociology of Education, 27*(1), 81–96.

———. (2010). A critical pedagogy of global space: Regeneration in and as action. In C. Raffo, A. Dyson, H. Gunter, D. Hall, L. Jones & A. Kalambouka (Eds.), *Education and poverty in affluent countries* (pp. 124–134). New York & London: Routledge.

Thornton, M. (2004). Corrosive leadership (or bullying by another name): A corollary of the corporatised academy. *Australian Journal of Labour Law, 17*(2), 161–184.

Thrift, N., & Williams, P. (Eds.). (1987). *Class and space*. London: Routledge.

Thrupp, M., & Willmott, R. (2003). *Educational management in managerialist times: Beyond the textual apologists*. Buckingham, UK: Open University Press.

Thurstone, L. (1938). *Primary mental abilities*. Chicago: University of Chicago Press.

Tizard, B., & Hughes, M. (2002 [1984]). *Young children learning* (2nd ed.). Oxford: Blackwell.

Toch, T. (2003). *High schools on a human scale: How small schools can transform American education*. Boston: Beacon.

Tooth, R., & Renshaw, P. (2012). Storythread pedagogy for environmental education. In T. Wrigley, P. Thomson & B. Lingard (Eds.), *Changing schools: Alternative ways to make a world of difference* (pp. 113–127). London: Routledge.

Tough, J. (1976). *Listening to children talk*. London: Ward Lock.

Townsend, P. (1979). *Poverty in the United Kingdom*. Harmondsworth, UK: Penguin.

Toynbee, P. (2003). *Hard work: Life in low-pay Britain*. London: Bloomsbury.

Tropp, A. (1957). *The school teachers: The growth of the teaching profession in England and Wales from 1800 to the present day*. London: Heinemann.

Troyna, B., & Siraj-Blatchford, I. (1993). Providing support or denying access? The experiences of students designated as "ESL" and "SN" in a multi-ethnic secondary school. *Educational Review, 45*(1), 3–11.

Turner, G. (1973). Social class and children's language of control age five and age seven. In B. Bernstein (Ed.), *Class, codes and control: Towards a theory of educational transmissions* (pp. 135–201). London: Routledge & Kegan Paul.

Tymms, P. (2004). Are standards rising in English primary schools? *British Educational Research Journal, 30*(4), 477–494.

U.S. Department of Education. (1998). *Promising results, continuing challenges: Final report of the National Assessment of Title 1*. Washington, DC: U.S. Department of Education.

Valencia, R. (2010). *Dismantling contemporary deficit thinking: Educational thought and practice*. New York: Routledge.

Valentine, C. (1971). The "culture of poverty": Its scientific significance and its implications for action. In E. Leacock (Ed.), *The culture of poverty: A critique* (pp. 193–225). New York: Simon & Schuster.

Veit-Wilson, J. (1986). Paradigms of poverty: A rehabilitation of B.S. Rowntree. *Journal of Social Policy, 15*(1), 69–99.

Vibert, A., Portelli, J., Leighteizer, V., with Forrest, M., & Will, B. (2001). *Student engagement in learning and school life: Case reports from project schools, Vol. 1, Part III: Nova Scotia*. Montreal: Ed-Lex, Faculty of Law, McGill University.

Vibert, A., Portelli, J., Shields, C., & LaRocque, L. (2002). Critical practice in elementary schools: Voice, community, and a curriculum for life. *Journal of Educational Change, 3*(2), 93–116.

Vicars, M. (2010). Girls, social class and literacy: What teachers can do to make a difference. *Discourse, 31*(2), 271–273.

von der Groeben, A. (2008). *Verschiedenheit nutzen: besser lernen in heterogenen Gruppen (Making use of diversity: Learning better in mixed groups)*. Berlin: Cornelsen.

Vygotsky, L. (1978). *Mind in society*. Cambridge, MA: Harvard University Press.

Wacquant, L. (2008). *Urban outcasts: A comparative sociology of advanced marginality*. Cambridge: Polity.

Walkerdine, V. (2010). Communal beingness and affect: An exploration in trauma in an ex-industrial community. *Body and Society, 16*(1), 91–116.

Warren, S. (2005). Resilience and refusal: African-Caribbean young men's agency, school exclusions, and school-based mentoring programmes. *Race, Ethnicity and Education, 8*(3), 243–259.

Wax, M., & Wax, R. (1971). Cultural deprivation as an educational ideology. In E. Leacock (Ed.), *The culture of poverty: A critique* (pp. 127–139). New York: Simon & Schuster.

Webb, R., & Vulliamy, G. (2001). Joining up the solutions: The rhetoric of inter-agency co-operation. *Children and Society, 15*, 315–322.

Wells, G. (1987). *The meaning makers: Children learning language and using language to learn*. London: Hodder & Stoughton.

Wertsch, J. (1990). The voice of rationality in a sociocultural approach to mind. In L. Moll (Ed.), *Vygotsky and education* (pp. 111–126). Cambridge & New York: Cambridge University Press.

Wexler, P. (1982). Structure, text and subject: A critical sociology of school knowledge. In M. Apple (Ed.), *Cultural and economic reproduction in education* (pp. 275–303). London: Routledge & Kegan Paul.

———. (1992). *Becoming somebody: Toward a social psychology of school.* London: Falmer.

Wilkinson, R., & Pickett, K. (2009). *The spirit level: Why more equal societies almost always do better.* London: Allen Lane.

Willes, M. (1983). *Children into pupils: A study of language in early schooling.* London: Routledge & Kegan Paul.

Williams, R. (1965). *The long revolution.* Harmondsworth, UK: Penguin.

———. (1985[1973]). *The country and the city.* London: Hogarth.

———. (1983 [1976]). *Keywords: A vocabulary of culture and society* (Rev. ed.). New York: Oxford University Press.

Willis, P. (1977). *Learning to labour.* Farnborough, UK: Saxon House.

Wrigley, T. (2000). *The power to learn: Stories of success in the education of Asian and other bilingual pupils.* Stoke, UK: Trentham.

———. (2003). *Schools of hope: Anew agenda for school improvement.* Stoke-on-Trent, UK: Trentham.

———. (2006). *Another school is possible.* Stoke-on-Trent, UK: Trentham.

———. (2007). Projects, stories and challenges: More open architecture for school learning. In S. Bell, S. Harkness & G. White (Eds.), *Storyline: Past, present and future* (pp. 166–181).Glasgow: Centre for Studies in Enterprise, University of Strathclyde.

———. (2008). School improvement in a neo-liberal world. *Journal of Educational Administration and History, 40*(2), 129–148.

———. (2011). "Rapidly improving results": Penetrating the hype of policy-based evidence. In H. Gunter (Ed.).*The state and education policy.* London: Continuum.

———. (2013). Rethinking school effectiveness and improvement: A question of paradigms. *Discourse: Studies in the Cultural Politics of Education. 34(1),* 31–47

Wrigley, T., & Kalambouka, A. (2012). *Academies and achievement: Setting the record straight.* Edinburgh: Changing Schools.

Wrigley, T., Thomson, P., & Lingard, B. (Eds.). (2012). *Changing schools: Alternative ways to make a world of difference.* London: Routledge.

Wyse, D., & Styles, M. (2007, April). Synethetic phonics and the teaching of reading: The debate surrounding England's Rose Report. *Literacy, 41*(1), 35–42.

Zipin, L. (2009). Dark funds of knowledge, deep funds of pedagogy: Exploring boundaries between lifeworlds and schools. *Discourse: Studies in the Cultural Politics of Education, 30*(3), 317–331.

Author Index

Subject Index

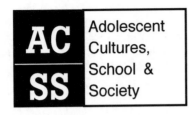

Adolescent Cultures, School & Society

Joseph L. DeVitis & Linda Irwin-DeVitis

GENERAL EDITORS

As schools struggle to redefine and restructure themselves, they need to be aware of the new realities of adolescents. Thus, this series of monographs and texts is committed to depicting the variety of adolescent cultures that exist in today's troubled world. It is primarily a qualitative research, practice, and policy series devoted to contextual interpretation and analysis that encompasses a broad range of interdisciplinary critique. In addition, this series seeks to address issues of curriculum theory and practice; multicultural education; aggression, bullying, and violence; the media and arts; school dropouts; homeless and runaway youth; gangs and other alienated youth; at-risk adolescent populations; family structures and parental involvement; and race, ethnicity, class, and gender/LGBTQ studies.

Send proposals and manuscripts to the general editors at:

Joseph L. DeVitis & Linda Irwin-DeVitis
Darden College of Education
Old Dominion University
Norfolk, VA 23503

To order other books in this series, please contact our Customer Service Department at:

(800) 770-LANG (within the U.S.)
(212) 647-7706 (outside the U.S.)
(212) 647-7707 FAX

or browse online by series at:

WWW.PETERLANG.COM